INSURANCE ETHICS FOR A MORE ETHICAL WORLD

RESEARCH IN ETHICAL ISSUES IN ORGANIZATIONS

Series Editor: Moses L. Pava

Associate Editor: Patrick Primeaux

Recent Volumes:

RESEARCH IN ETHICAL ISSUES IN ORGANIZATIONS
VOLUME 7

INSURANCE ETHICS FOR A MORE ETHICAL WORLD

EDITED BY

PATRICK FLANAGAN

St. John's University, New York, NY, USA

PATRICK PRIMEAUX

St. John's University, New York, NY, USA

WILLIAM FERGUSON

University of Louisiana at Lafayette, Lafayette, LA, USA

ELSEVIER
JAI

Amsterdam – Boston – Heidelberg – London – New York – Oxford
Paris – San Diego – San Francisco – Singapore – Sydney – Tokyo
JAI Press is an imprint of Elsevier

JAI Press is an imprint of Elsevier
The Boulevard, Langford Lane, Kidlington, Oxford OX5 1GB, UK
Radarweg 29, PO Box 211, 1000 AE Amsterdam, The Netherlands
525 B Street, Suite 1900, San Diego, CA 92101-4495, USA

First edition 2007

British Library Cataloguing in Publication Data
A catalogue record for this book is available from the British Library

ISBN-13:   978-0-7623-1333-4
ISBN-10:   0-7623-1333-1
ISSN: 1529-2096

For information on all JAI Press publications
visit our website at books.elsevier.com

Printed and bound in The Netherlands

07 08 09 10 11 10 9 8 7 6 5 4 3 2 1

Working together to grow
libraries in developing countries

www.elsevier.com | www.bookaid.org | www.sabre.org

ELSEVIER   BOOK AID International   Sabre Foundation

CONTENTS

LIST OF CONTRIBUTORS

James Barrese	Department of Risk Management, St. John's University, New York, NY, USA
Johannes Brinkmann	BI Norwegian School of Management, Oslo, Norway
Minnette A. Bumpus	Department of Management, School of Business, Howard University, Washington, DC, USA
Robert W. Cooper	College of Business and Public Administration, Darke University, Des Moines, IA, USA
Steve Diacon	Nottingham University Business School, Nottingham, UK
Christine Ennew	Nottingham University Business School, Nottingham, UK
William L. Ferguson	College of Business Administration, University of Louisiana at Lafayette, Lafayette, LA, USA
Patrick Flanagan	Department of Theology and Religious Studies, St. John's University, Queens, NY, USA
Kyoko Fukukawa	Bradford University School of Management, Bradford, UK
Joseph Heath	Department of Philosophy, University of Toronto, Ontario, Canada
Chalmer E. Labig	William S. Spears School of Business, Oklahoma State University, Stillwater, OK, USA

Rev Robert E. Lauder   Department of Philosophy, St. John's University, Queens, NY, USA

Martin J. Lecker   SUNY Rockland Community College, Suffern, NY, USA

Mary D. Maury   Department of Accounting and Taxation, St. John's University, Queens, NY, USA

Irene N. McCarthy   Department of Accounting and Taxation, St. John's University, Staten Island, NY, USA

Alfonso R. Oddo   Department of Accounting, Niagara University, Niagara, NY, USA

Daniel E. Palmer   Department of Philosophy, Kent State University, Warren, OH, USA

Patrick D. Primeaux   Department of Theology and Religious Studies, St. John's University, Queens, NY, USA

Victoria Shoaf   Department of Accounting and Taxation, St. John's University, Queens, NY, USA

Kenneth Zantow   College of Business, University of Southern Mississippi, Long Beach, MS, USA

STATEMENT OF PURPOSE

The purpose of the series is to explore the central and unique role of organizational ethics in creating and sustaining a flourishing, pluralistic, free enterprise economy. The primary goal of the research studies published here is to examine how profit seeking and not for profit organizations can be conceived and designed to satisfy legitimate human needs in an ethical and meaningful way.

Ethical Issues in Organizations encourages authors to submit rigorous research studies (essayistic or empirical) from a wide variety of academic perspectives including (but not limited to) business management, philosophy, sociology, psychology, religion, accounting, finance and marketing. Relevant book reviews are also invited.

Acceptable manuscripts probe important issues in organizational ethics and do so in ways that make original and substantial contributions to the existing business ethics literature. These studies are written in a clear and convincing style. The editorial board pledges timely editorial decisions and prompt publication.

Please send 3 copies of completed manuscripts to:

Dr. Moses L. Pava
Editor
Ethical Issues in Organizations
Yeshiva University
500 W. 185th St.
New York, NY 10033, USA

INTRODUCTION: INSURANCE ETHICS FOR A MORE ETHICAL WORLD

Patrick Flanagan, Patrick D. Primeaux, and William L. Ferguson

The insurance industry has been marked by exponential growth over the recent decade with more and more individuals and corporations appealing to the long-term security, which this service sector provides. As facts about ethical lapses and outright fraud emerge; however, the refuge that insurance companies were entrusted to provide may not be as embracing as first appears. As insurance CEOs and management teams are paraded before cameras into courtrooms, details about payoffs and kickbacks are disseminated, and financial reporting practices are scrutinized by authorities, public trust in this industry wanes. At best, public perception is tentative in light of recent scandals.

The insurance industry is not exempt from ethical dilemmas. To suggest otherwise would be to ignore the reaches of this industry. It is a part of the fabric of so much of life – health, property, auto, fire, to name a few. This is precisely the volatile topic that leaders in the academic and corporate world discussed at the Twelfth Annual International Conference Promoting Business Ethics held in October 26–30, 2005 at the Manhattan Campus of St. John's University strategically located in the heart of New York's Financial District.

Insurance Ethics for a More Ethical World
Research in Ethical Issues in Organizations, Volume 7, 1–7
Copyright © 2007 by Elsevier Ltd.
All rights of reproduction in any form reserved
ISSN: 1529-2096/doi:10.1016/S1529-2096(06)07001-5

The articles in this special volume of *Research in Ethical Issues in Organizations* have been selected from the many presentations at this conference. This conference is sponsored annually by the Vincentian universities in the United States: DePaul University in Chicago, Illinois; Niagara University in Niagara, New York; and St. John's University in Queens, New York. St. Vincent de Paul, the seventeenth century Roman Catholic saint who serves as the patron of these institutions, earnestly sought to remedy the plight of the casualties of self-serving commercial enterprises and individuals. DePaul did so by a disclosure and analysis of the problems experienced by the poor and proposals to alleviate their plight. Vincent's work continues today in a conference like this one where there is a synergistic effort on the part of academic and business leaders to deconstruct some of the more challenging ethical issues in the business sector and offer viable solutions to create a more ethical world.

This conference brought together the best of both worlds, resulting in a number of joint presentations by academic and business professionals, allowing for dynamism between scholarship and practice. The rich diversity of disciplines represented by the participants themselves (30 countries) enhanced the conference's international efforts to connect ethical theory and business practice.

Authors in this volume incorporate both sharp analysis and creative application. They examine delicate, sensitive ethical issues that have consumed media attention over the past few years. Some offer critically viable alternatives and suggestions for avoiding ethical lapses in the future. Others refer to insights from contemporary sources (movies and literature) in an effort not only to make poignant connections but also to demonstrate their import for the insurance industry.

Robert Cooper (Drake University, Des Moines, IA), asks the question whether or not the "extraordinary" events of 2004 have dramatically altered the insurance industry's ethical environment. In other words, are the recent activities in the insurance world indicative of a new cache of ethical issues facing the property-liability insurance industry or are they reflective of old business ethics practices recast in a new way. Cooper's paper here, "Spitzer's Allegations of Unethical/Illegal Behavior: Has the Insurance Industry's Ethical Environment Really Changed Dramatically?" received the 2005 Dean's Award from the reviewers as the best paper of the conference as well as a Special Recognition Award.

Cooper's research focuses on the events surrounding New York State Attorney General Eliot Spitzer's unmasking of unethical/illegal behavior in Marsh & McLennan, the world's largest provider of insurance brokerage and consulting services, and American International Group, Inc. (AIG), the world's largest commercial insurance company. Cooper reports on informative and strikingly interesting results from a 1989–1999–2005 survey conducted with Chartered Property Casualty Underwriter (CPCU), holders of the property-liability insurance industry's premier professional credential. After comparing the ethical issues of this highly publicized case with those regularly encountered in the insurance industry, he argues that while the context for insurance ethics might have changed, the key ethical issues have remained the same.

Mary Maury, Irene McCarthy, and Victoria Shoaf (St. John's University, Queens, NY) analyze the AIG scandal that Cooper introduces in the first article. They also received a Special Recognition Award. In their article, "AIG: Accounting and Ethical Lapses," they zero in on AIG's financial mismanagement which failed to account for loss and overrepresented its net worth. Additionally, the authors examine how AIG's CEO Maurice Greenberg, with really no sense of self-aggrandizement (they claim), violated insider trading rules encouraging traders late in the market day to buy AIG shares and pump up its price. Maury, McCarthy, and Shoaf review auditors' accounting procedures and analyze their lapses in light of corporate governance. Corporate governance, they assert, has the capacity to scrutinize financial reporting at many levels and thus promotes ethical behavior. In the end, in an age when business schools are seeking ways to help students see connections between ethical issues and the greater common good, discussion of this case, the authors would suggest, is a *sine qua non* for accounting education.

These two lead prize-winning articles might make readers pause and consider what similarities, if there are any, business ethics share with insurance ethics. James Barrese (St. John's University, Queens, NY) makes one connection by applying the perennial question about business ethics to the insurance industry in his article, "Insurance Ethics, An Oxymoron?" News about the insurance industry, Barrese demonstrates, has been rich with details about its fraudulent practices – committed not by claimants rather by industry participants. These practices, as he argues, are not limited to the violation of fiduciary relationships, perhaps because the insurance industry, unbeknownst to most, is not competitive.

Barresse appeals to the theory of corporate social responsibility (CSR) that has been in place since 1953, as a way of resolving present ethical tensions in the insurance industry. Where the emphasis of responsibility is to be placed in CSR is not always clear, on individuals or corporations or somewhere in between, is not always clear, yet CSR can serve as helpful template to resolve some of the polarities between insurance and ethics. All CSR theories, for the most part, for example, admit a basic respect for the law. Using CSR as an entry point for discussion of less apparent ethical issues facing insurance companies, namely concentration, market share persistence, interlocking ownership, and other incestuous industry practices, he illustrates how CSR might offer some insight for resolution of these ethical dilemmas.

Johannes Brinkmann (BI Norwegian School of Management, Oslo, Norway) proposes the concept of responsibility sharing as a way of framing the issues of insurance business ethics in his article "Responsibility Sharing: Elements of a Framework for Understanding Insurance Business Ethics." Responsibility, Brinkmann admits, is not an easy concept to explain, and attempts to do so by extrapolating from various appreciations of this notion and applying different concepts and typologies to the insurance industry and its customers. Shared responsibility involves shared risk and while initially challenging, could lead to a more accountable ethical environment.

Daniel E. Palmer (Kent State University, Warren, OH) addresses the exacting task of determining and assigning risk to potential insurance customers in his article "Insurance, Risk Assessment, and Fairness: An Ethical Analysis." While Barresse appeals to CSR theories, Palmer defers to the notion of fairness as a possible category from which to address ethical lapses in the insurance industry. Generally, Palmer admits this task involves considering the requested insurance programs, and then consulting statistical models for situating the individual's needs and concerns. This process, Palmer contends, is not without problems, both practical and philosophical ones, and turns to questions of fairness to address potential dilemmas. He deconstructs the present statistical risk assessment process and then argues the attributes of these structures must *fairly* represent the individual qua individual. Using philosophical understandings of the notion of "fairness," he seeks to weed out any statistical discrimination inherent in this classification process. In the end, Palmer offers both a helpful critique of the risk assessment process and provides a broader framework of ethical analysis for those in the insurance and regulation industry.

Joseph Heath (University of Toronto, Ontario, Canada) complements Palmer's article in discussing what he considers the most polarizing issue of insurance ethics: risk assessment. Heath's "Reasonable Restrictions on Underwriting" discusses two distinct approaches to risk classification. The first is the pure economical one that relies on a cost–benefit analysis to determine an appropriate rate. Quite contrarily, on another front, the author suggests, there are those philosophically grounded concerns with civil rights law that propose a standard fare for everyone. After discussing these extremes, Heath proposes a more limited right to underwrite, "one that grants the legitimacy of the central principle of risk classification, but permits specific deviations from that ideal when other important social goods are at stake."

Alfonso Oddo (Niagara University, Niagara University, NY), in his article, "Health Insurance: Economic and Ethical Issues," isolates what he understands to be the more critical economic and ethical issues in the health care insurance industry. Oddo surveys the landscape of health care spending and the huge increasing economic demands it is making on consumers as well as insurers. As he admits, it is becoming more and more difficult to offer quality health care at reasonable cost, and examines the cost of health care from a perspective of the institutions and individuals responsible for paying the premiums. This leads him to ponder the role of insurance in light of medical care provision for the insured and uninsured. One irony is that even if employees do have insurance, they are not always guaranteed what they need. Health care's rising costs create difficulties for everyone, particularly as employers are increasingly decreasing their own participate share. That may, as Oddo hedges, result in greater intervention by the U.S. government and result in the kinds of health care reform pursued in Canada and Europe.

Chalmer E. Labig (Oklahoma State University, Stillwater, OK) and Kenneth Zantow (University of Southern Mississippi, Long Beach, MS) extend Oddo's argument by addressing a relatively new issue in the health care insurance industry in their paper "A Medical Dilemma: How Should Physicians Respond to Patients' Questions About Pay?" The traditional dynamics of relationships between doctor, patient, and insurance company have been transformed with the introduction of managed care organizations (MCOs). MCOs reward doctors with financial incentives to ensure a given MCO's fiscal viability. This paper examines the ethical implications of these new fiduciary configurations from the perspective of patients who participate in these MCOs. Labig and Zantow's conclusions indicate that patients understand these incentives quite differently from health management personnel. From the patients' perspectives, they understand that these physicians pay incentives as perfectly ethical practices, as part of patient satisfaction and clinical expertise, when in fact they are based on revenue generation. Quite an interesting ethical dilemma in light of the introduction of recent pay disclosure regulations!

Kyoko Fukukawa (Bradford University School of Management, UK) together with Christine Ennew and Steve Diacon (Nottingham University Business School, UK) hone in on the customer perceptions, Labig and

Zantow refer to earlier. These authors present the results of their research seeking to understand why customers engage in aberrant consumer behavior (ACB) and how these actions can be a response to *perceptions* of corporate unfairness. The authors make clear that while consumers' judgments of the unfairness of the insurance industry may only be perceptions, they offer an evaluative window on the ethicalness of corporate activity in terms of pricing, product attributes, and customer relationships.

The next paper, "At the Movies with the Healthcare Industry," moves the ethical deception in the health insurance industry to the Hollywood screen. Minnette A. Bumpus (Howard University, Washington, DC) readily admits that motion pictures provide a valuable service by generating conversation about ethical issues. Films can enhance both undergraduate and graduate level teaching by demonstrating management concepts such as planning, decision-making, ethics and conflict resolution in ways, perhaps, a lecture cannot. Films like Winer's *Damaged Care* (2002), Cassavetes' *John Q* (2002), and Coppola's *The Rainmaker* (1997) that cast the health care insurance in a very unfavorable light offer viewers an opportunity to see decision-makers grapple with ethical dilemmas in particular settings. Bumpus offers not only a critical analysis of these three films but also practical strategies on how to incorporate them into the classroom. She concludes with suggestions on how environmental response strategies can be used to improve public perceptions of the health care industry.

Robert Lauder (St. John's University, Queens, NY) proposes the medical doctor and twentieth century novelist Walker Percy as a "prophetic figure for profit-makers." Lauder concedes that deferring to a novelist for insight into ethical behavior in the corporate world might be a stretch, but he is convinced that a review of Percy's work can offer much needed and, for far-too-long neglected, wisdom into appreciating the inestimable value of the human person. There is a value in attending to this "voice crying out in the desert" of what can be a reckless ethical environment in business. As Lauder demonstrates in his review of Walker Percy's work, the bottom line in business should not concentrate on profit margins, but in human persons living and working together respecting their and each others' meaningfulness and authenticity.

Martin Lecker (Rockland Community College, Suffern, NY) then examines a scintillating topic – "Workplace Romances: A Platonic Perspective." It is also a tenuous matter as people, like Boeing's CEO Harry C. Stonecipher, have been known to lose their jobs for engaging in relationships with co-workers while others risk demotion, dismissal, or sidelining. Lecker considers the dating policies of the 48 insurance companies that are part of the Fortune

500, if, in fact, there are any. He also reports his findings of a survey of 235 employees in the insurance industry in which he solicited observations about workplace romances, both positive and negative perceptions. Using Plato as a referent, he then considers the import this foundational philosopher offers to workplace romances concerning moderation, pleasure, happiness, and the good life. In the end, Lecker builds on his research and borrows from current literature to offer a viable code of ethics for the dynamics of romantic relationships in the workplace.

The papers selected for this volume of *Research in Ethical Issues in Organization* (REIO) represent the diversity, quality, and excellence of the conference presentations. A word of thanks is due to the conference coordinators: Marilynn Fleckenstein of Niagara University, Mary Maury of St. John's University, Patrick Primeaux, S.M. of St. John's University, and Patricia Werhane of DePaul University.

We are grateful to Moses Pava of Yeshiva University (New York), the series editor of REIO, for his ongoing participation in, and steady support of, the conference and for his invitation for us to serve as guest editors of this special volume. Gratitude is also extended to Ellen Thrower, Executive Director of the School of Risk Management, and Paul Lazauskas, Director of Conference Services (Manhattan Campus), of St. John's University for their generous participation and coordination of the logistics of this successful conference.

SPITZER'S ALLEGATIONS OF UNETHICAL/ILLEGAL BEHAVIOR: HAS THE INSURANCE INDUSTRY'S ETHICAL ENVIRONMENT REALLY CHANGED DRAMATICALLY?

Robert W. Cooper

ABSTRACT

Occasional, highly publicized examples of unethical behavior by executives of major businesses such as the unethical/illegal brokerage and financial reporting practices uncovered recently by New York Attorney General Eliot Spitzer's investigation of the insurance industry may be thought to have arisen from some rather unique set of ethical problems that differ significantly from the ethical dilemmas encountered daily by those working in the business. In reality, they did not. Instead, these highly publicized unethical activities on the part of leading brokerage firms and insurers are shown to be attributable to several of the same key ethical issues identified repeatedly by insurance professionals as presenting the greatest ethical challenges for those working in the insurance industry over the last decade and a half.

Insurance Ethics for a More Ethical World
Research in Ethical Issues in Organizations, Volume 7, 9–38
ISSN: 1529-2096/doi:10.1016/S1529-2096(06)07002-7

INTRODUCTION

Just like those employed in other areas of business, those working in the insurance industry face a variety of ethical dilemmas on a daily basis and often encounter various factors that present challenges to their efforts to resolve these dilemmas in an ethical manner. Likewise, just as other areas of business face occasional, sensational and highly publicized examples of unethical behavior by major corporations, so does the insurance industry. For example, during the last decade, many major companies in the U.S. life insurance industry faced (and settled) hundreds of millions of dollars in class action lawsuits and suffered a loss of the public trust due to alleged misrepresentation in the sale of vanishing premium life insurance products.

This decade, it has been the property-liability insurance industry's turn to face charges of unethical/illegal behavior on the part of its largest insurance companies and brokerage firms. The turmoil that began with a civil suit brought against the world's largest provider of insurance brokerage and consulting services, Marsh & McLennan Companies, by New York Attorney General Eliot Spitzer in October 2004 spread rapidly as many of the property-liability industry's largest brokerage firms and insurance companies also faced investigations and subsequent allegations of fraud and anti-competitive behavior for participating in a variety of bid rigging schemes and other unethical/illegal marketing-related activities. Responses to these charges led to ousters and resignations of key executives, more than a dozen criminal indictments and guilty pleas, numerous class-action lawsuits, settlements in which brokers have been required to return more than $1 billion to clients, and mass layoffs (Dankwa, 2006). Subsequently, a civil suit filed against the world's largest commercial insurance company, American International Group, Inc. (AIG), by Spitzer and New York Superintendent of Insurance Howard Mills in May 2005, alleging a number of types of improper financial reporting, not only led to ousters and resignations of key executives of AIG and other companies involved in the alleged activities, agreements by several executives to plead guilty to conspiracy to file false financial statements and other related charges, and a number of class-action lawsuits filed against AIG by its employees and others, but also resulted in a restatement of AIG's financial reports for 2000 through 2004 that produced a $3.924 billion (10.4 percent) reduction in net income for the 5-year period and a $2.264 billion (2.7 percent) reduction in its stockholders' equity in 2004 (Hulburt, 2005).

After describing more specifically the types of unethical/illegal behavior alleged in Spitzer's suits against leading insurers and brokerage firms, the paper reports the findings of a survey conducted during September 2005 with the assistance of the Chartered Property Casualty Underwriter (CPCU) Society and compares them with the findings of similar surveys of CPCUs – holders of the property-liability insurance industry's premier professional credential, the CPCU designation – conducted in 1989 and 1999 (Cooper & Frank, 1990, 2001) in an effort to examine the three following issues regarding the industry's changing ethical environment:

• What do insurance professionals perceive as being the key ethical issues facing those working in the property-liability insurance industry today and how do they relate to the unethical/illegal activities uncovered by Spitzer's investigation of the insurance industry?
• Has this last year of extraordinary turmoil associated with the allegations arising from Spitzer's investigation appeared to have brought about a change in the key ethical issues experienced by those working in the in-dustry today as compared with those faced by CPCUs six years ago?
• Has this last year of extraordinary turmoil associated with the allegations arising from Spitzer's investigation changed the perceptions of insurance professionals regarding the extent to which the key ethical issues are viewed as presenting problems for those working in the industry?

ALLEGED UNETHICAL/ILLEGAL INSURANCE BROKERAGE PRACTICES

Initial Charges – Marsh

From the time New York Attorney General Spitzer (2004b) filed a civil suit on October 14, 2004 against Marsh & McLennan Companies and Marsh, Inc. (Marsh) alleging "widespread fraud and antitrust violations in the procurement and broking of insurance" (Spitzer, 2004a, p.5), unethical/illegal behavior on the part of the largest brokers and insurers in the U.S. property-liability insurance industry has been a frequent topic of often heated discussion not only among those working in the industry, but also on the part of other important constituencies, especially insurance regulators and legislators, com-mercial lines customers, and the press (Stewart, 2005). The principal charges leveled against Marsh in Spitzer's suit (Spitzer, 2004b) were that Marsh:

• failed to serve the best interest of its clients as a result of conflicts of interest arising out of "contingent commissions" received from certain insurance companies for steering client business to them;

- disclosed the "contingent commission" arrangements to its clients in a false and misleading manner;
- conspired with certain large insurers to unreasonably restrain trade and commerce by, among other things:
  - providing clients seeking to purchase primary insurance with collusive, fictitious or otherwise non-competitive bids or other terms of sale;
  - allocating the opportunity to sell, and the sale of, insurance to clients; and
  - creating a scheme to pay Marsh to implement the unlawful conspiracy.
- engaged in various forms of bid rigging, such as:
  - the submission of fictitious or artificially inflated bids to create an illusion of competition among insurers;
  - arranging for insurers to refrain from bidding on certain accounts to limit competition; and
  - not shopping business that came up for renewal to guarantee the insurance remained with the current carrier.
- misrepresented services provided to its clients by claiming to consider the client's best interest in all placements, and to serve as the client's advocate and represent them, not the insurance companies, in negotiations.

Fig. 1 illustrates the most common situation uncovered by Spitzer's investigation of Marsh. As indicated, Marsh disclosed contingent commission agreements to clients in a false and misleading manner, secured fictitious or artificially inflated bids in order to create an illusion of competition among insurance carriers, and then, steered client business to selected insurers.

At the heart of Spitzer's allegations of fraud and anti-competitive behavior was Marsh's receipt of contingent payments resulting from placement service agreements (PSAs) and market service agreements (MSAs) entered into with certain major insurance companies. Despite important differences, Spitzer's complaint referred to Marsh's PSAs and MSAs as "contingent commissions," creating considerable confusion and attracting sharp criticism from the insurance industry where the term had been used for many years. With traditional contingent commission arrangements where payments have increasingly reflected primarily the underwriting profitability of the business placed with an insurer, the amount of a producer's commission under the arrangement could not be determined at the time of placement. Rather, the commission amount was contingent on a future assessment of the profitability of the business placed with the insurer as well as any changes in the contingent commission arrangement's terms made by the insurer between the time of placement and the time the amount of the commission was actually determined.

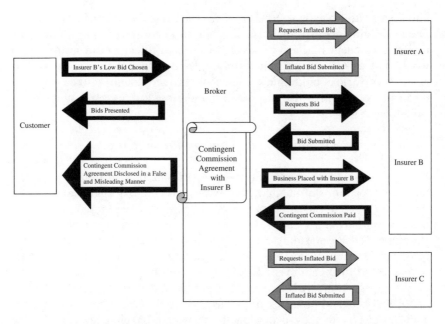

Fig. 1. The Most Common Situation Uncovered by Spitzer's Investigation of Marsh – the Disclosure of Contingent Commission Agreements to Customers in a False and Misleading Manner Combined with Securing Fictitious or Artificially Inflated Bids in Order to Create an Illusion of Competition among Insurance Carriers.

In contrast, Marsh's PSA and MSA payments tend to have been based on premium volume or growth. Under these terms, the commission amounts were not contingent in the traditional sense because they could be determined (or at least, closely estimated) at the time business was placed with the insurer. For example, exhibits to Spitzer's complaint indicated that the 2003 PSA with AIG risk management called for AIG to provide Marsh with a bonus of 2 percent of gross written premium for guaranteed cost new business and 3 percent of gross written premium for loss sensitive new business. For renewals, AIG agreed to pay a sliding scale of 1, 2 or 3 percent of renewal premiums depending upon whether Marsh's "renewal growth rate" was over 85, 90 or 95 percent, respectively. The PSA required AIG to provide Marsh with payment statements monthly and payments on a quarterly basis.

While "contingent commissions" were at the heart of Spitzer's allegations against Marsh, PSA and MSA payments alone were not sufficient grounds for the civil charges brought against Marsh for the fraudulent and anti-competitive behavior. Rather, it was their disclosure to clients in a false and misleading manner, their use in an unlawful conspiracy to restrain trade that steered client business to selected insurers rather than to insurers that would best serve the client's interests, and the incentive they provided for the creation of various bid rigging schemes by brokers to ensure their payment by insurers that provided the legal foundation for Spitzer's suit against Marsh.

Subsequent Charges – Universal Life Resources

While predominantly involving the property-liability insurance industry, Spitzer's allegations of unethical behavior involving bid rigging and lack of disclosure of "contingent commissions" spread to the employee benefits business on November 12, 2004 when a suit was filed against Universal Life Resources (ULR), a leading employee benefits consulting firm that provided brokerage services to Fortune 1000 corporations seeking group insurance coverages for their employees. Similar to the suit filed earlier against Marsh, this suit alleged that ULR had engaged in repeated and persistent fraudulent and illegal acts and practices, and conspired to unreasonably restrain trade and commerce, thereby depriving its clients and their employees of the opportunity to purchase insurance through the competitive process they desired and which ULR represented that it would provide (Spitzer, 2004c). More specifically, the principal charges were that ULR:

• failed to serve the best interest of its clients as a result of conflicts of interest arising out of undisclosed override payments and inflated communication fees received from certain insurance companies for steering client business to them;
• refused to disclose and instructed insurers not to disclose override payments and inflated communication fees to clients, and instructed insurers not to report these hidden payments on Schedule A of their annual statement;
• agreed with insurers to build the undisclosed fees paid by the insurers into the premiums charged to employees who purchased supplemental insurance;
• engaged in anti-competitive practices by colluding with select insurers to steer commercial clients' employee benefits programs to those insurers in exchange for payment of undisclosed override payments and inflated communication fees; declined to place business with insurers that refused to either enter into or refrain from disclosing these arrangements with ULR; and

- misrepresented services provided to their clients by claiming to consider their client's best interest in all placements; to serve as their client's advocate and represent them, not the insurance companies, in negotiations; and to recommend the carrier best suited to underwrite, administer and service the employee benefits program for the client's needs.

Fig. 2 illustrates the most common situation uncovered by Spitzer's investigation of ULR. As indicated, ULR entered into side agreements for override payments and inflated communication services fees with certain insurers, did not disclose these agreements to clients, instructed insurers not to disclose the override payments and inflated communication fees to clients and not to report them on Schedule A, directed business to insurers that participated in these arrangements, and refused to deal with insurers that did not comply with these arrangements.

ALLEGED IMPROPER INSURER FINANCIAL REPORTING

Just as the furor over the troublesome ethical situation in the brokerage segment of the industry began to die down in the spring of 2005, further findings of Spitzer's investigation of the insurance industry led to allegations of serious unethical/illegal activity in the management of some major insurance and reinsurance companies, especially with regard to the accuracy of their financial reporting activities. For example, in a suit (Spitzer & Mills, 2005) filed May 26, 2005 against AIG, along with both its recent Chairman and CEO Maurice "Hank" Greenberg and its recent CFO Howard Smith, Spitzer was joined by New York Superintendent of Insurance Howard Mills in alleging the defendants:

- in an effort to support the firm's stock price, engaged in at least two sham reinsurance transactions to give the investing public the impression that AIG had a larger cushion of reserves to pay claims than it actually did – transactions that Greenberg personally proposed and negotiated in phone calls with the then CEO of General Reinsurance Corporation, Inc. ("GenRe");
- hid losses from its insurance underwriting business by converting underwriting losses to capital losses;
- created false underwriting income – a scheme personally approved by Greenberg and Smith that involved falsely reporting the income from the purchase of life insurance policies as underwriting income;

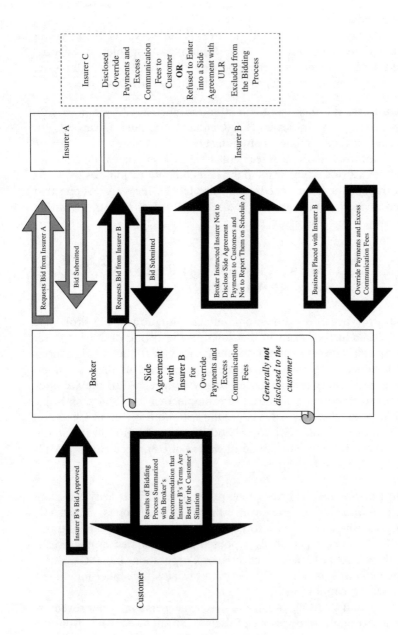

Fig. 2. The Most Common Situation Uncovered by Spitzer's Investigation of URL – Side Agreements for Override Payments and Inflated Communication Services Fees are not Disclosed to Customers by the Broker, Insurers are Instructed by the Broker not to Disclose these Additional Payments and Fees to Customers, Business is Directed to Insurers that Participate in these Arrangements, and the Broker will not Deal with Insurers that Refuse to Comply with these Arrangements.

- had for decades deliberately booked workers compensation insurance premiums as regular liability insurance revenue in an effort to reduce AIG's contributions to the state workers compensation system and avoid paying state taxes on those premiums; and
- repeatedly deceived the New York Insurance Department and other state regulators about its relationships with several offshore affiliate reinsurers.

THE PROPERTY-LIABILITY INSURANCE INDUSTRY'S CURRENT ETHICAL ENVIRONMENT

With the allegations of unethical/illegal behavior in the property-liability insurance industry having ranged far beyond the initial charges related to brokerage activities, the author approached the CPCU Society with a proposal to survey a sample of its members in an effort to determine whether this last year of extraordinary turmoil appeared to have changed the perceptions of insurance professionals regarding the key ethical issues facing those working in the industry.

2005 Survey Participants

Information regarding the property-liability insurance industry's current ethical environment was gathered using a 2-page questionnaire mailed to 3,000 CPCUs during September 2005. The 3,000 survey participants were selected from a list of CPCU Society members organized by functional title, reflecting the member's type of business, level of position and job function. Participants were selected at random from among the various functional title groups in proportion to the relative number of Society members in each group.

Completed surveys were received from 485 participants producing an overall response rate of 16 percent which was considerably lower than those experienced in past CPCU ethical issues surveys – response rates of 54 percent (810 responses from 1,500 CPCUs surveyed) obtained in the 1989 survey and 30 percent (451 responses from 1,500 CPCUs surveyed) in the 1999 survey. This low response rate was anticipated based on the authors' recent experiences with similar mail surveys conducted in other professions. While the response rate is too low to permit generalizations to be made regarding the views of all Society members, the findings are grounded in a sufficient number of responses to provide a sense of the ethical environment currently encountered in the property-liability insurance industry.

The Questionnaire

Since the principal purpose of the survey was to provide an indication of the key ethical issues and dilemmas facing the property-liability insurance industry today based on the perceptions of CPCUs in a variety of positions in the industry, the bulk of the survey form consisted of a list of 32 ethics-related statements that are reproduced in Table 1. The individuals surveyed were asked to rate each statement on a 5-point scale where 5 meant that it is a major problem today in the property-liability insurance industry and 1 meant that it is not a problem today in the industry.

The list of statements included in the survey form was identical to that contained in both the 1989 and 1999 questionnaires. Since the 32 statements included in the survey instrument are varied in their form of presentation (some reflect ethical conflicts that may be faced, many reflect unethical behaviors in response to ethical dilemmas, and a few are general situations which may give rise to ethical dilemmas as well as other problems), these statements will be referred to as "issues" to simplify the discussion in this paper.

Business versus Professional Issues

The first 28 issues listed in Table 1 reflect ethical issues and dilemmas facing businesses and their employees in general. However, professionals, particularly those who work with clients, also face a variety of other ethical issues arising out of the fiduciary nature of the professional–client relationship. This fiduciary relationship recognizes both the superior knowledge that professionals have and the role of client consent in the decision-making process. The professional analyzes the client's problem(s), formulates alternative courses of action, makes recommendations, and helps carry out the client's decision; the client, in turn, agrees or disagrees with the options and recommendations presented by the professional. Because the client must rely on and thus, trust the professional to provide informed options and recommendations that are in the client's best interest, the professional has special obligations to ensure that the trust is justified. These obligations give rise to a number of ethical responsibilities owed by professionals to their clients such as, keeping current with one's field, not undertaking tasks for which one lacks competence, being loyal to the client's interests and remaining independent and objective in one's judgment. Issues 29 through 32 were included in the survey form to provide an indication of how CPCUs, as professionals, view ethical issues of special relevance to professionals as compared with ethical issues of concern to businesses and their employees in general.

Table 1. CPCU Ethics Issues Survey Findings – All Respondents.

Issue	1989 Study		1999 Study		2005 Study		
	Mean	Rank	Mean	Rank	Mean	Rank	% 3, 4 or 5
1 Failure to provide products and services of the highest quality in the eyes of the customer	3.35*,**	3	2.70	8	2.61	7	50.4
2 Failure to provide prompt, honest responses to customer inquiries and requests	3.20*,**	4	2.91**	4	2.68	5	53.3
3 Making disparaging remarks about competitors, their products or their employees or agents	2.26	14	2.56†	10	2.56†	9	48.2
4 Misuse of proprietary information	1.87	24	2.16†	15	2.17†	20	32.4
5 Misuse of sensitive information belonging to others	1.80	27	2.14†	19	2.08†	23	30.0
6 Improper methods of gathering competitors' information	1.91	23	2.06†	22	2.08†	23	28.3
7 False or misleading representation of products or services in marketing, advertising or sales efforts	2.76	6	2.73	6	2.60	8	50.0
8 Conflicts between opportunities for personal financial gain (or other personal benefits) and proper performance of one's responsibilities	2.74	8	2.72	7	2.93†,*	3	60.5
9 Conflicts of interest involving business or financial relationships with customers, suppliers or competitors that influence, or appear to influence, one's ability to carry out his or her responsibilities	2.37	13	2.46	11	2.78†,*	4	55.5

Table 1. (*Continued*)

Issue	1989 Study		1999 Study		2005 Study		
	Mean	Rank	Mean	Rank	Mean	Rank	% 3, 4 or 5
10 Conflicts of interest involving the marketing of products and services competing with those of one's own company	1.92	22	2.08†	21	2.20†	17	34.3
11 Conflicts of interest that involve working for a competitor, customer or supplier without approval	1.68	31	1.72	31	1.77	30	17.7
12 Misuse of company assets/property	1.97	20	2.15†	17	2.20†	17	33.7
13 Insider trading/other security trading problems	1.85	26	1.89	30	2.19†,*	19	32.0
14 Giving excessive gifts or entertainment	1.87	24	2.01†	23	2.26†,*	15	36.6
15 Receiving excessive gifts or entertainment	1.78	29	1.96†	26	2.23†,*	16	36.2
16 Offering or soliciting payments or contributions for the purpose of influencing customers or suppliers	1.77	30	1.90	29	2.15†,*	21	31.4
17 Offering or soliciting payments or contributions for the purpose of influencing government officials	1.79	28	1.95†	27	2.05†	25	28.2
18 Offering or soliciting payments or contributions for the purpose of obtaining, giving or keeping business	2.04	18	2.15	17	2.35†,*	14	39.2
19 Offering or soliciting payments or contributions for the purpose of	1.30	32	1.40	32	1.62†,*	32	12.0

persuading employees of another company to fail to perform, or improperly perform, their duties

20 Offering or soliciting payments or contributions for the purpose of influencing legislation or regulations	1.97	20	2.16†	15	2.15†	21	33.0
21 Inaccuracy of books, records or reports	2.48*	10	2.30	13	2.55*	10	46.6
22 Abuse of expense accounts	2.23	16	2.44†	12	2.43†	13	44.3
23 Antitrust issues	2.45*,**	11	1.92	28	2.02	26	27.4
24 Relations with local communities	2.64*,**	9	2.12**	20	1.88	28	23.0
25 Office/agency closings and layoffs	2.41	12	3.04†,**	3	2.45	12	43.4
26 Discrimination	2.10	17	2.26†,**	14	1.95	27	25.4
27 Drug and alcohol abuse	2.25*,**	15	1.98**	25	1.69	31	15.5
28 Employee theft	1.99**	19	2.00**	24	1.80	29	15.9
29 Lack of knowledge or skills to competently perform one's duties	3.39**	2	3.31**	1	2.95	2	63.6
30 Failure to identify the customer's needs and recommend products and services that meet those needs	3.41*,**	1	3.20**	2	3.04	1	68.2
31 Failure to be objective with others in one's business dealings	2.75**	7	2.66	9	2.52	11	46.8
32 Misrepresenting or concealing limitations in one's abilities to provide services	2.88**	5	2.89**	5	2.67	6	50.7

* = significantly greater than the 1999 CPCU study value at the .05 level.
** = significantly greater than the 2005 CPCU study value at the .05 level.
† = significantly greater than the 1989 CPCU study value at the .05 level.

In addition to the 32 issues to be rated, the survey form also contained two open-ended questions. First, survey participants were asked to indicate (and rate on a 5-point scale) any other ethical issues not already listed in the form that present problems in the property-liability insurance industry. Also, they were asked to indicate what they feel is the most important specific ethics problem or issue facing those who work in the property-liability insurance industry today. These two questions were included principally to provide a crosscheck on the completeness of the list of 32 ethical issues and on the ratings provided for those issues.

Finally, participants were asked to indicate whether they were a senior manager, middle manager or not in management, and whether they work in an agency, brokerage, insurance company, reinsurance or other type of organization. These questions were included to permit an analysis of whether the perceptions of the key ethical issues differed significantly by level within the organization and/or the type of organization within which respondents work.

Survey Findings – All Respondents

Table 1 shows the mean ratings for each of the 32 ethical issues based on the individual ratings given to each issue by all of the CPCUs responding to the 2005 survey (as well as those for the 1989 and 1999 surveys to be discussed later). The table also shows the rank of each issue based on the size of the issue's mean rating. Finally, the table indicates the percentage of the respondents who rated each issue 3, 4 or 5. Thus, for example, Issue 1 (failure to provide products and services of the highest quality in the eyes of the customer) was rated 2.61 on average by all survey respondents, had the seventh highest mean rating among the 32 ethical issues listed in the survey form, and was rated 3, 4 or 5 by 50.4 percent of the respondents.

Eleven ethical issues received mean ratings greater than 2.50. All these issues were rated 3, 4 or 5 by 46 percent or more of the CPCUs responding to the survey and 8 received these ratings from 50 percent or more of the respondents, suggesting that they are perceived as presenting real problems for the industry. In descending rank by mean rating, these 11 key ethical issues are:

• failure to identify the customer's needs and recommend products and services that meet those needs (Issue 30);
• lack of knowledge or skills to competently perform one's duties (Issue 29);

- pursuit of personal financial gain or other personal benefits interfering with the proper performance of one's duties (Issue 8);
- conflicts of interest involving business or financial relationships with customers, suppliers or competitors that influence, or appear to influence, one's ability to carry out his or her responsibilities (Issue 9);
- failure to provide prompt, honest responses to customer inquiries and requests (Issue 2);
- misrepresenting or concealing limitations in one's abilities to provide services (Issue 32);
- failure to provide products and services of the highest quality in the eyes of the customer (Issue 1);
- false or misleading representation of products or services in marketing, advertising or sales efforts (Issue 7);
- making disparaging remarks about competitors, their products or their employees or agents (Issue 3);
- inaccuracy of books, records or reports (Issue 21); and
- failure to be objective with others in one's business dealings (Issue 31).

As might be expected, the CPCUs responding to the survey rated two of the issues related to the ethical responsibilities of professionals, but not of businesses and their employees in general (Issues 30 and 29), as being on average of greatest concern to the industry today. The other two issues directly related to professional ethical responsibilities (Issues 32 and 31) were also rated among the top-eleven ethical issues facing those currently working in the property-liability insurance industry. As shown in Table 2, two of these professional issues – failure to identify the customer's needs and recommend products and services that meet those needs (Issue 30), and failure to be objective with others in one's business dealings (Issue 31) – encompass several examples of the unethical/illegal activities engaged in by Marsh and ULR as they breached their promises to work for their clients' best interests.

Seven issues of interest to businesses and their employees in general also qualified as key ethical issues by being rated on average greater than 2.50 by the CPCUs responding to the survey. As shown in Table 2, various unethical/illegal activities engaged in by Marsh and ULR are closely related to five of these seven key ethical issues (Issues 1, 2, 7, 8 and 9). Moreover, Table 2 indicates that two of the seven key ethical issues of interest to businesses and their employees in general describe certain aspects of the unethical/illegal behavior alleged in the AIG suit – inaccuracy of books, records and reports (Issue 21) and pursuit of personal financial gain or other personal benefits

Table 2. Relationship between the Unethical Activities Uncovered by Spitzer's Investigation of Marsh, ULR and AIG and Eight of the Eleven Key Ethical Issues Identified in the 2005 CPCU Study.

Key Ethical Issues	Marsh – Contingent Commission Arrangements	ULR – Undisclosed Override Payments and Communication Fees	AIG – Improper Financial Reporting
Failure to provide products and services of the highest quality in the eyes of the customer (Issue 1)	- Steering business to preferred insurers rather than to those who would serve the best interests of the client - Colluded with select insurers to steer commercial clients' business to pre-selected insurers by avoiding, limiting, misrepresenting and/or rigging bids	- Steering business to preferred insurers rather than to those who would serve the best interests of the client - Colluded with select insurers to steer commercial clients' business to those insurers in exchange for payment of undisclosed override payments and communication fees - Ceased doing business with insurers who refused to make the required payments and/or who disclosed them to clients	
Failure to provide prompt, honest responses to customer inquiries and requests (Issue 2)	- Described contingent commission arrangements to clients and the public in a false and misleading manner	- Refusal to disclose override payments and communication fees to clients - Instructed insurers not to disclose these payments and fees to customers	
False or misleading representation of products or services in marketing, advertising or sales efforts (Issue 7)	- Described contingent commission arrangements to clients and the public in a false and misleading manner - Misrepresented services	- Agreeing with insurers to build undisclosed payments and fees paid by the insurers into the premiums charged to employees who purchased	

Conflicts between opportunities for personal financial gain (or other personal benefits) and proper performance of one's responsibilities (Issue 8)	promised to their clients, such as to serve their best interests in insurance placements, serve as clients' advocates in negotiations, and recommend the carrier best suited to underwrite, administer and service the insurance program based on the client's needs - Conflict between steering business to preferred insurers in exchange for contingent commissions and recommending those insurers who would serve the best interests of the client	supplemental insurance - Misrepresented services promised to their clients, such as to serve their best interests in insurance placements, serve as clients' advocates in negotiations, and recommend the carrier best suited to underwrite, administer and service the insurance program based on the client's needs - Conflict between steering business to preferred insurers in exchange for payment of undisclosed override payments and communication fees and recommending those insurers who would serve the best interests of the client	- In an effort to support the firm's stock price, engaged in at least two sham reinsurance transactions to give the investing public the impression that AIG had a larger cushion of reserves to pay claims than was actually the case
Conflicts of interest involving business or financial relationships with customers, suppliers or competitors that influence, or appear to influence, one's ability to carry out his or her responsibilities (Issue 9)	- Conflict between steering business to preferred insurers in exchange for contingent commissions and recommending those insurers who would serve the best interests of the client	- Conflict between steering business to preferred insurers in exchange for payment of undisclosed override payments and communication fees and recommending those insurers who would serve the best interests of the client	- In an effort to support the firm's stock price, engaged in at least two sham reinsurance transactions to give the investing public the
Inaccuracy of books, records or reports (Issue 21)			

Table 2. (*Continued*)

Key Ethical Issues	Marsh – Contingent Commission Arrangements	ULR – Undisclosed Override Payments and Communication Fees	AIG – Improper Financial Reporting
			impression that AIG had a larger cushion of reserves to pay claims than was actually the case - Hid losses from its insurance underwriting business by converting underwriting losses to capital losses - Created false underwriting income – a scheme that involved falsely reporting the income from the purchase of life insurance policies as underwriting income - Deliberately booked workers compensation insurance premiums as regular liability insurance revenue in an effort to reduce AIG's contributions to the state workers compensation system and avoid paying state taxes on those premiums - Repeatedly deceived the New York Insurance Department and other state regulators about its relationships with several offshore affiliate reinsurers

Failure to identify the customer's needs and recommend products and services that meet those needs (Issue 30)	- Steering business to preferred insurers rather than to those who would serve the best interests of the client - Misrepresented services promised to their clients, such as to serve their best interests in insurance placements, serve as clients' advocates in negotiations, and recommend the carrier best suited to underwrite, administer and service the insurance program based on the clients' needs - Colluded with select insurers to steer commercial clients' business to pre-selected insurers by avoiding, limiting, misrepresenting and/or rigging bids	- Steering business to preferred insurers rather than to those who would serve the best interests of the client - Misrepresented services promised to their clients, such as to serve their best interests in insurance placements, serve as clients' advocates in negotiations, and recommend the carrier best suited to underwrite, administer and service the insurance program based on the clients' needs - Colluded with select insurers to steer commercial clients' business to those insurers in exchange for payment of undisclosed override payments and communication fees
Failure to be objective with others in one's business dealings (Issue 31)	- Steering business to preferred insurers rather than to those who would serve the best interests of the client	- Steering business to preferred insurers rather than to those who would serve the best interests of the client - Ceased doing business with insurers who refused to make the required payments and/or who disclosed them to clients

interfering with the proper performance of one's duties (Issue 8). With regard to the latter issue, the suit filed by Spitzer and Mills against AIG pointed out that the alleged fraudulent financial reporting undertaken in an effort to support the price of AIG's stock reflected a conflict of interest involving personal financial gain in that "both Greenberg and Smith had a direct personal interest in AIG's stock price; both held hundreds of thousands of shares of AIG stock. For example, the value of Greenberg's holdings increased or decreased approximately $65 million for every dollar AIG stock moved" (Spitzer & Mills, 2005, p. 2).

While the remaining 21 issues were not viewed as presenting particularly significant problems for those working in the industry by as large a percentage of the respondents as was the case for the key ethical issues, all but the four lowest ranked (Issues 11, 19, 27 and 28) were rated 3, 4 or 5 by 20 percent or more of the respondents, and 12 of the 21 lowest ranked issues received this rating from 30 percent or more of those CPCUs responding to the survey. This suggests that these issues, while not viewed as presenting particularly widespread problems, are sufficiently pervasive that they should not be ignored by management. Managers and supervisors need to be alert to identify and handle, on an individual basis, those situations that present reasonably significant challenges to ethical behavior in the workplace.

Survey Findings for Different Groups of CPCUs

Although the findings discussed previously indicated how all the CPCUs responding to the 2005 survey perceived the various ethical issues overall, they did not indicate whether different groups of respondents had different perceptions of the extent to which a particular issue presented problems for those working in the industry. Table 3 indicates where perceptions of key ethical issues differed significantly among CPCUs responding to the survey who are involved in different functions, at different organization levels and in different types of business organizations.

A COMPARISON WITH THE 1989 AND 1999 SURVEY FINDINGS

Table 1 provides a comparison of findings of the issue means and ranks for all respondents to the 1989, 1999 and 2005 surveys. Several points regarding the findings of the three studies are noteworthy. First, while differences do exist in the order of the 32 ethical issues based on their means, the

Table 3. 2005 Study Findings for Different Groups of CPCUs.

Key Ethical Issues	Functions – Underwriting, Claims, Marketing and Risk Management	Organization Levels – Senior Management, Middle Management and Not in Management	Types of Business Organizations – Agency, Brokerage Firm and Insurance Company
Failure to provide products and services of the highest quality in the eyes of the customer (Issue 1)	Marketing and Risk Management Groups perceived this issue as presenting significantly greater problems than did the Claims Group	Not in Management Group perceived this issue as presenting significantly greater problems than did the Middle Management Group	Brokerage Firm Group perceived this issue as presenting significantly greater problems than did the Insurance Company Group
Failure to provide prompt, honest responses to customer inquiries and requests (Issue 2)			
Making disparaging remarks about competitors, their products or their employees or agents (Issue 3)	Marketing and Underwriting Groups perceived this issue as presenting significantly greater problems than did the Claims Group		
False or misleading representation of products or services in marketing, advertising or sales efforts (Issue 7)			
Conflicts between opportunities for personal financial gain (or other personal benefits) and proper performance of one's responsibilities (Issue 8)			
Conflicts of interest involving business or financial relationships			Brokerage Firm Group perceived this issue as

Table 3. (*Continued*)

Key Ethical Issues	Functions – Underwriting, Claims, Marketing and Risk Management	Organization Levels – Senior Management, Middle Management and Not in Management	Types of Business Organizations – Agency, Brokerage Firm and Insurance Company
with customers, suppliers or competitors that influence, or appear to influence, one's ability to carry out his or her responsibilities (Issue 9)			presenting significantly greater problems than did the Insurance Company Group
Inaccuracy of books, records or reports (Issue 21)			
Lack of knowledge or skills to competently perform one's duties (Issue 29)			
Failure to identify the customer's needs and recommend products and services that meet those needs (Issue 30)			
Failure to be objective with others in one's business dealings (Issue 31)		Senior Management Group perceived this issue as presenting significantly greater problems than did the Not in Management Group	
Misrepresenting or concealing limitations in one's abilities to provide services (Issue 32)	Marketing and Risk Management Groups perceived this issue as presenting significantly greater problems than did the Claims Group		Brokerage Firm Group perceived this issue as presenting significantly greater problems than did the Insurance Company Group

correlation coefficients calculated from the mean ratings of the three studies were .873 for the 1989 and 1999 studies, .868 for the 1999 and 2005 studies and .756 for the 1989 and 2005 studies. These rather high positive correlation coefficients, especially those for the two pairs of consecutive studies, suggest that the order of the ethical issues was actually quite similar overall for the three studies.

Second, as shown in Table 4, a number of similarities exist with respect to the top-ranked issues identified in the three studies – that is, between the 11 key ethical issues identified in the 2005 study and the 10 key ethical issues

Table 4. Key Ethical Issues in 2005 that were also Key Ethical Issues in 1989 and/or 1999.

Issue	2005 Study Ranks	1999 Study Ranks	1989 Study Ranks
1 Failure to provide products and services of the highest quality in the eyes of the customer	7	8	3
2 Failure to provide prompt, honest responses to customer inquiries and requests	5	4	4
3 Making disparaging remarks about competitors, their products or their employees or agents	9	10	
7 False or misleading representation of products or services in marketing, advertising or sales efforts	8	6	6
8 Conflicts between opportunities for personal financial gain (or other personal benefits) and proper performance of one's responsibilities	3	7	8
9 Conflicts of interest involving business or financial relationships with customers, suppliers or competitors that influence, or appear to influence, one's ability to carry out his or her responsibilities	4		
21 Inaccuracy of books, records or reports	10		10
29 Lack of knowledge or skills to competently perform one's duties	2	1	2
30 Failure to identify the customer's needs and recommend products and services that meet those needs	1	2	1
31 Failure to be objective with others in one's business dealings	11	9	7
32 Misrepresenting or concealing limitations in one's abilities to provide services	6	5	5

identified and reported for the 1989 and 1999 surveys:

- The same two issues related to ethical responsibilities of professionals (Issues 29 and 30) ranked first and second in all three studies;
- Nine of the top-ten issues identified in the 1999 study (Issues 1, 2, 3, 7, 8, 29, 30, 31 and 32), including all four of the issues related to ethical responsibilities of professionals, also rank among the top-eleven issues in the 2005 study;
- Nine of the top-ten issues identified in the 1989 study (Issues 1, 2, 7, 8, 21, 29, 30, 31 and 32), including all four of the issues related to ethical responsibilities of professionals, also rank among the top-eleven issues in the 2005 study; and
- Eight of the ten key ethical issues identified in both the 1989 and 1999 studies (Issues 1, 2, 7, 8, 29, 30, 31 and 32), including all four of the issues related to ethical responsibilities of professionals, are identical to eight of the eleven key ethical issues identified in the 2005 study.

These findings suggest that the key ethical issues facing the property-liability insurance industry today are quite similar to those in 1989 and 1999. However, two issues, Issues 9 and 21, were identified as new key ethical issues in the 2005 study. Issue 9 – conflicts of interest involving business or financial relationships with customers, suppliers or competitors that influence, or appear to influence, one's ability to carry out his or her responsibilities – was not perceived as being a key ethical issue by the CPCUs responding to the 1989 and 1999 surveys, and Issue 21 – inaccuracy of books, records or reports – was not perceived as being a key ethical issue by those responding to the 1999 survey.

Finally, as indicated in Table 1, the extent to which particular issues were perceived as presenting problems for those working in the property-liability insurance industry changed significantly (at the .05 level) over the past 6 years for 18 of the 32 issues studied. Nine issues, including the following three of the top-eleven issues identified in the 2005 study, were perceived as presenting *a greater problem* for the industry today than in 1999:

- pursuit of personal financial gain or other personal benefits interfering with the proper performance of one's duties (Issue 8);
- conflicts of interest involving business or financial relationships with customers, suppliers or competitors that influence, or appear to influence, one's ability to carry out his or her responsibilities (Issue 9); and
- inaccuracy of books, records or reports (Issue 21).

As shown in Table 2, all three of these issues are related to unethical activities uncovered by Spitzer's investigation of Marsh, ULR and/or AIG. Fig. 3 indicates that in contrast to this finding of greater problems being presented to those working in the industry over the past six years, two of these issues, Issues 8 and 9, had experienced no significant change in the extent to which they were perceived as presenting ethical problems for the property-liability insurance industry from 1989 to 1999, and Issue 21 was perceived as presenting less of a problem in 1999 than in 1989.

Nine issues, including the following four of the top-eleven issues identified in the 2005 study, were seen as presenting *less of a problem* for those working in the industry today than in 1999:

• failure to provide prompt, honest responses to customer inquiries and requests (Issue 2);
• lack of knowledge or skills to competently perform one's duties (Issue 29);
• failure to identify the customer's needs and recommend products and services that meet those needs (Issue 30); and
• misrepresenting or concealing limitations in one's abilities to provide services (Issue 32).

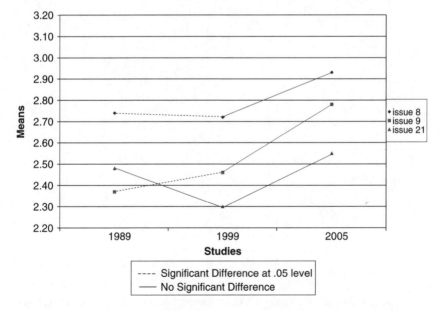

Fig. 3. Key Ethical Issues Perceived as Presenting Greater Problems in 2005 than in 1999.

As shown in Table 2, two of these four key ethical issues perceived as presenting less of a problem to those working in the industry in 2005 than in 1999 – Issues 2 and 30 – encompass several examples of the unethical activities uncovered by Spitzer's investigations of Marsh and ULR. Fig. 4 indicates that these two ethical issues were already perceived as presenting significantly less of a problem for the industry in 1999 than in 1989, and have continued this downward trend in recent years despite the highly publicized examples of unethical/illegal behavior on the part of some major brokers and insurers.

According to the survey respondents, the remaining 14 issues, including the following four of the top-eleven issues identified in the 2005 study, experienced *no statistically significant change* (at the .05 level) in the extent to which they were perceived as presenting problems for those working in the property-liability insurance industry in 1999 and 2005:

- failure to provide products and services of the highest quality in the eyes of the customer (Issue 1);
- making disparaging remarks about competitors, their products or their employees or agents (Issue 3);

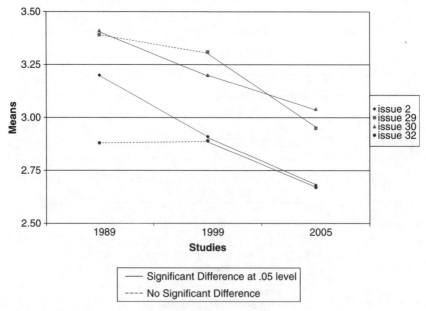

Fig. 4. Key Ethical Issues Perceived as Presenting Less of a Problem in 2005 than in 1999.

- false or misleading representation of products or services in marketing, advertising or sales efforts (Issue 7); and
- failure to be objective with others in one's business dealings (Issue 31).

As shown in Table 2, three of these four key ethical issues that experienced no significant change from 1999 to 2005 – Issues 1, 7 and 31 – describe certain aspects of the unethical behavior uncovered by Spitzer's investigation of Marsh and ULR. Fig. 5 indicates that two of these three issues (Issues 7 and 31) had previously shown no significant change from 1989 to 1999. However, Issue 1 – failure to provide products and services of the highest quality in the eyes of the customer – experienced a significant reduction in the extent to which it was perceived as causing ethical problems for the industry from 1989 to 1999 before showing no significant change over the past six years.

These findings suggest two points regarding the impact that Spitzer's highly publicized allegations against several major insurance brokers and companies appear to have had on the industry's ethical environment. First,

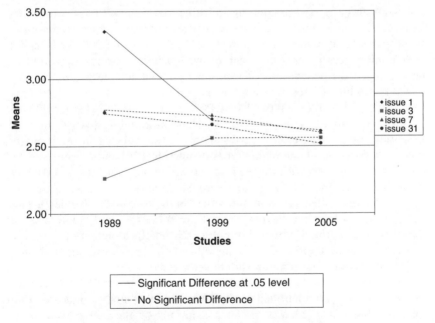

Fig. 5. Key Ethical Issues Perceived as Presenting Essentially the Same Degree of Problems in 1999 and 2005.

despite the sensationalism surrounding Spitzer's allegations of unethical/ illegal behavior in the insurance industry, eight of the eleven key ethical issues identified in the 2005 study, including five issues mentioned earlier as being closely related to Spitzer's allegations against Marsh and ULR (Issues 1, 2, 7, 30 and 31), were perceived as presenting either less of a problem or essentially the same degree of challenge to those working in the industry today as in 1999. Second, three key ethical issues shown earlier to be related to Spitzer's allegations of unethical/illegal activities engaged in by executives and other employees of Marsh, ULR and/or AIG were identified in the 2005 study as presenting greater problems for the industry today than in 1999. This suggests that in some cases, the extraordinary turmoil associated with Spitzer's investigation appears to have had a rather significant, yet quite focused, negative impact on the industry's ethical environment during the past year.

SUMMARY OF KEY FINDINGS AND IMPLICATIONS

This paper has reported the findings of three surveys of CPCUs concerning their perceptions of the key ethical issues encountered by those working in the property-liability insurance industry in 1989, 1999 and 2005 in an effort to determine whether this last year of extraordinary turmoil appeared to have changed the perceptions of insurance professionals regarding the key ethical issues facing those working in the industry.

Analysis of the data from the 2005 CPCU study led to the identification of 11 of 32 issues that were perceived by those responding to the study as presenting the greatest ethical problems for those working in the industry today. Comparison of the major types of unethical behavior uncovered by Spitzer's investigation with these 11 key ethical issues indicates that each of Spitzer's alleged unethical activities is an example of, and thus, related to, one or more of 8 of the key issues identified in the 2005 study (Table 2). This suggests that rather than having arisen from some seemingly unique set of ethical problems, the recent highly publicized unethical activity appears to be attributable to several of the same ethical challenges encountered on a daily basis by those working in the industry today.

Comparison of the 11 key ethical issues identified in the 2005 study with the key ethical issues identified in the 1989 and 1999 studies indicated that there has been little change in the perceptions of the key ethical issues encountered in the industry today as compared with 1989 and 1999. Nine of the top-ten issues identified in the 1989 study, nine of the top-ten issues identified in the 1999 study and eight of the top-ten issues identified in both the 1989 and 1999 studies correspond to issues included among the 2005 study's eleven key ethical issues. Examination of the information in Table 2 indicates that each of the major unethical activities uncovered by Spitzer's investigation of the insurance brokerage business is an example of, and thus, related to, one or more of six of the eight key ethical issues (Issues 1, 2, 7, 8, 30 and 31) identified in all three CPCU studies. Similarly, the most controversial and highly publicized allegation of unethical behavior leveled against AIG by Spitzer and Mills, the use of improper financial reporting in an effort to support the firm's stock price, is an example of one of the key ethical issues (Issue 8) identified as existing in 1989, 1999 and 2005. This suggests that for the most part, the recent highly publicized unethical activity appears to be attributable to several of the same ethical challenges commonly encountered by those working in the industry over the past decade and one half.

Finally, with regard to the extent to which the key ethical issues are perceived as presenting problems for those working in the industry, 8 of the 11 key ethical issues identified in the 2005 study were found to present less of a problem or about the same degree of problem as in 1999, suggesting that Spitzer's allegations over the past year of unethical/illegal behavior on the part of certain insurance brokers and companies do not appear to have had as broad a negative impact on the industry's ethical environment as might have been anticipated. However, the identification of two new key ethical issues in 2005 as well as the perception of three key ethical issues as presenting greater ethical problems for the industry in 2005 than in 1999 suggest that instead, Spitzer's allegations appear to have had a rather focused negative impact on the industry's ethical environment during the past year, reflecting especially the close relationship of these three key ethical issues with Spitzer's charges of conflicts of interest leveled against major brokerage firms, and inaccurate financial reporting and improper pursuit of personal financial gain leveled against certain insurers and their executives.

REFERENCES

Cooper, R. W., & Frank, G. L. (1990). Ethics in the property-liability insurance industry. *CPCU Journal, 43*, 224–238.

Cooper, R. W., & Frank, G. L. (2001). Key ethical issues facing the property and casualty insurance industry: Has a decade made a difference. *CPCU Journal, 54*, 99–111.

Dankwa, D. (2006). Investigations spawn disclosures, fee changes. *Best's Review Property & Casualty, 106*(9), 31.

Hulburt, H. M. (2005). Financial reinsurance and the AIG/General Re Scandal. *CPCU eJournal, 58*(11), 5.

Spitzer, E. (2004a). *Testimony of New York Attorney General Eliot Spitzer.* Subcommittee on Financial Management, the Budget and International Security, Committee on Governmental Affairs, U.S. Senate, Washington, DC, November 16.

Spitzer, E. (2004b). *Complaint: The people of the State of New York against Marsh & McLennan Companies, Inc. and Marsh Inc.* Supreme Court of the State of New York, County of New York, New York, October 14. Available at http://www.oag.state.ny.us/press/2004/oct/oct14a_04_attach1.pdf

Spitzer, E. (2004c). *Complaint: The People of the State of New York against Universal Life Resources, dba ULR; Universal Life Resources, Inc. dba ULR Insurance Services; Douglas P. Cox; and Benefits Commerce.* Supreme Court of the State of New York, County of New York, New York, November 12. Available at http://www.oag.state.ny.us/press/2004/nov/nov12a_04_attach1.pdf

Spitzer, E., & Mills, H. (2005). *Complaint: The People of the State of New York against American International Group, Inc., Maurice R. Greenberg and Howard I. Smith.* Supreme Court of the State of New York, County of New York, New York, May 26. Available at http://www.oag.state.ny.us/press/2005/may/Summons%20and%20Complaint.pdf

Stewart, G. (2005). Sobering Survey. *Best's Review Property & Casualty, 106*(6), 116.

AIG: ACCOUNTING AND ETHICAL LAPSES

Mary D. Maury, Irene N. McCarthy, and
Victoria Shoaf

ABSTRACT

*American International Group, Inc. (AIG) has recently been charged
with reporting bogus transactions that hid losses and inflated its net
worth. The New York State Attorney General Eliot Spitzer alleges that
AIG inflated reserves used for paying claims by millions of dollars and
that AIG's CEO Maurice Greenberg repeatedly directed AIG traders late
in the day to buy AIG shares to prop up its price, among other allegations.
We examine the accounting errors for which AIG and Greenberg are
being charged and analyze the opportunities missed by the auditors to
detect problems, within the framework of corporate governance. That is,
we evaluate the corporate environment that supported these lapses and
provided an environment conducive to the perpetration and acceptance of
fradulent reporting. We discuss how corporate governance not only promotes better financial reporting, but provides a level of scrutiny that
encourages more ethical behavior at all levels of the corporate hierarchy,
and we discuss the imperative for accounting education.*

Insurance Ethics for a More Ethical World
Research in Ethical Issues in Organizations, Volume 7, 39–53
Copyright © 2007 by Elsevier Ltd.
ISSN: 1529-2096/doi:10.1016/S1529-2096(06)07003-9

INTRODUCTION

According to the AIG website, "American International Group, Inc. (AIG) is the world's leading international insurance and financial services organization, with operations in more than 130 countries and jurisdictions. ... In the United States, AIG companies are the largest underwriters of commercial and industrial insurance" (http://ir.aigcorporate.com). *Business Insurance* (2004) recognizes AIG as "one of the nation's most profitable companies"; it earned $11 billion last year alone. It is also listed as number 3 of the top 10 companies on The Forbes Global 2000 List (2000) which is based on a composite ranking from four metrics: sales, profits, assets, and market value (http://www.forbes.com). Why, then, has it become the poster child of malfeasance in the insurance industry? A *Wall Street Journal* article dated March 28, 2005, pointed out that "accounting at AIG is being investigated by the SEC, Justice Department, the New York attorney general and New York state insurance regulators, besides its own board" (Langley, Solomon, Francis, & McDonald, 2005). Additionally, according to Squeo and Francis (2005) the FBI is now "conducting a wide-ranging inquiry into the insurance industry" (p. A-3), which could extend into related industries such as banking and finance as a result of the developments at AIG.

On March 31, 2005, AIG acknowledged that its accounting for a number of transactions was improper (Anderson, 2005). In May, the company stated, after an extensive internal review, that it would restate more than 4 years of financial statements, reducing its net worth by $2.7 billion (McDonald & Francis, 2005). That admission caused the rating services to downgrade AIG's long-term counterparty credit and senior debt ratings and that of its subsidiaries (Ha & Hay, 2005).

In many ways, the story of AIG's legal troubles is intrinsically tied to the fortunes of Maurice R. (Hank) Greenberg, who has been at its helm since 1967; he oversaw an organization whose profits rose under his leadership from $14 million in 1967 to $11 billion in 2004. Despite this formidable record, he was removed as chief executive "with a heavy heart" by unanimous consent of AIG's board on March 13, 2005, while remaining as chairman, only to be forced to resign from the company entirely by March 28, 2005 (Eichenwald & Anderson, 2005).

Greenberg was by all accounts unlike any of the other chief executives who have gotten themselves in trouble. He was not trying to increase his personal wealth or hide a failing company as were many of the characters in the news of late (such as Lay, Ebbers, Rigas, Kozlowski). Instead, Murray (2005) describes him as "a man of great pride who cared deeply about the company he ran." Unfortunately, according to Murray, rather than being comfortable taking the long view, he obsessed about the daily fluctuations in the company's stock price and was thus led astray. "Mr. Greenberg knew better than anyone that the transactions were merely short-term fixes. But there's no evidence that he sold stock in the short term, and therefore no reason to think he personally benefited. Instead, his actions were more likely rooted in his pride – an intense desire to succeed by the measures the market set for him" (Murray, 2005).

In an article about Greenberg in *Fortune*, the authors note that his most frequent quote is "All I want in life is an unfair advantage" (Leonard, Elkind, & Burke, 2005). Greenberg is known to be regarded by most people, even his enemies – of which he made more than a few – as a business genius. However, he has a strong personality to go with it "To be sure, Greenberg was famously brutal with competitors, employees, analysts, customers – even members of AIG's board .... He ran roughshod over state insurance regulators. But all that was viewed as part of his genius, evidence of how much smarter and tougher he was than anyone else" (Leonard et al., 2005).

In the press release put out by Elliot Spitzer, the New York State Attorney General, upon filing the lawsuit against AIG and its top managers for a pattern of fraud at AIG on May 26, 2005, he stated that "The irony of this case is that AIG was a well-run and profitable company that didn't need to cheat. And yet, the former top management routinely and persistently resorted to deception and fraud in an apparent effort to improve the company's financial results" (Office of the Attorney General, 2005b).

WHAT WENT WRONG?

The insurance business is structured in such a way that companies generally lose money writing policies but earn their profits by investing the premiums they collect. Greenberg, however, emphasized that underwriting was their most important business, and Wall Street rewarded AIG's record of making money on underwriting with a premium multiple, indicating that the market also valued underwriting profits more highly than unpredictable investing results. They used large amounts of reinsurance to grow.

Reinsurers are the behind-the-scenes companies, frequently located in offshore islands such as Bermuda and Barbados that are outside of the jurisdiction of U.S. regulators and with no corporate income tax. They also have laws that are less strict about establishing reserves for anticipated losses. These offshore islands allow discounting of the loss reserves based on the premise that losses will be paid out over time. Insurance companies are not required to book the entire amount of potential loss through the income statement immediately as they are in the United States, but can report instead a discounted amount, based on the time value of money, thereby needing a smaller amount of loss reserves. Thus, reinsurers sell insurance to insurers, lessening their risk and thereby letting them shrink their booked reserves.

AIG regularly used these reinsurance companies to keep its reserves down, especially on some of the more risky policies that it was willing to write for such risks as expropriation of property by foreign governments and terrorism. AIG used reinsurance companies for as much as 70% of its premiums, while competitors only utilized reinsurers for about 10% of their premiums. This policy, while causing the company to give up some of its profits, allowed it to continue to grow using its limited capital (Leonard et al., 2005).

One of the issues that came under investigation was whether AIG was using reinsurance companies that it controlled while treating them as separate entities to minimize its risk exposure. The question was whether these were really loans and whether assets and liabilities were swapped to smooth out earnings. The biggest acknowledgment of "improper" accounting involved a finite reinsurance transaction with Berkshire Hathaway's General Re unit using a sham risk-free swap of insurance assets that allowed AIG to artificially inflate its premium growth and temporarily boost claims reserves in order to keep the analysts happy. "The AIG/General Re deal, in two separate transactions in late 2000 and early 2001, shifted $500 million of expected claims to AIG from Gen Re, along with $500 million of premiums. AIG recorded the premiums as revenue and added $500 million to its reserves to show its obligation to pay claims" (Ha & Hays, 2005, p. 7). Ha and Hays also report that AIG admitted that its Gen Re deal should have been recorded as loans, not as insurance, due to lack of evidence of risk and that the company has since said, "They will now be listed as deposits rather than consolidated net premiums" (p. 7).

As the investigations and scrutiny increased, AIG began an extensive review of its books and records in preparation for its 2004 Annual Report. On May 1, 2005, AIG issued a news release that stated: "The findings of that review, together with the results to date of investigations conducted by outside counsel at the request of AIG's Audit Committee and in consultation with AIG's independent auditors, PricewaterhouseCoopers LLP have resulted in AIG's decision to restate its financial statements for the years ended December 31, 2003, 2002, 2001, and 2000, the quarters ended March

31, June 30 and September 30, 2004 and 2003 and the quarter ended December 31, 2003" (AIG, 2005). It also announced that it expected to file its 2004 Form 10-K by May 31, 2005.

Among the items listed in its news release was an anticipated decrease of approximately 3.3% in AIG's unaudited consolidated shareholders' equity of $82.87 billion at December 31, 2004. There would also be corrections of accounting errors totaling approximately $2.0 billion, as well as fourth quarter changes in estimates – tax accruals, deferred acquisition costs, contingencies, and allowances – totaling approximately $700 million.

In the news release AIG revealed that "The restatement will correct errors in prior accounting for improper or inappropriate transactions or entries that appear to have had the purpose of achieving an accounting result that would enhance measures important to the financial community and that may have involved documentation that did not accurately reflect the nature of the arrangements." In many cases, these improper entries resulted from "top level" adjustments, which were possible because of "certain control deficiencies, including (i) the ability of certain former members of senior management to circumvent internal controls over financial reporting in certain circumstances, (ii) ineffective controls over accounting for certain structured transactions and transactions involving complex accounting standards and (iii) ineffective balance sheet reconciliation processes. These deficiencies are 'material weaknesses' as defined by the Public Company Oversight Board's Auditing Standards No. 2. Consequently, management has concluded that AIG's internal control over financial reporting was ineffective as of December 31, 2004."

The news release contained a list of many of the expected changes, which included reclassifying realized capital gains to net investment income, increasing expense deferrals, decreasing reserves to shift income between reporting periods or among business segments. Some other changes that were noted included:

- *Foreign currency translation* did not in some cases comply with the functional currency determination;
- *Life settlements* designed to assist life insurance policyholders to monetize the existing value of life insurance policies; AIG determined that certain aspects of its prior accounting for this business were incorrect, but the appropriate treatment is still being discussed by AIG and PWC with the regulatory authorities;
- *Deferred acquisition costs* (DAC) reflected incorrect application of accounting principles regarding DAC, and adjustments to reduce the DAC

asset are necessary. Cumulative effect of adjustments will be approximately a $200 million decrease in stockholders' equity; and
• *SICO deferred compensation*: The internal review determined that AIG should have been expensing amounts attributable to deferred compensation granted to certain AIG employees by SICO, a private holding company that owns approximately 12% of AIG's common stock.

In addition to this aforementioned plethora of troubles that AIG unearthed, on April 26, 2005, the office of the New York State Attorney General issued a press release stating that AIG was to be audited for alleged misreporting of workers' compensation premiums. It alleges that there was a practice that lasted for a decade despite challenges from AIG insiders repeatedly challenging its legality, involving the booking of premiums for workers' compensation coverage as premiums for general liability coverage (Office of the Attorney General, 2005a).

In reviewing this litany of transgressions, one would have to agree with the article in *Fortune* magazine that aptly states: "A simple, mystifying question looms over all this: Why? Why would such an iconic corporate figure – Spitzer calls him 'the most powerful businessman in the world,' and it's only a slight stretch – engage in so many deceptions that ultimately made little difference to his company's rise? After sifting through the questionable transactions, AIG reduced its net worth by $2.26 billion – a decrease of only 2.7% and less than the company makes in a typical quarter. The games Greenberg is accused of playing were intended to address mundane problems: a short-term stock decline, the failure of a new business venture, an analyst's criticism that AIG was under-reserved for potential losses" (Leonard et al., 2005, 17).

WHERE WERE THE AUDITORS?

As the picture of accounting improprieties and allegations of illegal acts at AIG unfolds, it is evident that not all of AIG's transgressions are recent. However, only recently did its auditors, PricewaterhouseCoopers, balk at approving its reports until the accused CEO Greenberg was removed from the board (Kadlec, 2005). In the post-Enron era, with increased scrutiny of internal controls and every phase of external auditing, the question arises as to how this number of accounting errors could have been missed.

In the 2004 *10-K*, the new AIG management team seems ready and willing to heap the blame for past transgressions on the officers named in the charges, who had stepped down or been fired by the company; they are clearly eager to clear the air and start afresh. In the *Management Discussion & Analysis*, the new management asserts:

> Certain of AIG's controls within its control environment were not effective to prevent certain members of senior management, including the former Chief Executive Officer and former Chief Financial Officer, from having the ability, which in certain instances was utilized, to override certain controls and effect certain transactions and accounting entries. In certain of these instances, such transactions and accounting entries appear to have been largely motivated to achieve desired accounting results and were not properly accounted for in accordance with GAAP. Further, in certain of these instances, information critical to an effective review of transactions, accounting entries, and certain entities used in these transactions and accounting entries, were not disclosed to the appropriate financial and accounting personnel, regulators and AIG's independent registered public accounting firm. As a result, discussion and thorough legal, accounting, actuarial or other professional analysis did not occur. This control deficiency is based primarily on these overrides.

In effect, the new management exonerates the auditors, among others, who were apparently misled by the former CEO and CFO. While PricewaterhouseCoopers may be pleased with this pass – and has not, to date, been named in any law suits related to the misstatements (Glater, 2005) – pointing the finger somehow misdirects the question. Is not the purpose of the recent focus on improving the quality of audits and other aspects of corporate governance to circumvent a situation where one or more top-level employees can "cook the books"?

The overbearing manner in which Greenberg exercised his role as CEO was certainly a key factor in the fraud at AIG, but the overall weakness in corporate governance allowed the fraud to flourish. There is empirical evidence in the accounting literature (e.g., Dechow et al., 1996; Beasley, 1996; Farber, 2005) indicating that weak corporate governance is associated with financial reporting fraud. Farber (2005) finds that the weaker governance associated with reporting frauds includes few outside board members, few audit committee meetings, few financial experts on the audit committee, and the role of the CEO on the board of directors. We believe that these and other factors operative at AIG – such as its size and success, the encouragement of ruthless and competitive behavior, the closeness of the relationship with the auditors – provided an environment conducive to the perpetration and acceptance of fraudulent reporting.

While others in the insurance industry were moving toward recruiting more outside directors "with the CEO having a more limited degree of involvement" (Bowers, 2004), AIG's board was still composed of internal (management executive) directors and outside directors selected by

Greenberg. Hence, the board lacked the element of independence that might have been useful in directing and assessing the company's management and in protecting the shareholders' interests. The board was clearly dominated by Greenberg. Indeed, board members, as well as AIG executives and former executives, also served on the board of Starr International, one of three other organizations headed by Greenberg. Starr International provided a deferred compensation package to AIG executives, and when the propriety of using Starr International as a compensation vehicle was raised, the board even declined Greenberg's suggestion to put it to a shareholder vote (Francis & McDonald, 2005a), indicating the strength of Greenberg's influence. Since the *10-K* restatement, institutional investors have expressed their desire for AIG to reform its board with independent directors (Lubin, Langley, & Francis, 2005). Indeed, one of the proxy-advisory firms hired by AIG's new management recommended removing 10 of the 15 board members, retaining only the new CEO, the interim Chairman, and the 3 board members appointed after Greenberg's departure (Francis, 2005a) – a recommendation which AIG has not, to date, acted upon.

One reason that Greenberg may have succeeded unquestioned and unchecked in his domination of the corporate environment and the undercutting of balanced corporate governance at AIG is the tremendous success of the company. The company's success brought praise and financial rewards to its executives and directors, secure employment to lower level employees, and wealth to its shareholders. With such success, scrutiny by the board (and the auditors, regulators, and others) undoubtedly became lax; there was no apparent need to be concerned for the welfare of comfortable, contented shareholders. The reliance on success to maintain domination without criticism may even have precipitated the fraudulent behavior. As previously noted, there was no need to augment the company's already good profits, and there was no personal gain obtained by Greenberg or other executives from maintaining the stock price. In 1987, one of the factors documented by The National Commission on Fraudulent Financial Reporting (the Treadway Commission) as underlying accounting frauds was a need to meet specific performance expectations – in this case, perhaps, Greenberg's own preoccupation with Wall Street expectations and maintaining the ascent of his dominion.

With such a dominating CEO, the tone at the top likely permeated the corporate culture, and the competitive tone is probably best exemplified by Greenberg's favorite quotation, noted above. Numerous anecdotes have appeared since the charges were released showing the encouragement of ruthless and competitive behavior by AIG's management team. For instance, lower level employees apparently engineered the practice of under contributing to worker's compensation funds and underpaying taxes on workers' compensation premiums, thus shifting the burden to its competitors and other firms. Greenberg is said to have supported the practice and laughed at an underling's observation that "if we were legal, we wouldn't be in business" (Coy, 2005). This interchange suggests a bond among management levels in a corporate community, a winning-side arrogance and sense of entitlement.

The auditors may also have been bound to the AIG community by a common history. Five of the top executives, including the chief financial officer, were formerly employed by PricewaterhouseCoopers (Tuckey, 2005). As such, the executives certainly knew the audit procedures, possibly some members of the audit team, and vice versa. The possible impairment of independence by hiring from the audit firm is implied by its prohibition in the Sarbanes-Oxley Act of 2002. While these events pre-dated that law, and may not have directly affected independence, they certainly must have contributed to the level of comfort the auditors felt with AIG, along with AIG's size and level of success.

Even if the auditors were comfortable in the environment and lax in scrutinizing AIG's financial reports, however, it would have been extraordinary for them to have missed errors of the magnitude indicated by the 2004 *10-K* restatement. In fact, the release of this document, with its pointed accusations, caused Greenberg to issue his own 51-page "white paper" that defends the accounting decisions made while he was CEO of AIG and asserts that they were made with the assistance and knowledge of auditors from PricewaterhouseCoopers. At the same time, he accuses the current management of inflating the charges against income in the restatement in order to make future performance look better (Francis & McDonald, 2000b). Indeed, others have suggested that the "frightened AIG board" may have over-reacted to the legal actions brought by New York State Attorney General Eliot Spitzer (Melloan, 2005).

How could PricewaterhouseCoopers and AIG's accounting and financial team, many of whom participated in drafting the original documents, now decide that such a massive restatement was necessary? One problem is that the accounting guidelines are not specific.

Corporate accounting, contrary to popular belief, is chock-full of judgment calls .... But most people don't know how flexible corporate accounting can be, particularly in an insurance company .... Restatements in such a complex world aren't extraordinary, for reasons, like honest mistakes, that are not criminal in nature. Merely adjusting the amount of earnings set aside for loss reserves – a judgment call based on guesses about what damage the future holds – can make a world of difference (Melloan, 2005).

It is not unusual to find differences in judgment, and in the face of the allegations of fraud made against it, AIG and PricewaterhouseCoopers may have decided to make much more conservative choices than they did in the previous statements. To some extent, it is credible that at least some of the alleged "accounting errors" represent only a difference in judgment.

It may be prudent, however, to question the use of accounting judgment. In the allegation of fraudulently reporting a transaction with General Re as reinsurence, for instance, instead of a loan, Greenberg's "white paper" says: "The process for determining whether a finite reinsurance contract qualifies for reinsurance accounting has historically been complex and highly subjective" (Parekh, 2005). It goes on to point out that even the new rules being discussed by the National Association of Insurance commissioners would permit AIG's original treatment of it. Greenberg's judgment appears to be that if there is no "bright line" excluding the transaction from reinsurance accounting, then it should be allowed. This rules-based approach, ever seeking the loophole, is exactly what the Securities Exchange Commission (SEC) has denounced in recent publications and communications with the Financial Accounting Standards Board (FASB). The SEC has requested that the FASB adopt a more principles-based or objectives-based approach to setting accounting standards, so that judgment, when exercised, would be to determine whether the objectives of the standard in reflecting the economic reality are met – not to determine whether the rules are technically, however minimally, implemented (see, for instance, SEC, 2003). In Greenberg's case, the transaction did not have the essential economic elements of reinsurance, including transfer of risk, so good judgment should have dictated a different accounting treatment.

Certainly, PricewaterhouseCoopers auditors were familiar with the weak corporate governance at AIG – the dependency of the board members and the CEO's domineering style. It would have been remarkable if they had not also have been aware of the executives' ability to make top-down adjustments, and indeed, they apparently did know about the actual exercise of those "overrides" described in AIG's 2004 *10-K* but judged them to be immaterial (Francis, 2005b). In short, the auditors knew that the means and opportunity for fraud were overtly present in the corporate environment at AIG; only the motive was absent. The apparent lack of motive, given AIG's success, seems to have hypnotized the board, the auditors, and the regulators into accepting accounting treatment that skimmed the "bright lines" of accounting rules. Whether these transgressions represent crimes, or merely instances of poor judgment, remains to be decided by the courts.

Interestingly, in the aftermath of the furor caused by the charges being brought against Greenberg and AIG and the subsequent 2004 *10-K* restatement, AIG is continuing to follow a rules-based approach toward redeeming the corporate culture. That is, the company almost appears to be following a corporate governance checklist in developing its new Corporate Governance Committee, a Code of Conduct, and a corporate-level compliance framework, as the 2005 *Proxy Statement* indicates. The discussion on the improvement of the ethical climate – referred to as the "compliance function" – appears under "Regulatory Matters" in the new CEO's letter to the shareholders. However, as Verschoor (2005) points out, most of the improvements merely bring AIG up to the minimum requirements, and in fact, "AIG seems to be embracing a more ethical structure only because of legal requirements" (p. 18). Falling within the "bright lines" of the rules will not bring about the lasting change to its corporate culture that AIG needs.

WHAT CAN WE DO?

Avoiding future situations like the one currently unfolding at AIG – and its predecessors at Enron, Worldcom, and the like – requires more than compliance with minimum standards of corporate governance after the fact. It may require a complete overhaul, beginning with the housecleaning and subsequent maintenance of our corporate governance framework and then reaching back to the beginning in the business education of our corporate leaders.

In the current post-Enron environment, companies are falling all over themselves to hire ethics officers, announce ethics codes, set up whistle-blower hotlines, and launch ethics training. As at AIG, these efforts often reflect a compliance, check-box attitude toward corporate governance. Indeed, in some cases, these changes are part of deferred prosecution arrangements. In other cases, they stem from the 2002 Sarbanes-Oxley legislation. More important to the overhaul of corporate governance, perhaps, is the ethics framework created by the 2004 revision of the Organizational Sentencing Guidelines. These guidelines say that if firms want leniency during a prosecution, they must have an effective ethics program in place. More fundamentally, however, the guidelines say that companies must create an *organizational culture that encourages ethics* (Kelly, 2005). In other words, companies need a willingness to look at the culture that allows or even encourages unethical behavior, such as that at AIG.

Almost two decades ago, the Treadway Commission outlined the components of an effective system of internal controls recognizing the critical role of internal controls over financial reporting. The foundation of that framework is a strong control environment, including *tone at the top*. Castellano and Lightle (2005) suggest that a cultural audit would provide a means for assessing the tone at the top and the attitude toward internal controls and ethical decision-making. The authors propose that the board of directors, through the audit committee, should retain an outside firm to conduct a cultural audit every three years. External auditors should include in their internal control assessments and risk management profiles a process designed to assess *tone at the top* and the resulting impact on a company's culture. The authors cite three issues that need to be addressed:

- the degree to which preoccupation with meeting the analyst's expectations permeates the organizational climate;
- the degree of fear and pressure associated with meeting numerical goals and targets; and
- the compensation and incentive plans that may encourage unacceptable, unethical, and illegal forms of earnings management.

Such a cultural audit at AIG would immediately have revealed the aspects of the corporate environment conducive to fraud. Of course, it is unlikely that AIG would have pursued such an audit unless it were required legally or by industry regulators. We believe that the presence of such a requirement would make it difficult for companies to maintain a weak corporate governance and would, in essence, force the housecleaning that may be necessary.

While immediate action is necessary to restore corporate governance, the longer view dictates that we focus on the education of our future leaders. The recent scandals have raised a serious question about the accounting education that public accountants obtain. Waddock (2005) believes that business schools must focus on integrity at the individual, company, and societal levels – that is, on business in society, not just business in economy. She suggests that future accountants receive a "mindful accounting education" that includes awareness of their belief systems, consciousness of consequences, and the capablity of thinking broadly about the impact of their actions and decisions. The function of accounting education should be that ethics, accuracy, and transparency are integral to accounting, not something to consider only when dilemmas arise. She states that it is the integrated relationship of ethics and accounting that business schools have generally failed to recognize. Further, to assume the role of a "professional," future accountants must assume responsibility for the welfare of others, not just themselves. Waddock believes that accountants must be able to make decisions based on principles and relationships – that they will not be operating from conventional levels of moral reasoning, but from post-conventional levels that will require them to view situations from a variety of perspectives that include all stakeholders and society as a whole (Rest, Narvaez, Bebeau, & Thomas, 1999).

Business schools have been under pressure to improve their teaching of ethics in the wake of corporate scandals over the last few years (Mangan, 2004). In January 2004, business schools and the Business Roundtable, an association of CEOs, joined together to form a new ethics institute to be housed at the University of Virginia's Darden Graduate School of Business Administration. The independent center, the Business Roundtable Institute for Corporate Ethics, was backed by $2.7 million from the business group; its function will be to conduct research, create courses, and lead executive seminars on business ethics. R. Edward Freeman, the institute's academic director and a leading ethics expert, argues that there is nothing new about today's corporate scandals. He believes they reflect the broad, longstanding problem in business that managers are often judged almost completely by how much they increase profits and add value for shareholders. The Institute is a first step toward convincing business schools to take that information and overhaul their curricula, which is what is really needed.

There is some evidence that the teaching of ethics is becoming more central to business education. For instance, Columbia's revamped program, The Individual, Business and Society: Tradeoffs, Choices and Accountability, is no longer a separate course with its own final and grade (Alsop, 2005). Columbia now requires its professors to weave in ethics in the content of its core courses. The revised ethics program also features many activities outside the classroom, such as a morality play, guest lecturers, and panel discussions. Columbia claims its approach of blending ethics with social responsibility and corporate governance is not an attempt to teach students right from wrong but rather to give students strategies for protecting their integrity in the workplace. Harvard Business School's new required course, Leadership and Corporate Accountability (Alsop, 2005) also places ethics within a larger framework, using the case-study format. The course includes sections on personal values and leadership, governance issues and the legal, ethical, and economic responsibilities of companies to their stakeholders. Harvard is still committed to a stand-alone course, citing the crowding out of ethics discussion in management courses, and the lack of training of faculty members in ethics and law and inability to incorporate them well.

In contemplating what can be done in business education, we believe that Waddock (2005) said it best "Until business schools teach future accountants and leaders how deep the connections are between business, society, nature, and the world, corporations will continue to be run by hollow leaders who have no sense of ethics or responsibility. Accounting for performance is likely to remain too narrowly focused to be helpful in today's demanding environment."

We believe that the combination of improved ethics education in business schools and the introduction of cultural audits of businesses would have a profound effect on improving corporate governance and decreasing the risk of fraudulent financial reporting.

REFERENCES

AIG. (2005). AIG nears completion of internal review; will restate results, provides update of internal review and timing of Form 10K (May 1). Accessed 9/15/05. http://ir.aigcorporate.com/phoenix.zhtml?c = 76115&p = irol-newsArticle&ID = 703645&highl

Alsop, R. (2005). MBA track/focus on academics, careers and other B-school trends. *Wall Street Journal*, April 12, p. B4.

Anderson, J. (2005). Insurance giant calls its accounting improper. *The New York Times*, May 31, p. A-1.

Beasley, M. (1996). An empirical analysis of the relation between the board of director composition and financial statement fraud. *The Accounting Review, 71*, 443–465.

Bowers, B. (2004). Governing principals. *Best's Review, 104*(10), 29–32.

Castellano, J., & Lightle, S. (2005). Using cultural audits to assess tone at the top. *The CPA Journal*. Available at: http://www.nysscpa.org/printversions/cpaj/2005/205/p6.htm

Coy, P. (2005). Spitzer may get his day in court. *Business Week*, June 13 (3937), p. 40.

Dechow, P., Sloan, R., & Sweeney, A. (1996). Causes and consequences of earnings manipulation. An analysis of firms subject to enforcement actions by the SEC. *Contemporary Accounting Research, 13*, 1–36.

Eichenwald, K., & Anderson, J. (2005). How a titan of insurance ran afoul of the government. *The New York Times*, April 4, p. C-1.

Farber, D. (2005). Restoring trust after fraud: Does corporate governance matter? *The Accounting Review, 80*(2), 539–561.

Francis, T. (2005a). Moving the market: Advisory firms offer mixed view of AIG's board. *Wall Street Journal*, July 26, p. C3.

Francis, T. (2005b). Moving the market: Tracking the numbers/outside audit: AIG's accounting errors raise questions about auditors' duties. *Wall Street Journal*, June 3, p. C3.

Francis, T., & McDonald, I. (2005a). Greenberg calls into question AIG's restatement; ousted chief defends accounting decisions. *Wall Street Journal*, July 15, p. C4.

Francis, T., & McDonald, I. (2005b). Moving the market: Greenberg defends AIG's accounting, rebuts allegations. *Wall Street Journal*, August 5, p. C3.

Glater, J. (2005). For the auditors of A.I.G., a delicate balancing act. *The New York Times*, May 3, p. FC6.

Ha, M., & Hay, D. (2005). AIG admits 'improper accounting' on Gen Re deal. *National Underwriter, P&C, 109*(13), 6.

Kadlec, D. (2005). Down ... but not out. *Time, 165*(25), 50–53.

Kelly, M. (2005). The ethics revolution. *Business Ethics, 19*(2), 6.

Langley, M., Solomon, D., Francis, T., & McDonald, I. (2005). SEC subpoenas senior executives in probe at AIG. *Wall Street Journal*, March 28, p. A-1.

Leonard, D., Elkind, P., & Burke, D. (2005). All I want in life is an unfair advantage. *Fortune, 152*(3), 76–96.

Lubin, J., Langley, M., & Francis, T. (2005). Moving the market: AIG talks to big holders about board's composition. *Wall Street Journal*, June 20, p. C3.

Mangan, K. (2004). Business schools and corporate CEOs team up to start ethics institute (January 15). Available at: chronicle.com/temp/email.php?id = fha2vg9whk7 × 72oov8-arapvlw b0xjulm

McDonald, I., & Francis, T. (2005). AIG to restate over four years to fix errors. *Wall Street Journal*, May 2, p. C-1.

Melloan, G. (2005). As lawyers invade accounting, clarity flees. *Wall Street Journal*, August 9, p. A11.

Murray, A. (2005). Greenberg lost sight of the long view. *Wall Street Journal*, June 22, p. A-2.

Office of the Attorney General. (2005a). Press release: AIG to be audited for alleged misreporting of workers' compensation premiums (April 26). Accessed 9/15/05 http://www.oag.state.ny.us/press/2005/apr/aig_wc.pdf

Office of the Attorney General. (2005b). Press release: State suit cites pattern of fraud at AIG, former CEO Hank Greenberg directed and approved illegal transactions. (May 26). Accessed 9/15/05 http://www.oag.state.ny.us/press/2005/may/may26a_05.html

Parekh, R. (2005). Greenberg challenges AIG restatements. *Business Insurance, 39*, 3–4.

Rest, K., Narvaez, D., Bebeau, M., & Thomas, S. (1999). *Postconventional moral thinking: A Neo-Kolbergian approach*. Mahwah, NJ: L. Erlbaum Associates.

Securities Exchange Commission (SEC). (2003). Study pursuant to section 108(d) of the Sarbanes-Oxley Act of 2002 on the adoption by the United States financial reporting system of a principles-based accounting system. Accessed 9/15/05 http://www.sec.gov/news/studies/principlesbasedstand.htm

Squeo, A., & Francis, T. (2005). AIG investigation sparks FBI probe of insurance firms. *Wall Street Journal*, May 5, p. A-3.

The Forbes Global 2000 List. (2000). Accessed 9/15/05 http://www.forbes.com/2005/03/30/05f2000land.html

Tuckey, S. (2005). Greenberg slams AIG earnings restatement. *National Underwriter, P&C, 109*(31), 31.

Verschoor, C. (2005). AIG remediation emphasizes compliance, but not ethics. *Strategic Finance, 87*(3), 17–18.

Waddock, S. (2005). Hollow men and women at the helm ... hollow accounting ethics? *Issues in Accounting Education, 20*(2), 145–150.

INSURANCE ETHICS, AN OXYMORON?

James Barrese

ABSTRACT

The insurance industry often experiences criticism for unethical and frequently illegal activities. This document suggests that insurers operate in an uncompetitive environment and that the nature of insurer operations leads otherwise ethical individuals in the direction of questionable ethical decisions throughout the operations of an insurance company.

The question of ethics and the insurance industry arises frequently. Often it is the industry expressing ethical concerns about fraudulent claims but it is also in the form of agent behavior. However, having even the slightest acquaintance with the news in the past year, one cannot escape the feeling that the largest fraud problem plaguing the insurance industry is the fraud committed by industry participants rather than by claimants.

A considerable literature exists on the notion of corporate social responsibility (CSR). The CSR theories range from a description of corporation responsibility as lower than that of individuals (Carr, 1996) to theories that assign greater social responsibilities to corporations (Carroll, 2000). The existence of the various theories highlights the point that there is no fixed standard for evaluating the ethical behavior of corporations. Still, the

Insurance Ethics for a More Ethical World
Research in Ethical Issues in Organizations, Volume 7, 55–81
ISSN: 1529-2096/doi:10.1016/S1529-2096(06)07004-0

notion that corporate responsibility requires obedience to the laws is a minimum in all but the most extreme CSR theories.

The recent proliferation of lawsuits against leading insurance companies and renowned industry leaders, for multi-year illegal activities, is an obvious signal that the industry has a share of ethical issues to address. Because the popular press almost daily reports examples of unethical or questionable insurance industry behavior, the focus of this selective survey is on some less obvious ethical issues facing the industry. Specifically, we focus on concentration, market share persistence, interlocking ownership, and other incestuous industry practices.[1] We also summarize and suggest extensions to some of the studies of incentives driving the behavior of insurance companies and their employees in a direction that violates their fiduciary responsibilities.

Welfare economics provides a model for social utility that is the basis for antitrust laws. The existence of these laws and the Court's historical interpretation of these laws demonstrates society's acceptance of the notion that anticompetitive structures are unacceptable even when the attainment of an anticompetitive position is through efficient and legal means (Caves, 1987). We provide circumstantial evidence that the insurance industry is not competitive and has maintained an anticompetitive structure for a long period.

One of the most important roles of the insurance industry, its raison dètre, is to pay contractual claims when a loss occurs. It is often the case that the precise responsibility for a loss is not certain and a negotiation results. Evidence suggests that the negotiated results reflect the naturally aligned interests of insurers and their employees, sometimes at the expense of providing justice to policyholders. We extend the discussion of the conditions affecting the insurer biases.

1. CORPORATE ETHICS AND THE CSR CONCEPT

Defining the terms "values," "ethics," and "social responsibility" is an almost impossible task yet the first two often are interchanged. Ethics is the science of human duty; values are set of individual or expressed group beliefs that provide a basis for action. The debate over CSR, which references both ethical behavior and values, started with the 1953 publication of Bowen's "Social Responsibilities of Businessman."

The debate over the legitimacy of CSR raises fundamental questions that, too often, are ultimately unanswerable. Why do corporations exist? To whom are corporations responsible? What does it mean to be socially responsible? How can social performance be measured? Should economic performance be sacrificed for social performance? Workable solutions can be obtained but answers based on positive rather than normative concepts are not available to answer many of these questions.

Social responsibility is a balancing act: business must balance economic performance, ethical performance, and social performance. Controversy arises when activities that enhance one type of performance reduce performance in other areas. One extreme admits almost no constraint on the profit motivation except compliance with the rules set by the existing law. For example, Carr (1996) holds that ethically questionable individual action, such as lying about the quantity or quality of mileage on a used car, is permissible in business. The individual Jekyll/Hyde employee's duty as the agent of their employer overrides their individual ethical objections to such practices. At the other extreme, Miller and Ahrens (1993) suggest social welfare should be the primary goal, even, without qualification, if profit suffers. Less extreme positions recognize the balancing nature of the issues but approach the balance from different directions – Friedman (1996) stresses profit performance as the goal that trumps other goals and accepts the profit requirement but insists that business should be sensitive to the effect of its actions on multiple stakeholders.

One view of corporate responsibility is that behavior dedicated to something other than profit maximization, staying within the realm of law, is a violation of the fiduciary obligations of employees and is therefore unethical. This view is consistent with the expression of Friedman (1996) that "the business of business is business." Friedman defends this position based on assumptions that markets operate efficiently and that business executives, who are neither democratically elected nor accountable to the general public, should not impose their own vision of the public good on the society by strength of their access to a corporate treasury. Moreover, he holds that the managerial sacrifice of business profits for the sake of promoting social ends violates the rights of the shareholders; it is tantamount to theft. Drucker (1973) goes only a small step further: "the first responsibility of a professional, was spelled out clearly, 2,500 years ago, in the Hippocratic oath of the Greek physician: *primum non nocere*-'Above all, not knowingly to do harm'" (quoted in Jennings, 2003, p. 48). Critics counter that business depends on society for resources and services that enhance the likelihood of corporate profit. These exchange-facilitating services include, but are not limited to supplying two very special rights to assist business in performing its role: potential immortality and limited liability. In return for these special privileges being granted to business, corporations have a responsibility to fulfill to the society.

Debate not only centers on whether the social responsibility of business is satisfied by the provision of goods that offer a net consumer surplus, it also involves the related question of whether the appropriate charge for corporate resource use is sufficiently covered by corporate taxes; alternative views are provided by Bowie (1995) and Lippke (1996).

A more extreme suggestion is that the special legal status of corporations, which is created by the state as the representative of society, and the consequent possibility of large size, the modern corporation should be considered as a public rather than a private organization, so that it can be held to a higher legal and moral accountability than the traditional business enterprise (Miller & Ahrens, 1993).

In addition to theoretical criticisms of the notion of CSR, some raise practical criticisms: the social contract varies from region to region, changes as society changes, does not specify to what extent the corporation should be considered a public vs. a private enterprise and how that may vary with the size of the enterprise; definitions vary according to the context and cultural situation.[2]

The appropriateness of CSR depends on one's view of the role of business in society. Critics of CSR take the view that business designed for a single purpose: to make money for its owners (Friedman, 1970; Lantos, 2001). CSR proponents view business is an integral part of the society with responsibilities to expend time, energy, and money, even at the expense of its owners, in order to fulfill those responsibilities (Bowen, 1953; Balabanis, Phillips, & Lyall, 1998; Key & Popkin, 1998). These divergent views of business' role within society ultimately lead to two different perspectives on the appropriateness of CSR.

The basic idea of Friedman's reasons is that the money to pay for activities deemed "socially responsible" must come from somewhere. If the manager raises prices, then he is "taxing" the consumer for the activities; if not the consumer, then the shareholders, since the costs involved in pursing corporate social responsibility will reduce the retained earnings of the owners. Or, the employees may be taxed since their pay or benefits may not increase or may even decrease. In other words, for Friedman, business operations are a zero sum game. To pursue one activity is to take away from another; and in the case of corporate social responsibility, the manager would be acting as a government. This leads, Friedman asserts, to an erosion of the market system.

Common expressions of CSR theories are referred to as the "charity principle" and the "stewardship principle." The first, a modern version of noblese oblige, suggests that the more fortunate should assist the less fortunate. The second requires businesses and wealthy individuals to see themselves as caretakers, not just as shareholders of financial resources, of society's resources – holding property in trust for the benefit of society as a whole. The laws set a floor for behavior but, unable to anticipate every contingency, they are limited in scope; they suggest what aught be done to balance competing interests and rely for compliance on fear of punishment rather than on an expectation of behavior consistent with moral conviction.

Acceptance of CSR requires a normative judgment. Those who are not prepared to make such judgments will not accept the legitimacy of the positive positions taken in the remainder of this document because the positions require an acceptance of the normative notion that corporations owe a duty to society that is separate from its duty to shareholders. We base our acceptance of this public duty on the basis of the State's grant to corporations of eternal existence and limited liability for shareholders. Evaluating industry behavior in a CSR context permits such statements as "the oil industry has taken CSR ... more seriously than other industries. ... The banking industry is lagging in this respect" (Armstrong & Sweeney, 2002). We know of no CSR study of the insurance industry.

The focus of this paper is on two issues in which the insurance industry fares poorly. In some ways the issue of ethics is difficult when discussing insurance because discrimination is the essence of the business. If a good driver and bad driver are charged an average premium, the company may soon find that it is insuring only bad drivers (the notion adverse selection). For this reason insurers discriminate between drivers on the basis of their historical driving record. Still, society deems some forms of discrimination reprehensible and prohibits discrimination on these bases; race is one such example. Ladd (1998) notes that even though loan default rates are higher for black applicants than white, banking lenders cannot use race as a factor in deciding whether to accept a loan application. Companies that use proxies to accomplish discrimination correlated with prohibited discrimination factors clearly behave unethically; such is the case, for example, where the bias is on the basis of factors that are group defined rather than individually defined. The groups we use as examples in this note are gender and age. The second issue we address is the likelihood of anticompetitive behavior by firms in the industry.

2. SELECTED ETHICAL ISSUES OF INSURER OPERATIONS: CLAIM HANDLING BIAS AND ANTICOMPETITIVE INDUSTRY STRUCTURE

Discrimination against groups of people is both morally and legally prohibited. Such discrimination is common in the insurance industry but is arguably not the policy of the companies. The ethical question relates to the absence of effective measures by firms to prevent the application of these biases in the face of cost efficiencies they grant to the firms. The second issue, the anticompetitive structure of the insurance industry is more complex because there is a weaker theoretical tie between structural measures describing the industry and the certainty of an anticompetitive result. Absent a "smoking gun" evidencing anticompetitive behavior that harms consumers, there is a questionable legitimacy to expecting firms in the industry to take action to reduce the suggestive structural measures.

2.1. Group Claim Handling Bias

Doerpinghaus, Schmidt, and Yeh (2003) investigate the notion that insurers may ignore the natural biases of their employees when those biases work to the advantage of the insurer at the expense of the policyholder to whom the insurer owes a fiduciary responsibility. Other than sales issues, these biases are most evident in the claim adjustment process yet, with few exceptions, claim-handling practices are little researched. The exceptions focus on how organizational characteristics affect consumer perceived service quality, or how claim-handling expenses affect insurer total costs (Doerpinghaus, 1991; Barrese, Doerpinghaus, & Nelson, 1995; Browne & Wells, 1999). Others have analyzed the effect of the legal system on the claims process, including the plaintiff's willingness to litigate or settle, and circumstances under which an attorney is more likely to be involved in the negotiations (Cummins & Tennyson, 1996; Kritzer, 1998; Kritzer & Krishnan, 1999).

An ethical direction is taken in the Doerpinghaus et al.'s (2003) article; it provides information on the potential for bias associated with personal demographic characteristics and state liability rules on claims adjuster assessment of fault. Examining data for bodily injury liability claims in which two cars were involved, they study the percentage of fault assigned by the claims adjuster against the insured defendant. They exclude cases that report either 100 percent or 0 percent fault assessed against the insured defendant because these cases may involve less opportunity for claims adjuster judgment. The results show higher assessed fault against female, young, and elderly insured defendants, all else remaining equal.

Acting as profit-maximizing firms, insurers attempt to minimize overall costs for any given level of revenue. One method of reducing claims administration costs is to use formal and informal standards or "rules-of-thumb" for claims adjusting, rather than to uniquely negotiate each claim. Such rules are likely to exist when the cost of arguing over the distribution of financial responsibility exceeds the benefit to the insurer of engaging in the argument. When such economic incentives exist, insurer management need not articulate the standards to have the standard applied relatively consistently because adjuster biases will yield the consistent outcome. We believe the insurer has an ethical obligation to ensure that the cost of adjuster biases is not borne by the insureds.

Ross (1970) identified the use of informal claims adjusting patterns, presenting evidence that certain accident conditions tend toward particular outcomes. These outcomes are so well known that almost every driver is aware of the "rule-of-thumb." Thus, regardless of who is at fault, there is a presumption that a driver who hits another vehicle from behind is likely to be held responsible for the accident. Rule-of-thumb decision-making may offer the potential benefits of lower premiums (through greater efficiency in claims adjusting), but it may come at the expense of selected individuals or groups of consumers. The potential for informal standards to affect *groups* of consumers identified through means other than the factors of an accident is troubling.

The application of the economics of discrimination to insurance markets, following Becker's (1957) seminal work, focused predominately on race, considering such issues as availability (Klein, 1997), price (Harrington & Niehaus, 1998), and service (Chan, 1998). Doerpinghaus et al. (2003) extend the insurance discrimination literature by considering gender and age effects on assignment of fault.

A. Gender Bias
The adjuster, the insured defendant, and the claimant are influenced consciously or unconsciously by the risk and negotiation preference of both self and others. Individuals who are more risk averse would accept lower-valued settlements with certainty rather than subject themselves to larger risky judgments. If claims adjusters could identify (consciously or unconsciously) more risk-averse claimants, they would effect lower settlements. Similarly, claims adjusters would offer lower settlements to less aggressive negotiators, given that the psychic and perhaps economic costs of extended negotiations are higher for this group.

Evidence suggests that women on average are more risk averse and less aggressive negotiators than men, all else remaining equal. Halek and Eisenhauer (2001) test the effects of various demographic characteristics, including gender and age, on relative risk aversion. They find that women demonstrate greater relative risk aversion than men, both regarding pure and speculative risks. This is consistent with Sorrentino (1992), and others (Levin, Snyder, & Chaptman, 1988; Powell & Ansic, 1997) who find that women demonstrate preference for a moderate payoff with certainty over a higher payoff with uncertainty.

Researchers have also observed gender differences in negotiations. Women are more conflict averse in dispute settlement, and negotiate less successful outcomes than men (see Doerpinghaus et al. (2003) for a survey of prior research on these topics). In negotiations, women, relative to men, prefer being perceived as fair-minded or reasonable, men have a relatively higher orientation toward maximizing economic outcome; women have greater self-doubt about their perceptions and therefore may perceive lower settlements as fair. The causes of gender differences in risk attitude and negotiating styles are difficult to establish. Pervasive stereotypes may drive behaviors. Whether due to innate differences or because of behavioral expectations, claims adjusters seem to understand that the cost of an error against women is less likely to be challenged.

B. Age Bias

Evidence suggests that the elderly (i.e., persons age 65 or older) on average demonstrate greater risk aversion relative to the population at large (Halek & Eisenhauer, 2001). The evidence shows decreasing risk aversion with age increases until age 65 when the relationship reverses: individuals over age 65 demonstrate greater risk aversion than others. In addition to greater risk aversion, tenuous negotiating skills in the elderly may coincide with physical fragility and dependency (Doerpinghaus et al., 2003).

Age effects on auto claims management are relevant where there is (1) an age difference between insured defendant and claimant; (2) where one or both parties is/are very young – less than 22 years old; and (3) where one or both parties is/are elderly – age 65 or older. Claimants or insured defendants on the extremes of the age continuum (i.e., younger than 22 or ages 65 and older) are expected to differ from those in-between (i.e., the middle-aged, ages 22–64). Claims adjusting bias would favor a middle-aged insured defendant who is sued by a younger claimant, per Halek and Eisenhauer (2001) and Riley and Chow (1992), since risk aversion declines with age (up to age 65). In addition, middle-aged individuals have the advantage of greater experience with negotiation. Note that both the very young and the very old are also likely to be viewed as being more often at fault, given the generally higher frequency of accidents at these ages. Given the evidence to date, we expect higher average fault assessment against very young and elderly insured defendants, all else remaining equal.

Controlling for true fault, the evidence suggests that female, elderly, and young drivers are assessed a higher percentage of fault than are others, all else remaining equal. In addition, during the middle years (between ages 22 and 64), relatively older insured defendants are assessed relatively less fault than are relatively younger insured defendants. Doerpinghaus et al. (2003) provide some support for this alternative explanation: while both male and female insured drivers are assessed traffic violations about 70 percent of the time that they are in accidents, male drivers account for a much higher percent of the severe violations than do women. This is consistent with true fault being greater for males while assessed fault is greater for females, and is also consistent with the explanation of gender bias in claims handling.

Ladd (1998) notes that discriminatory behavior undertaken for pure profit-maximizing purposes may be illegal; i.e., even though loan default rates are higher for black applicants than white applicants, the lender cannot use race as a factor in deciding whether to accept a loan applicant. Variations in insurance claim management practices by gender and age might meet the legal definition of discrimination and therefore be prohibited under current laws.

Initial mortgage lending studies have found strong differences in the likelihood of loan denial between whites and blacks, but insufficient control data weakened the results. Legal changes in 1975 altered data reporting requirements for lending institutions, promising a richer data set for empirical testing. The Federal Reserve Bank of Boston ultimately conducted a comprehensive study that incorporated *all* data available to lenders at the time of loan application and corroborated earlier evidence of difference in loan denial rates by race. The insurance evidence reported here demonstrates the need for richer data sets on insurer claims management practices as well as incorporation of demographic factors into analysis of insurer practices. Both the mortgage lending and insurance claims adjusting fields have begun to move toward online systems of doing business that are independent of personal decision makers. Claims adjusting online involves a series of double-blind settlement offers between the insurer and claimant (or the claimant's attorney on behalf of the claimant). Demographic factors do not enter into negotiation. In fact, it is possible that the claims adjuster and attorney/claimant never meet. Similar systems are used in mortgage lending and may have a role in reducing the effects of personal bias in business decision-making.

2.2. Concentration in the Insurance Industry

The economic case for the superiority of free markets depends on the existence of competition to promote the public interest. The existence of monopoly power may lead to lower levels of production and higher product prices. The sources of monopoly power include entrance or exit barriers. Economic barriers insulate existing firms from potential competition. Product differentiation, economies of scale, predatory practices, and advertising are often identified as important barriers that limit competition. In addition, collusion that restricts market output is said to be socially inefficient.

The implication that concentration is not in the interests of society sees its most forceful expression in the 1945 U.S. v. Aluminum Co. of America (ALCOA) decision; it found a high market share a legal offense even though the market share was seen to be a consequence of the company's production efficiency (Alcoa, 1945). Alcoa was convicted because it had succeeded. Alcoa was convicted of monopolizing the market for primary ingot aluminum with almost 90 percent of the market despite the fact that the firm was not found guilty of illegally excluding competition, conspiracy, charging excessive prices, or earning an excessive rate of return.[3] While writers do not unanimously support the appropriateness of the Alcoa decision the case demonstrates the suspicion of high market shares held for long periods of time. The time dimension noted in *Alcoa* is particularly relevant for our study of the property-liability (P&L) insurance industry, which finds high market share concentration levels with persistent market share leaders over time, and both concentrated and interlocking ownership relationships; circumstantial features of a non-competitive industry.

Despite a historic validity to the claim that the insurance industry is collusive, academic researchers differ from popular opinion regarding the industry competitiveness.[4] This paper describes circumstantial evidence supporting popular opinion in personal lines. In the commercial lines, an inability to completely define the relevant market impedes coming to a similar conclusion. However, the popular press contains strong recent evidence of anticompetitive behavior in the commercial lines.[5]

The traditional structure–conduct–performance (SCP) paradigm considers the association of concentrated markets with collusive behavior or superior market performance. SCP studies typically follow one of two concentration paths; the most common studies investigate market share concentration, another path investigates ownership concentration. SCP market share studies of the P&L insurance industry conclude that it is competitively structured in most lines, with numerous firms, relatively easy entry, and satisfactory concentration levels, though popular claims persist that the industry is not competitive (Kopcke & Randall, 1991).

Long-run market power requires barriers to the entry of competitors. There are three types of entry or exit barrier: natural, legal, and strategic (Armentano, 2000). Evidence suggests that natural and legal barriers in the insurance industry are not sufficient to grant market power to existing firms. Scale and scope economy studies of the insurance industry are not consistent; most find evidence of cost or technical efficiencies. A survey of 14 frontier efficiency studies of the insurance industry reports that 11 of the studies find cost efficiency results and 5 find technical efficiencies (Cummins & Weiss, 1998). Estimates of cost efficiencies are reported for the life insurance (Grace & Timme, 1992; Cummins & Zi, 1998) but limited studies exist for the P&L industry (an exception is Doherty, 1981). Legal barriers, which include licensing and industry specific laws and regulations that create an entry cost constraint, provide consumers with fewer choices and protect inefficiencies and the profit margins of existing suppliers. Yet, to satisfy other social goals States require that insurers be licensed and conform to the rules promulgated by the State (McKenzie, 2001). State regulation both raises entry barriers and defines the geographic boundary of the market but reviewers conclude that legal barriers are not a prohibitive constraint in the insurance industry (Cummins & Weiss, 1991).[6]

Strategic barriers include both legal firm specific actions, such as product differentiation, and illegal or unethical collusive constraints. Among the latter, firm specific strategies that can raise entry barriers include the threat of predatory or limit pricing. Strategic barriers created by cooperation among firms in an oligopolistic market include price-fixing, the misuse of trade associations, preventing price discounts, and agreements to divide the market (Bulow, Geanakoplos, & Klemperer, 1985b). The insurance industry is often accused of these types of activity. Bulow, Geanakoplos, and Klemperer (1985a) also provide an entry barrier rationale for a frequent feature of the insurance industry, the existence of excess capacity. If imperfect competition is present, excess capacity provides the firm with a credible threat to use against cartel-violating competition or new entrants.

Ownership concentration, following the Berle-Means (1932) paradigm relating ownership concentration and profitability, is less frequently seen in insurance studies. Berle and Means (1932) concluded that share ownership was becoming increasingly dispersed and implications of this corporate evolution, separating the management and ownership functions, form the foundation of modern financial theory. Countless articles have replicated or extended these studies and most empirical works continued to find declining ownership by the directors and officers of corporations but an exhaustive survey comparing 1935 and 1995 reaches the opposite conclusion (Holderness, Kroszner, & Sheehan, 1999). Recent work links the concentration of power in the hands of those governing corporations with reductions in firm value. For example, Bebchuk and Cohen (2004) note that participants in the corporate governance debate suggest shareholder value is negatively affected by their inability to effectively threaten management because this inability affects the probability of an acquisition and the expected acquisition premium. Others discussing the entrenchment theory suggest that entrenched management has a higher ability to pursue goals other than value maximization.[7]

A. Market Share Concentration

The US P&L insurance industry has thousands of firms, a large number even after correcting for the fact that many of the thousands of firms are subsidiaries of holding companies that exercise tight coordination. After controlling for grouping there are 1,117 P&L insurers in 2002.[8] However, the top ten firms account for almost 44 percent of 2002 industry premiums and the top 25 firms account for 63 percent of these revenues. The market share of each of the smallest 1,000 insurers is less than or equal to 0.1 percent of the industry total.[9]

The focus on market share concentration in the industrial organization literature is due to a disagreement about the causal direction of the link between industry concentration and competitiveness. Higher concentration levels imply greater opportunities for operating a cartel effectively because members will find it easier to detect price-cutting (Stigler, 1964) and many empirical studies, following the tradition of Bain (1951), find a positive though often weak link between concentration and profit rates. Critics (Demsetz, 1973; Baumol, 1982) question the presumption that market share concentration is suggestive of market power; they argue that the causal structure is as likely to be from performance to structure rather than from structure to performance.[10] DeVany and Kim (2002) also criticize reliance on concentration indices, arguing that these static measures, computed using point-in-time market shares, give a false sense of market stability. They argue that market share leaders in a competitive industry change rapidly and often. Persistence in the concentration and composition of market leadership bring into question the notion that a market is competitive.

Despite the question regarding the causal direction of the relationship between concentration indices and performance, a relatively high market share concentration is a necessary, though not a sufficient condition to demonstrate a lack of competition. Absent concentration in an industry with more than a few firms, a collusively equal distribution of the market is unrealistic given the advantages to each member from cheating on the cartel agreement. This view is reflected in the US Department of Justice (US DOJ) use of market share concentration data as a starting point for analyzing competitive impact in horizontal merger cases. The US DOJ presumes adverse competitive effects when a merger will cause the four firm concentration ratio (CR_4) to exceed 35 percent and the Herfindahl–Hirshman index (HHI) to exceed 1,000.[11]

Measures of market concentration require two distinct dimensional specifications: definition of the product and the geographic area. Because most products are not perfectly homogeneous the product definition includes the range of products that consumers perceive as close substitutes. For regulatory and practical reasons, personal lines consumers have few choices; insurance for a specific risk is addressed by policies insurers consider in a particular line of business. For example, insurance to cover potential damage to a car is addressed by an automobile insurance policy while a homeowner policy covers the potential damage to a home. Because the policies are not substitutes, this distinction serves to set a product definition limit to these markets. Reliance on the "line of business" to set the product definition limits of the market is less reliable for commercial lines. Business risk managers have a wider variety of loss financing tools available, many of these alternatives are not insurance products or not in the market share measures available (e.g., loss financing derivatives and premiums paid to a captive are not in the market share data).

Identifying the state as the relevant geographic area for insurance is more complicated. The geographic area must include all suppliers of a good who are actual or potential competitors. To write business in a state, the actual competitors must be licensed by and use forms and rates complying with state filing regulations. Potential competition is difficult to identify. Though 1,112 insurance groups or unaffiliated companies operate in the US of the lines of business identified by each state fewer than 200 firms typically have sales in a state.[12] Because legal entry barriers are low, it has been argued that the large number of insurers not operating in a state provides a competitive constraint. This argument is limited by the fact that industry sales are concentrated in the hands of about 100 insurers, and most of these insurers operate in all states. Still, this potential competitor dilemma complicates the notion that the market definition for insurance is no larger than the boundaries of the state.

A further geographic boundary complication exists because the market for some lines also depends on the size and mobility of consumers. Personal lines insurance, including auto and homeowners insurance, are products whose demand and policy format are set by State regulations and lending requirements while a corporate insurance policy may cover exposures in more than one state.[13] Thus, not only do business insurance lines face competition from alternative risk transfer tools, it is unlikely that the corporate premiums insurers report as being in a particular state is attributable only to exposures situated in that state. While we rely on state boundaries to define the geographic market area in this study, we recognize the limitations created by this definition.

Table 1 reports the 2002 direct premium written by insurers in 5 selected lines of insurance, they account for 73 percent of the industry total. The table also lists average state concentration and persistence measures.

The CR_4 and HHI columns report the average of the state values. Regardless of the concentration measure, on average the personal lines are more concentrated than the commercial lines. By-state and by-line analysis demonstrates that the combination of CR_4 and HHI values in most states and lines exceeds the combination cited by the US DOJ as presumptive of adverse competitive effects.[14]

For multiple years, the insurance industry concentration levels in many states exceed the presumptively adverse combination of a high CR_4 and HHI. The pattern is least frequent in commercial lines but this perception may have more to do with the difficulty of correctly defining the geographic and cross-price elasticity issues that define these markets.

Table 1 also reports two values characterized as measuring persistence. As suggested by DeVany and Kim (2002), an absence of competition is reflected by an industry with the same market share leaders for an extended period of time. Column 6 reports the number of top four 2002 firms that were in the top four in a selected number of other time periods covering a 17-year period: 2002, 2000, 1995, 1990, and 1985.[15] The second "Persistence" column reports the number of states in which at least three of the top four 2002 firms also held one of the top four positions in each of the other four periods considered. For example, for private passenger auto, in 18 of 51 states the top four firms in

Table 1. DPW, CR_4, HHI and Persistence, Selected Lines (Group & Unaffiliated Insurers, 2002 ($B)).

Line of Business	DPW		CR_4	HHI	Persistence 85–02	
	$Billions	%			4	4:3
Private passenger auto	1,721.8	36.5	0.541	1,021	18	47
Homeowners	448.8	9.5	0.564	1,118	18	43
Workers compensation	576.7	12.2	0.478	1,090	0	6
Commercial multiperil	365.3	7.7	0.353	586	0	1
Commercial auto	334.6	7.1	0.301	421	0	3

2002 were also the top four firms in 2000, 1995, 1990, and 1985. In 47 states, the top four 2002 firms occupied at least three of the top positions in the earlier years. The table demonstrates that persistence is more common in personal than in commercial lines.[16] In none of the states were the top four 2002 commercial lines firms market leaders for each of the earlier periods. The dramatic difference between the personal and commercial lines persistence and concentration values reflects market definition issues. Because we cannot solve this problem of correctly identifying the commercial lines market, we report values for an investigation of the commercial lines but do not consider them to be accurate estimates of those segments of the P&L industry.

Market share concentration is a concern if it has economic or welfare implications; these include the existence of excess profit. Most industry studies of the relationship between market share concentration and the rate of return earned on equity capital are straightforward, not so in the insurance industry where identifying the market ROE is possible for only part of the industry. In the US P&L insurance industry, 33.7 percent of the firms are non-stock firms that account for 48.5 percent of industry premiums earned. In addition, many stock insurers are closely held, making market data less reliable. In the spirit of the ROE measure, the National Association of Insurance Commissioners (NAIC) reports a by-line and state measure characterized as the return on net worth (RNW).[17] RNW is an imperfect ROE proxy because it relies on the statutory accounting principle (SAP) annual statement but the measure has the advantage that it can be computed for any insurer.[18]

Table 2, which compares the RNW for the P&L industry and the ROE for all industries, reveals one of the curiosities of the insurance industry: the reported measure of profit consistently trails industry averages yet the share price of insurance company stocks exceeds the performance of the market over the same time period. The seemingly low returns may reflect a relatively low risk level for the insurance industry but we also question the method of measuring industry profit.[19] If the RNW measure accurately reflects the relative level of industry return, the reason for the existence of excess capacity is an unanswered conundrum with a possible answer in the strategic barrier suggestion of Bulow et al. (1985a).

Table 2.   Comparison of ROE and RNW.

	2002	2000	1995	1993–2002
ROE: forbes magazine all industry	10.2	14.6	14.0	13.1
RNW: NAIC property/casualty insurance	1.7	6.6	8.8	7.0

Consistent with most insurance industry studies, by-line regressions of the measures of market share concentration for each state on the state average RNW do not reveal statistically significant relationships.[20] As noted by critics of the SCP market share-concentration approach, this absence of a statistical relationship is consistent with both a competitive and a collusive industry structure.

B. Insurer Ownership Concentration

Berle and Means' (1932) survey of the ownership and control of US corporations concluded that share ownership was becoming increasingly dispersed. Later investigators felt that the 1932 study was an early snapshot of the evolution of the corporate form and countless articles have replicated or extended these studies. Most empirical works continued to find declining ownership by the directors and officers of corporations but an exhaustive survey comparing 1935 and 1995 reaches the conclusion that the trend has recently been reversed (Holderness et al., 1999).

Implications of this corporate evolution identified by Berle and Means (1932), separating the management and ownership functions, form the foundation of modern financial theory. Gordon (1940), Williamson (1964), and others observe that the separation of firm ownership and control pits the preferences of owners against those of managers. Jensen and Meckling (1976) observe that conflicting incentives among the parties generates agency costs incurred in to reduce incentive conflicts; these agency costs reduce corporate performance. The incentive alignment theory suggests higher levels of equity ownership by managers may increase corporate performance because it aligns the financial incentives of the manager and other equity owners. Bebchuk and Cohen (2004) provide a summary of the entrenchment argument, which describes the entrenchment of managers under different board organization structures, implies that levels of equity ownership by management sufficiently high to render unlikely the replacement of managers by other shareholders may decrease corporate performance (also see, Kamerschen, 1968). The utility preferences of the owner–managers may work against the incentive to maximize profit, substituting goals such as the maximization of compensation, market share, or industry leadership (Morck, Shleifer, & Vishny, 1989). Consistent with the entrenchment hypothesis, Fama and Jensen (1983) suggest increased ownership concentration decreases financial performance because it raises the firm's cost of capital as a result of decreased market liquidity. While disagreement exists about the reasons why managers might be motivated to deviate from a profit-maximization goal, theories suggest that managerial utility is correlated with firm size (Marris, 1963). Larger firms are likely and often more able to provide managers with higher levels of salary, power, and status. Combining these conflicting hypotheses, Stultz, Walking, and Song (1990) and Morck et al. (1989) argue that the effect of the incentive alignment hypothesis is dominant for low levels of managerial ownership but for higher levels, about 5 percent managerial ownership, the entrenchment effect is dominant. They argue that the relationship again reverses for managerial ownership levels higher than 30 percent.

Studies of managerial ownership typically focus on ownership by the firm's directors and executive officers (D&O) and tend to exclude financial service firms. Holderness et al. (1999) do not exclude the financial service sector but they concentrate only on firms organized using the stock form. The relative importance of non-stock firms in the insurance industry means that any study of the control exerted by a small group of insurance company shareholders must understate true industry control levels. Table 3 provides a descriptive view of insurance industry ownership patterns using a sample of firms obtained from the Securities Exchange Commission's (SEC) Edgar database for firms in NAICS code 6331 (Fire, Marine and Casualty Insurance). For comparison, the table also lists information for other industries drawn from Holderness et al. (1999).[21] Mean managerial ownership rose for all industries from 12.9 percent in 1935, to 21.1 percent in 1995. Dividing their sample into broad industry categories, Holderness et al. (1999) report a similar pattern for the Finance, Insurance, and Real Estate (FIRE) sector though the level of managerial ownership for this sector is reported to be

Table 3. Ownership Concentration Patterns.

	1935	1995	2002 Shareholders	
			D&O	Plus Other Significant
All Industries	12.9%	21.1%		24.8[a]
FIRE (%)	8.4%	17.4%		
Insurance (%)			19.6%	52.7%

[a]Holderness, Kroszner, and Sheehan (1999) report the 1935 and 1995 values; the authors compute insurance values for 2002 including, for comparison purposes, the "plus other significant shareholder" value for all industries with 2001 "Blockholder data" provided by Andrew Metrick, htmhttp://finance.wharton.upenn.edu/~metrick/data.htm (viewed September 21, 2004). This data suggests a director and officer level closer to 3.8 than to the 21.1 percent reported in Holderness. This anomaly raises a question about what is measured by HKS or about the accuracy of the Metrick data. Still, the total blockholder percentage falls well below that of the insurance industry.

lower than the overall average in each time period: 8.4 percent in 1935 and 17.4 percent in 1995.

Managerial ownership for the insurance companies in this study, at 19.6 percent, is not dissimilar from Holderness's FIRE finding for 1995. For at least two reasons, however, this estimate of the concentration of corporate control is conservative. First, in the insurance industry we find a very significant level of ownership concentration if other large shareholders, those holding a block of more than 5 percent of the firm's stock, are added to the holdings of management and directors.[22] The last row in Table 3 reports the average ownership of this more inclusive set of close decision makers as 52.7 percent.

In addition to stock measurement issues, two additional insurance industry features imply that the listed estimates of stock concentration understate the true measure of control by a small group. The first feature is the importance of the mutual organizational form; mutual shareholders legally own the firm but the directors and officers control the firm because policyholder block voting is almost impossible for a sizeable firm.[23] Recognizing that one of the largest insurers is a mutual, a firm that is persistently among the top four market share leaders, it is clear that the exclusion of this group of firms leads to an understated measure of the control of industry by a small group of individuals. The other industry feature implying that the coordination of behavior in the insurance industry could be accomplished with ease is the degree of interrelated ownership of insurance company stock. The authors provide evidence of a potential pattern of linkages through large ownership holdings of individuals, families, and funds.[24] The connections are based on the 10K reporting requirement that firms reveal beneficial owners of 5 percent or more of the firm's stock.[25]

Mathiesen (2002) provides an exhaustive survey of the recent empirical literature building on Berle and Means (1932) study; many investigate a link between firm performance and ownership patterns.[26] These empirical studies use a variety of measures as a proxy for performance but the studies have inconsistent results. Table 4 reports revenue weighted regression outcomes for the insurance industry that relate 2002 firm risk levels and ownership concentration to two measures of performance, the return on equity and Tobin's Q.[27]

The results are consistent with the pattern hypothesized by Stultz, Walking, and Song (1990) and Morck et al. (1989). The incentive alignment hypothesis appears dominant for lower ownership levels while the entrenchment hypothesis dominates for high levels of ownership concentration. That is, the models find higher levels of firm performance at low ownership levels but performance is either neutral or decreasing at higher levels of ownership concentration.

Table 4. Revenue Weighted Regressions for ROE and Tobin's Q.

	Return on Equity		Tobin's Q	
	Coefficient	Significance	Coefficient	Significance
Constant	1.249	0.402	0.242	0.155
Beta	4.009	0.047	0.684	0.004
Leverage				
Liquidity				
Ownership 25–50%	4.560	0.000	0.258	0.067
Ownership 50–80%	0.622	0.793	−0.474	0.102
Ownership > 80%	1.538	0.431	−0.722	0.002
Adjusted R^2	0.201		0.377	

C. SCP Conclusion

This section develops a set of circumstantial evidence suggesting that the US P&L industry is able to exercise monopoly power. The issue is important because of a discontinuity between an almost unanimous collection of studies of the insurance industry that suggest the industry is competitive and an equally firm conviction to the contrary that is popularly held. We focus on state markets and specific lines of business to develop measures typical of the SCP approach and find concentration levels that would raise concerns for the US Justice Department in merger cases. Consistent with the existing literature, we find insignificant relationships between profit levels and the CR_4 and HHI concentration measures. However, pursuing the approach of Berle and Means we observe concentrated and interlocking ownership relationships that add to both competitive and social concerns. Consistent with the management entrenchment hypothesis, empirical estimates reveal a negative relationship between ownership concentration and Tobin's Q. The data raise a social concern about the potentially coordinating role for mutual fund managers who are shown to be part of an industry network characterized by concentrated and interlocking ownership relationships. Justice Brandeis warned that the concentration of ownership is important not only for its implications about the competitiveness of the industry but also for its implications about the distribution of societal wealth, power, and welfare.[28]

In sum, we find that average by-state and by-line CR_4 and HHI market share concentration levels exceed those that raise concerns for the US Justice Department in merger cases but we do not find a positive relationship between these measures and industry profit levels. This empirical outcome is consistent with both a competitive and a collusive market. We find market share leadership persistence that has lasted for decades in personal lines. This persistence is consistent with the exercise of entry barriers. We believe it is unlikely that the persistence pattern is fully accounted for by an alternative theory: consumer status quo bias. Finally, the results of a NEIO study suggest that the auto insurance market is weakly oligopolistic. Empirical issues prevent developing broader conclusions for commercial lines. The section does not supply conclusive evidence of the exercise of monopoly power in the P&L industry but the data provide circumstantial evidence that such a claim is not irresponsible.

3. SUMMARY

This paper describes a subset of ethically questionable insurance industry practices: anticompetitive collusion and gender and age biases.

Collusion ...

Initial mortgage lending studies have found strong differences in the likelihood of loan denial between whites and blacks, but insufficient control data weakened the results. Legal changes in 1975 altered data reporting requirements for lending institutions, promising a richer data set for empirical testing. The Federal Reserve Bank of Boston ultimately conducted a comprehensive study that incorporated *all* data available to lenders at the time of loan application and corroborated earlier evidence of difference in loan denial rates by race. The insurance evidence reported here demonstrates the need for richer data sets on insurer claims management practices as well as incorporation of demographic factors into analysis of insurer practices. Both the mortgage lending and insurance claims adjusting fields have begun to move toward online systems of doing business that are independent of personal decision makers. Claims adjusting online involves a series of double-blind settlement offers between the insurer and claimant (or the claimant's attorney on behalf of the claimant). Demographic factors do not enter into negotiation. In fact, it is possible that the claims adjuster and attorney/claimant never meet. Similar systems are used in mortgage lending and may have a role in reducing the effects of personal bias in business decision-making.

NOTES

1. The usage of "incestuous" is consistent with the following of Webster's definition reference: "resembling incest between people or groups so closely related as to

make such activity improper or unethical; as, an incestuous coziness between the management of a company and its union."

2. For a sample of significant statements in the evolution of the CSR, see Table 2, "Significant Documents: Best Practice in Corporate Governance Reporting" (Armstrong & Sweeney, 2002).

3. Aluminum ingot prices had fallen from over $2.00 a pound in the 1890s to less than 22 cents a pound at the time of the trial, and Alcoa's average rate of return for 50 years was just over 10 percent on invested capital. The firm was guilty of monopoly by virtue of its success; maintenance of a high market share was a sufficient violation of the antitrust law. Judge Learned Hand explained that it was Alcoa's "skill, energy, and initiative" that "excluded" competitors in aluminum production. If Alcoa had been less efficient there would have been "more competition" and no violation of the antitrust law.

4. For the popular opinion, see National Marketing Services. "Insurance Industry Outlook 2004 Study." http://www.nationalmarketing.com/Markets/outlook_2004_ overview.asp?node = 5&sNode = 4&Exp = Y viewed July 23, 2004. Also see Consumer Reports. "Surviving the 'hard market' in homeowners insurance."

5. See "Spitzer making good on plan for wide insurance probe," http://money. cnn.com/services/tickerheadlines/djh/200410191651DOWJONESDJONLINE000944. htm viewed October 19, 2004.

6. State regulations also impose exit barriers. See, for example, "Coalition for Auto Insurance Competition Implores New Jersey State Government to Urgently Address Auto Insurance Availability." (June 4, 2004) http://www.collision-insight. com/news/20020604-coalition.htm, viewed July 20, 2004.

7. See, Fahlenbrach, Rüdiger. "Shareholder rights and CEO compensation." University of Pennsylvania. Working paper. (2003) http://assets.wharton.upenn.edu/ ~rfahlenb/Papers/Rights_and_comp11022003.pdf (viewed Sept. 18, 2004).

8. Groups or unaffiliated insurers. *Best's Aggregates and Averages*, 2002 Edition. Oldwick, NJ: A.M. Best Company and *AM Best Pick-a-Page* software, 2003.

9. The market share concentration is from "Property and Casualty Insurance Industry 2002 Market Share Report by State and Countrywide." http://www.naic. org/research/Research_Division/Stats/2002_PC_MktShare.pdf. Viewed August 6, 2004. There are a variety of concentration measures. Two of the more common are the n-firm market share and the Hirfindahl–Hirschman Index. Bikker and Haaf (2002) summarize the relationship between 10 measures of concentration and provide policy makers guidelines for choosing the concentration index based on the situation. But, Donsimoni, Geroski, and Jacquemin (1984) argue "there is no such thing as an optimal index of concentration, both because different industries behave differently as well as because no obvious widely accepted normative judgments exist to guarantee its optimality."

10. Mathiesen (2002) summarizes empirical studies of the hypothesis that performance is a function of ownership concentration (the performance hypotheses) or that ownership concentration is a function of firm performance (the ownership hypotheses). Some performance hypotheses suggest that higher levels of managerial ownership have a positive impact on firm performance; some suggest the impact is negative; and some studies allow for both positive and negative impacts in various ownership ranges. Each of the ownership hypotheses, however, associates higher

levels of firm performance with higher levels of ownership concentration. The hypothesized link between ownership and performance is discussed in Holderness et al. (1999) and partially by Mayers, Shivdasani, and Smith (1997) for the insurance industry.

11. US Department of Justice. "Horizontal Merger Guidelines." April 8, 1997. http://www.usdoj.gov/atr/public/guidelines/horiz_book/hmg1.html viewed May 2, 2004. See especially Section 2.0.

12. Approximately, half of the insurers operate in one or two states; 13 have a positive DPW in all states.

13. Master Commercial General Liability (CGL) policies designed to cover multiple locations allocate property-based premium to states in an arbitrary way. Allocation is still more difficult when liability exposures are covered. The impossibility of identifying a "correct allocation" is mentioned in conversation with the NY State tax department, a group with an interest in the correct allocation because it affects premium tax revenues. (For a copy of the CGL policy, see the *CPCU Handbook of Insurance Policies* Insurance Institute of America (2003).)

14. The number of states exceeding both a 35percent CR_4 and a 1,000 HHI, by line, are personal auto, 23 states; homeowners, 15 states; commercial multiple peril, 9 states; workers compensation, 10 states; and commercial auto, 11 states. By-state, by-line information is provided for a selection of years. (Data available from the authors.)

15. An alternative is to use a rank correlation measure, such as the Spearman R statistic. The valid computation of this statistic requires a comparison of the entire distribution of firms rather than isolating the leaders. For example, if the top four firms in 2002 were ranked 1, 2, 8, and 3 in the prior time period, the rank correlation would be -1.5, a nonsensical value.

16. Consumer choice, rather than firm or collusive behavior may be the cause of the persistent leadership for a period of time, but theory suggests that persistent market share leadership is a possible barrier to the entry of competitors. Zeckhauser and Samuelson (1989) suggest that insured are unlikely to change insurers, even after negative experiences, because they believe the alternatives will be no better and that incurred search costs will not be recouped.

17. See Bailey (1969) for a still relevant critique of the formula and the problem of measuring profitability. The unfortunate consequence is that results are adjusted in different ways, reducing the credibility of results. See Cummins and Tennyson (1992) for a review of other approaches to addressing insurance profit measurement.

18. Insurance company annual statements do not report data in a format conducive to matching the revenue and costs of its product and it is theoretically difficult to determine an allocation of equity or investment income to specific lines or states. Losses are reported by line for the policy years written but not by line and state. In addition, frequent changes in loss reserves suggest significant variation in expected losses or purposeful reporting issues (Bradford & Logue, 1997). Revenues are reported by-line and by-state but not by the year of the initial policy. Recognizing the difficulties, insurance industry studies typically rely on the practical solution of measuring performance by comparing the aggregate losses and expenses incurred in a calendar year with the premiums earned in that year. The mismatch between current year revenue values, the loss protection purchased by that revenue, and the

resulting profit generated reduces the confidence of conclusions drawn from the use of single year values. The difficulty of correctly identifying revenue, loss, and associated investment streams creates a need for imperfect proxies to measure profit in the insurance industry.

19. The ROE and RNW comparison is culled from National Association of Insurance Commissioners. "Profitability by Line by State in 2002." *Research Quarterly*, (Kansas City: 2003) page 14.

20. Regressions of the state average RNW on CR_4 and HHI yield significant positive relationships in most lines. However, the addition of a state size adjustment variable – either state personal income as a proxy for effective in-state demand or the state population – renders the CR_4 and HHI coefficients insignificant.

21. Insurance company data are drawn from the SEC forms 10-K and 14A for 2002; Appendix 4 lists the sample. The corporate entities in the sample had revenues of $224.6 billion, more than half of the $422.1 billion total 2002 industry premium.

22. The 2002 D&O control of AIG voting stock, for example, is reported on their 10-K as 3.3 percent. However, two related entities own an additional 16 percent and members of the AIG management control these other entities. In addition, at least one mutual fund owns 5.2 percent of AIG stock, this external ownership generally adds to the voting block of the directors and officers bringing the total share percentage controlled by a relatively small group to 24.5 percent.

23. Policyholders are allowed minimal participation in electing a mutual insurance company's board of directors. In New York, mutual life insurance policyholders are allowed one vote regardless of the number or value of their policies. Policyholders have the right to oppose the administrative ticket if they submit a petition signed by at least 500 eligible voters. To obtain a list of eligible voters, the policyholders interested in opposing the administrative ticket must file a petition, signed by 25 eligible voters, with New York's Superintendent of Insurance. After overcoming these two blocks, the insurer's board of directors can require voting by ballot only rather than by proxy.

24. The list of other funds holding significant blocks of insurance company stock is large. For the sample subset of 22 large insurers, 32 funds are involved as significant owners.

25. If the fund owns less than five percent SEC rules do not require that the ownership be identified but the fund manager may have a role at the shareholder meetings. To understand the possible significance of ownership when less than five percent of the firm is owned, the stock holdings of two funds were obtained from the SEC and the insurers in each firm's portfolio identified. Not surprisingly, the funds owned over 80 insurance companies and shares in over 60 of these other companies are owned by both funds. Finally, the stock of some insurers is held in the investment portfolio of other insurers, including mutual insurers.

26. See http://www.encycogov.com/ for Mathiesen's (2002) dissertation. The document summarizes 94 studies produced between 1966 and 2000 linking performance and ownership percentages. Of the 94 articles reviewed, 31 are event studies. The 63 non-event studies employ samples ranging from 43 to 4,202 firms.

27. We follow the suggestion of DaDalt, Donaldson and Garner (2003) and use the simple computation of q described by Chung and Pruitt (1994) to avoid loosing observations in a data set that is already small (However, though the set of observations is small these groups encompass almost 700 individual firms over 25 percent of industry

sales with another 15 percent accounted for by two large mutual companies.). For ease of interpretation, we invert q so that an increase in q implies an increase in market's evaluation of the value of the firm relative to the firm's book value.

28. Brandeis, speaking primarily of the then relevant problem of interlocking corporate directorates, believed the smaller the group controlling business activity the more likely the actions of the group would be coordinated rather than competitive. "The practice of interlocking directors is the practice of many evils. ... Applied to rival corporations, it tends to the suppression of competition ... applied to corporations which deal with each other, it tends to disloyalty and violation of the fundamental law that no man can serve two masters. In either event, it tends to inefficiency for it removes incentives and destroys soundness of judgment." Pujo committee report, 1913; quoted in Miller (1997).

REFERENCES

Armentano, D. T. (2000). *Barriers to entry.* http://www.mises.org/fullstory.asp?control = 509, visited April 22, 2004.

Armstrong, A., & Sweeney, M. (2002). Corporate governance disclosure: Demonstrating corporate social responsibility through social reporting. *New Academy Review, 1*(2), 33–51.

Bailey, R. A. (1969). A review of the little report on rates of return in the property and liability insurance industry. *Proceedings of the Casualty Actuary Society, 56*(106), 133–141 and Author's review of the discussion. *Proceedings of the Casualty Actuary Society, 56*(106), 155–163.

Bain, J. S. (1951). Relation of profit-rate to industry concentration: American manufacturing, 1936–1940. *Quarterly Journal of Economics, 65,* 293–324.

Balabanis, G., Lyall, J., & Phillips, H. (1998). The impact of social corporate responsibility on the economic performance of the large British firms. *European Business Review, 28*(1), 25–45.

Barrese, J., Doerpinghaus, H. I., & Nelson, J. M. (1995). Do independent agent insurers provide superior service? The insurance marketing puzzle. *Journal of Risk and Insurance, 62,* 297–308.

Baumol, W. (1982). Contestable markets: An uprising in the theory of industry structure. *American Economic Review, 72*(1), 1–15.

Bebchuk, L. A., & Cohen, A. (2004). The costs of entrenched boards. *John M. Olin Center for Law, Economics, and Business.* Discussion paper no. 478.

Becker, G. S. (1957). *The economics of discrimination.* Chicago: University of Chicago Press.

Berle, A., & Means, G. (1932). *The modern corporation and private property.* New York: Macmillan.

Bikker, J., & Haaf, K. (2002). Measures of competition and concentration in the banking industry: A review of the literature. *Economic & Financial Modeling, 9,* 53–98.

Bowen, H. R. (1953). *Social responsibilities of the businessman.* New York: Harper & Row.

Bowie, N. (1995). New directions in corporate social responsibility. In: W. M. Hoffman & R. E. Frederick (Eds), *Business ethics: Readings and cases in corporate morality,* (3rd ed.). New York: McGraw-Hill.

Bradford, D. F., & Logue, K. D. (1997). The influence of income tax rules on insurance reserves. *National Bureau of Economic Research,* Working paper 5902.

Browne, M. J., & Wells, B. P. (1999). Claims adjudication in the personal automobile insurance residual market. *Journal of Risk and Insurance, 66,* 275–290.

Bulow, J. I., Geanakoplos, J. D., & Klemperer, P. D. (1985a). Holding idle capacity to deter entry. *Economic Journal, 95,* 178–182.

Bulow, J. I., Geanakoplos, J. D., & Klemperer, P. D. (1985b). Multimarket oligopoly: Strategic substitutes and complements. *Journal of Political Economy, 93,* 488–511.

Carr, A. Z. (1996). Is business bluffing ethical? In: S. B. Rae & K. L. Wang (Eds), *Beyond integrity: A Judeo-Christian approach* (pp. 55–62). Grand Rapids, MI: Zondervan Publishing.

Carroll, A. B. (2000). The four faces of corporate citizenship. In: J. E. Richardson (Ed.), *Business ethics 00/01* (pp. 198–203). Guilford, CT: Dushkin/McGraw-Hill.

Caves, R. (1987). *American industry: Structure, conduct and performance* (6th ed.). Englewood Cliffs, NJ: Prentice-Hall.

Chan, T. S. F. (1998). Consumer complaints, racial discrimination, and distribution channels in private passenger insurance. *Journal of Insurance Regulation, 17,* 24–41.

Chung, K., & Pruitt, S. (1994). A simple approximation of Tobin's q. *Financial Management, 23,* 70–74.

Cummins, J. D., & Weiss, M. A. (1991). The structure, conduct, and regulation of the property-liability insurance industry. In: R. W. Kopcke & R. E. Randall (Eds), *The financial condition and regulation of insurance companies* (pp. 117–154). Boston: Federal Reserve Bank.

Cummins, J. D., & Weiss, M. A. (1998). *Analyzing firm performance in the insurance industry using frontier efficiency methods.* Working paper, Wharton Financial Institutions Center.

Cummins, J. D., & Zi, H. (1998). Measuring economic efficiency of the US life insurance industry: Econometric and mathematical programming techniques. *Journal of Productivity Analysis, 10,* 131–150.

Cummins, J. D., & Tennyson, S. (1992). Controlling automobile insurance costs. *Journal of Economic Perspectives, 6*(2), 95–115.

Cummins, J. D., & Tennyson, S. (1996). Moral hazard in insurance claiming: Evidence from automobile insurance. *Journal of Risk and Uncertainty, 12,* 29–50.

DaDalt, P., Donaldson, J., & Garner, J. (2003). Will any q do? *Journal of Financial Research, 26*(4), 535–551.

Demsetz, H. (1973). The structure and ownership and the theory of the firm. *Journal of Law and Economics, 26,* 375–390.

DeVany, A., & Kim, C. L. H. (2002). *Concentration measures and antitrust in the motion picture industry: Why the Herfindahl Index fails as a measure of competitiveness.* Working paper, Irvine: University of California.

Doerpinghaus, H. I. (1991). An analysis of complaint data in the automobile insurance industry. *Journal of Risk and Insurance, 58,* 120–127.

Doerpinghaus, H. I., Schmidt, J., & Yeh, J. J. (2003). Personal bias in automobile claim settlement. *Journal of Risk and Insurance, 70*(2), 185–205.

Doherty, N. (1981). The measurement of output and economies of scale in property-liability insurance. *Journal of Risk and Insurance, 48*(3), 390–402.

Donsimoni, M., Geroski, P., & Jacquemin, A. (1984). Concentration indices and market power. *Journal of Industrial Economics, 32*(4), 419–434.

Drucker, P. F. (1973). *Management: Tasks, responsibilities, practices.* New York: HarperCollins Publishers.

Fama, E. F., & Jensen, M. C. (1983). Separation of ownership and control. *Journal of Law and Economics, 26*, 301–325.

Friedman, M. (1970). The social responsibility of business is to increase its profits. *The New York Times Sunday Magazine*, September.

Friedman, M. (1996). The social responsibility of business is to increase profits. In: S. B. Rae & K. L. Wong (Eds), *Beyond integrity: A Judeo-Christian approach* (pp. 241–245). Grand Rapids, MI: Zondervan Publishing.

Gordon, R. A. (1940). Ownership and compensation as incentives to corporate executives. *Quarterly Journal of Economics, 54*(3), 455–473.

Grace, M. F., & Timme, S. G. (1992). An examination of cost economies in the United States life insurance industry. *Journal of Risk and Insurance, 59*(1), 72–103.

Halek, M., & Eisenhauer, J. G. (2001). Demography of risk aversion. *Journal of Risk and Insurance, 68*, 1–24.

Harrington, S. E., & Niehaus, G. (1998). Race, redlining and automobile insurance prices. *Journal of Business, 71*, 433–469.

Holderness, C. G., Kroszner, R. S., & Sheehan, D. P. (1999). Were the good old days that good? Changed in managerial stock ownership since the great depression. *Journal of Finance, LIV*(2), 435–469.

Jensen, M. C., & Meckling, W. H. (1976). Theory of the firm and managerial behavior, agency costs, and ownership structure. *Journal of Financial Economics, 3*, 305–360.

Jennings, M. (2003). *A business tale, a story of ethics, choices, success and a very large Rabbit.* Arizona: Thomson.

Kamerschen, D. R. (1968). The influence of ownership and control on profit rates. *American Economic Review, 58*(3), 432–447.

Key, S., & Popkin, S. J. (1998). Integrating ethics into the strategic management process. *Management Decision, 36*, 331–338.

Klein, R. W. (1997). Availability and affordability problems in urban homeowners insurance markets. In: G. W. Squires (Ed.), *Insurance redlining: Disinvestment, reinvestment and the evolving role of financial institutions*. Washington, DC: Urban Institute Press.

Kopcke, R. W., & Randall, R. E. (Eds). (1991). The financial condition and regulation of insurance companies: An overview. In: *The financial condition and regulation of insurance companies* (pp. 1–18). Boston: Federal Reserve Bank.

Kritzer, H. M. (1998). Contingent-fee lawyers and their clients: Settlement expectations, settlement realities, and issues of control in the lawyer–client relationship. *Law and Social Inquiry, 23*, 795–821.

Kritzer, H. M., & Krishnan, J. K. (1999). Lawyers seeking clients, clients seeking lawyers: Sources of contingency fee cases and their implications for case handling. *Law and Policy, 21*, 347–375.

Ladd, H. F. (1998). Evidence on discrimination in mortgage lending. *Journal of Economic Perspectives, 12*, 41–62.

Lantos, G. (2001). The boundaries of strategic corporate social responsibility. *Journal of Consumer Marketing, 18*, 595–630.

Levin, I. P., Snyder, M. A., & Chaptman, D. P. (1988). The interaction of experiential and situational factors and gender in a simulated risky decision-making task. *Journal of Psychology, 122*, 173–181.

Lippke, R. L. (1996). Setting the terms of the business responsibility debate. In: R. A. Larmer (Ed.), *Ethics in the workplace: Selected readings in business ethics*. Minneapolis/St. Paul, MN: West Publishing Company.

Marris, R. (1963). A model of the 'managerial' enterprise. *The Quarterly Journal of Economics*, *77*(2), 185–209.

Mathiesen, H. (2002). *Managerial ownership and financial performance*. Ph.D. dissertation, series 18.2002, Copenhagen Business School, Denmark.

Mayers, D., Shivdasani, A., & Smith, C. W. Jr. (1997). Board composition and corporate control: Evidence from the insurance industry. *The Journal of Business, 70*(1), 33–62.

McKenzie, R. B. (2001). Monopoly: A game economists love to play – badly! *Southern Economics Journal, 70*(4), 1–20.

Miller, F. D., & Ahrens, J. (1993). The social responsibility of corporations. In: T. I. White (Ed.), *Business ethics: A philosophical reader* (pp. 187–204). Upper Saddle River, NJ: Prentice-Hall.

Miller, G. (1997). Interlocking directorates and the antitrust laws. *The Colorado Lawyer, 26*(3), 11–17.

Morck, R., Shleifer, A., & Vishny, R. W. (1989). Alternative mechanisms for corporate control. *The American Economic Review, 79*(4), 842–852.

Powell, M., & Ansic, D. (1997). Gender differences in risk behaviour in financial decision making: An experimental analysis. *Journal of Economic Psychology, 18*, 605–628.

Riley, W. B. Jr., & Chow, K. V. (1992). Asset allocation and individual risk aversion. *Financial Analysts Journal, 48*(6), 32–37.

Ross, H. L. (1970). *Settled out of court: The social process of insurance claims adjustments*. Chicago: Alpine Pub.

Sorrentino, R. M. (1992). Risk-taking in games of chance and skill: Informational and affective influences on choice behavior. *Personality & Social Psychology, 62*, 522, 524–526.

Stigler, G. L. (1964). A theory of oligopoly. *Journal of Political Economy, 72*, 44–61.

Stultz, R. A., Walking, R. M., & Song, M. H. (1990). The distribution of target ownership and the division of gains in successful takeovers. *Journal of Finance, 45*(3), 817–833.

U.S. v. Aluminum Co. of American (ALCOA). (1945). 148 F.2d 416(2d Cir.).

Williamson, O. (1964). *The economics of discretionary behavior: Managerial objectives in a theory of the firm*. Englewood Cliffs, NJ: Prentice-Hall.

Zeckhauser, R., & Samuelson, W. (1989). Status quo bias and insurance markets. *John Liner Review, 3*, 38–45.

RESPONSIBILITY SHARING (ELEMENTS OF A FRAMEWORK FOR UNDERSTANDING INSURANCE BUSINESS ETHICS)

Johannes Brinkmann

ABSTRACT

This contribution suggests a preliminary, broad definition of responsibility and presents different dimensions of the concept. Next, the concept of shared responsibility is developed by combining different criteria to a number of typologies. These concepts and typologies are then illustrated with reference to the relationship between insurance customers and the insurance industry. The paper concludes with formulating some next steps for future empirical studies of interdependent insurance marketing and insurance consumer ethics.

If being responsible and taking responsibility is considered to be good, should sharing responsibility be considered as even better? Can sharing responsibility among two or more parties often be more constructive than *not* sharing it, in taking either *too little* responsibility or *too much* responsibility at the expense of others? What type of industry is most suitable for illustration if one wants to ask such questions in detail and from different angles? At least the last question is easy to answer: there are few better

Insurance Ethics for a More Ethical World
Research in Ethical Issues in Organizations, Volume 7, 83–111
ISSN: 1529-2096/doi:10.1016/S1529-2096(06)07005-2

candidates than the insurance business, with responsibility sharing as its core idea (the fact that both the topic and the chosen example of an industry contain a clear tension between ideals and realities, such as solidarity versus opportunism, makes the topic only more challenging).

With such thoughts in mind, this contribution drafts a conceptualization of responsibility sharing, using the insurance business as an illustration. Hopefully, by such a combination the contribution can be of double use for an improved understanding of both responsibility sharing and of what one could call insurance business ethics.

Insurance is marketed and consumed as an intangible product.[1] Within a social science frame of reference,[2] insurance as a product can be described as follows:

"In spite of its significance for people's lives, insurance is a product that most buy with little appreciation. They spend large sums of money to purchase something they have little knowledge about and therefore cannot adequately assess with respect to price and features. The only material thing they obtain at the outset is a piece of paper: a legal contract that they rarely read and even more rarely understand. They do understand that embedded in the contract is a promise to pay if something goes wrong. However, the details are typically obscure and most hope that they will not have to collect on the promise, since they can only do so if a loss has been suffered. They are buying trust in an abstract system, a peace of mind and taken-for-grantedness that if the worst happens there will at least be financial compensation ... Insurance is an expensive product directed at long-term, imagined futures ... Many insurance products must be sold proactively ... (promoted) by marketing (in)security, the need to consume more because of dreaded futures ... Insurance is also unique because consumers are actually a part of the product: the product consists of all members of the risk pool that the insurance company differentiates, packages and sells ..." (Ericson et al., 2003, pp. 4–5).

The present paper can also be read as a contribution to business ethics, marketing ethics and consumer ethics,[3] using the insurance industry as an example. A few examples of articles published in business ethics or business journals can be mentioned briefly, not least as sources of a few further references. Eastman and Eastman (1996, 1997) offer a limited summary of the literature and references to a few studies of ethically disputable insurance marketing.[4] Cooper and Frank (2005) try to describe the moral climate changes in the US life insurance industry between 1990 and 2003 using insurance professionals' responses to a 32-item ethical issues instrument.[5] Gowri (2004) reviews (in a paper about "moral externalities") some literature about discrimination and exclusion of populations from insurance coverage, in other words insurance de-marketing. There is a paucity of publications which one could label insurance consumer ethics. The few examples are, mainly looking at different explanations for clear differences in insurance fraud tolerance, such as social-situational context, insurance industry perceptions (Tennyson, 1997), insurance contact experience (Tennyson, 2002, cf. also Coalition ... against Insurance Fraud, 1997); policy-holder, agent and company traits (Dean, 2004) or more generally situational explanations (Brinkmann, 2005a) or moral-sociological ones (Brinkmann & Lentz, 2006), all with some empirical data and with a few further literature references.

In some contrast to such publications (and more in line with the criminologist-holistic works of Ericson and co-authors),[6] the present paper is primarily concerned with insurance as a commercial arrangement of responsibility *sharing*, i.e. looking at companies and at consumers, insurance consumers and insurance companies *not* one at a time, but as interdependent.[7]

The structure of the paper is as follows. The next section will suggest a preliminary, broad definition of responsibility and present different dimensions of the concept. Afterwards, the concept of shared responsibility is developed by combining different angles and criteria to a number of typologies. These concepts and typologies are then illustrated with reference to the relationship between insurance customers and the insurance industry.

RESPONSIBILITY AS A RELATIONAL CONCEPT

Responsibility is by connotation a *relational* concept, even without an explicit focus on responsibility sharing. This means that responsibility represents or even identifies the obligations *of someone* (an actor) towards *someone else* (at least one other actor), either because one's actions have consequences for this *someone* or because actions and consequences are critically evaluated by *someone else* (at least one other actor). Such a relational concept of responsibility is emphasized in an essay by Lenk and Maring (1993), who define responsibility as a mixture of interdependent components,using a sequence of such components rather than an ordinary nominal definition format:

"Someone (a subject with or bearer of responsibility) is responsible *for* something (actions, action consequences, states, tasks etc.) *in* relation to an addressee and *towards* a (sanctioning, judging) institution, *according to* a (prescriptive, normative) criterion, in the *context* of a given responsibility

and action domain ..." (p. 229, author's translation, here and elsewhere in the paper).[8]

Car-owner liability insurance serves as a good example. The subject's actions with consequences are covered, and responsibility exists towards other drivers and their insurance companies, all of which is in accordance with valid legislation administered by responsible institutions, perhaps with some moral responsibility towards other stakeholders in addition to legal responsibility, depending on the action context.

The relational connotation also underlies common definitions of Corporate Social Responsibility and what one could call Consumer Social Responsibility,[9] which is more or less analogous to the standard reference to four dimensions of corporate social responsibility as a property of actors *in* relation to stakeholders or of stakeholder relations. This could then be expressed as "... a consumer's obligation to maximize his/her positive impact on stakeholders ... and to minimize his/her negative impact. There are four kinds of social responsibility: legal, ethical, economic and philanthropic ..." (following the formulations of Ferrell et al., 2002, p. 73).[10]

This paper's title suggests the need to discuss *shared* corporate and consumer responsibility, in order to maximize positive and to minimize negative impacts, rather than of sole responsibility. In the long run, corporations "need" consumer–customers (at least some) and consumer–customers need corporations (at least some), as allies for sustainable, shared responsibility taking. Neither corporations nor consumers are "alone". They are parts of a relationship, or, sociologically speaking, they could be viewed as almost *being* their relationships. In addition, an (idealistic) assumption of this paper is that such relations or such interdependency should not be used for mutual blame placing or for a denial of responsibility, but as a *common* ground and as a good reason for some kind of solidarity, i.e. for *shared* responsibility taking.

ASPECTS AND DIMENSIONS OF MORAL RESPONSIBILITY

"To speak of one single concept of responsibility, one single meaning of *the* responsibility does not cover all the various interpretations and frames of reference appropriately" (Lenk & Maring, 1993, p. 230).[11] One way of doing justice to responsibility in a given situation is to apply the relational or component-definition referred to above. Another way is to distinguish among different aspects or dimensions of responsibility. There is only space here for addressing a few of such possible distinctions, as an opportunity to transcend the possible narrowness of "one size fits all" definitions. The same main distinctions that are briefly described here are also summarized in Exhibit 1 (and in Appendix Exhibit A).

(1) A first kind of definitional narrowness assumes explicitly or implicitly that responsibility is faced or ascribed (rather than chosen). As an alternative, one could distinguish (with Kaufmann, 1995) between typical

Exhibit 1

Criteria (and author)	Short Description of Suggested Alternatives and/or Possible Typologies
Responsibility taking vs. responsibility ascription (Kaufmann, 1995)	• Self-obligation versus • Penal law, civil law, non-fault liability versus • Power, success, trust-related political and task responsibility
Responsibility for past vs. future outcomes (Bayertz, 1995)	• Retrospective, ex post attribution of responsibility versus • Prospective, ex ante concepts of responsibility, focusing on anticipation of future states and proactive behaviour
Responsibility vs. accountability (Kaufmann, 1995)	• "Non-programmable" responsibility (Verantwortlichkeit), requiring cognitive, moral and communicative competence versus • Clearly task- and role-related responsibility (= accountability)
Insider vs. outsider perspective (Bierhoff, 1995)	• Measurable willingness to take responsibility as a personality variable • Responsibility refusal: denial of emergency; blaming the victim; passing on responsibility to others • Heider's five levels of responsibility attribution: association, causality, predictability, intentionality and justification • Excuses and justifications (referring to denial of intentionality and/or predictability of consequences; acceptance of cause-effect)

Note: For further examples cf. Appendix Exhibit A.

situations where responsibility is ascribed, by others and/or by norms[12] and situations where a moral subject takes responsibility, by self-obligation. Both facing and taking responsibility are a question of conditions. Kaufmann distinguishes accordingly, by conditions, between *moral-philosophical* responsibility (qua self-obligation) and *legal* responsibility (usually qua ascription, ranging from penal law responsibility, to civil law to non-fault liability/responsibility). Kaufmann's third category of *political responsibility* relates to power and power abuse, success and failure, trust and control, including concepts of vicarious responsibility (where e.g. a leader resigns and thus takes responsibility for a lower-level employee's actions or failures).

(2) Many definitions of responsibility represent classical, "retrospective" responsibility concepts. Such concepts focus negatively on damages, while modern and "prospective" responsibility concepts rather would focus positively, on avoiding possible future damages and on minimizing risks, on keeping or creating desirable situations. Modern concepts pay relatively less attention to active action than to necessary omissions, and less to good or bad intentions than (rather or exclusively) to likely or factual consequences (see Bayertz, 1995, pp. 24–26, 45–47).[13]

(3) A clear definition of responsibility could conceal that responsibility itself can be more or less clear. In other words, clarity is not a necessary condition of responsibility. In this sense, many definitions of responsibility (cf. note 11 above) look somewhat biased, in favour of responsibility specification. Instead, a distinction between task- and role-related responsibility (or "accountability") versus vague, almost non-programmable responsibility can often be fruitful. Whenever one takes leadership responsibility beyond any easy definition and control possibilities the main role norm asks for "responsibility" ("Verantwortlichkeit" in the original German text), for self-obligation and for non-programmable willingness to act when it comes to specific responsibilities, i.e. it requires both "cognitive, moral and communicative, trust-building capabilities" (Kaufmann, 1995, p. 88, present author's free translation; cf. with similar thoughts but different formulations Petersen's work, 2002, referred to below and in Appendix Exhibit A).

(4) Responsibility appears differently from the "inside" and from the "outside", i.e. from the responsible subject's or actor's point of view and from the standpoint of a more or less qualified and more or less critical outside observer. Whenever such a difference in perspective exists, it is a good rule to delay moral judgment and to first describe and understand factors and processes, such as willingness and refusal or denial of

responsibility, attribution and neutralization, *before* casting stones at assumed sinners, who may or may not be responsible (cf. for a few aspects Exhibit 1 and for a details Bierhoff, 1995).

As a summary of the above and Exhibit 1, it is possible to distinguish four basic dimensions of responsibility for consideration in analyses of responsibility in relationships:

- taken versus ascribed responsibility;
- ex ante versus ex post-responsibility;
- vague versus specified responsibility; and
- insider-view versus outsider-view responsibility.

Insurance customers can often choose to *take* responsibility for their risks by deciding to stay self-insured or by signing up for voluntary insurance coverage. Alternatively, they may behave more or less responsibly without or "within" an insurance contract, in many cases probably as a response to responsibility *ascriptions* from insurance companies and their marketers (for mutual ascription of responsibility and for taking of joint responsibility cf. the sections below). In particular, the distinction between *retrospective* and *prospective* responsibility gives a better understanding of the insurance business, which is based on a specific *combination* of retrospective and prospective responsibility concepts. These are represented by prospective-"predicting" insurance statisticians, prospective contract designers and underwriters and retrospective claims-handlers.

Bayertz's "modern" responsibility concept expresses the classical core of the insurance business: minimizing the likelihood or risk of losing money when compensating for random incidents, using a mix of good predictions, avoidance of irresponsible customers and asking a premium which covers the agreed-on damage compensation, with a certain profit. Kaufmann's (and Petersen's) distinction between (rather unlimited) *responsibility* and (rather limited) *accountability* is potentially useful for empirical studies of gaps between potentially unlimited insurance customer expectations and normally limited insurance products.[14] Such gaps between customers' and companies' perceptions and expectations can also serve as an illustration of the fourth distinction, between *insider* and *outsider responsibility concepts*, with a whole range of more or less traditional psychological explanations of ideals, denial, attribution and ex post-rationalization.

The potential inspirational value of the concepts and distinctions introduced above requires some translation into empirical approaches. One could examine possible typological combinations. For example, using taking versus ascribing and prospective versus retrospective responsibility concepts, or of prospective versus retrospective and vague versus specified responsibility concepts, in the creation of four-cell tables.

Most important is to transcend more or less hidden assumptions of one-actor-responsibility in moving towards looking for shared responsibility in actor-relationships. Perhaps there are already some assumptions to start with, that sharing equal taking responsibility seems easier than ascribed sharing of it. In other words, to take responsibility for a common future seems easier than for a common past, to agree on shared vague responsibility seems easier than on specified sharing, and constructing responsibility jointly from inside seems easier than from outside.

For the time being, it could be a good start to add an additional component to the Lenk and Maring (1993) definition of responsibility referred to and adopted above, such as: "Someone ... is responsible, *alone or who together with whom*, for something in relation to an addressee and towards an institution, according to a (prescriptive, normative) criterion, in the context of a given responsibility and action domain ..." (present author's italics). For example, insurance marketers "together with" insurance customers co-operate to protect insurance as a social institution against self-destruction.

SHARED RESPONSIBILITY
ELEMENTS OF A FRAMEWORK

A shared responsibility framework will be drafted here as a combination of several complementary theory fragments, in particular Sykes and Matza's (1957) Moral neutralization techniques, Smith's Ethics continuum framework (1993, 1995), the Prisoners' dilemma (Rapoport & Chammah, 1965; Poundstone, 1992; http://www.prisoner-dilemma.com), Zimmerman's (1991) thoughts about Collective Responsibility and Petersen's (2002) view of an Erosion of Responsibility.

Moral Neutralization Techniques as a Kind of Responsibility Sharing

This first theory fragment claims essentially that individuals, such as consumers, protect their self-image by "moral neutralization", with five alternative "techniques": denial of responsibility, denial of injury, denial of the victim, condemnation of the condemner and appeal to higher loyalties

(Sykes & Matza, 1957, cf. also Vitell & Grove, 1987 and Brinkmann, 2005a). In the context of the present paper it is tempting, in any case, to re-label these techniques as "techniques of responsibility sharing"[15] by:

- denying the causality or harmful effect conditions of one's own responsibility and hence *reducing one's own responsibility (share)*; or by
- either explaining the victim's loss as just retaliation given the circumstances or by refocusing attention and appointing the victim a responsible subject (or at least a hypocrite), hence *increasing the victim's responsibility (share)*; or by
- introducing *additional responsibility (to share)* by referring to additional stakeholder relations.

The Marketing Ethics Continuum
As a Continuum of Responsibility Sharing

As a second theory fragment one can consider Craig Smith's suggestion to conceptualize marketing ethics along a *caveat venditor* versus *caveat emptor* continuum (see Smith & Quelch, 1993; Smith, 1995). Smith's continuum has an underlying assumption of responsibility sharing. The two extreme situations in Smith's continuum leave "all" responsibility *either* to assumed "sovereign" consumers (i.e. "emptor's" responsibility of watching his/her own interests) *or* to corporations-as-sellers (i.e. "venditor's" responsibility of not hurting consumer interests). The range of different, more or less typical situations *between* these two extremes is most interesting, with more or less even responsibility sharing (cf. Exhibit 2, loosely inspired by Smith's typology in Smith and Quelch, 1993, p. 21 and in Smith, 1995, p. 89).

Conditional Responsibility Sharing

Moral neutralization can sometimes turn into potentially endless mutual blaming among two or more parties. One way of getting out of such a stalemate situation could be to take a closer look at possible tacit conditions of responsibility sharing. Such a condition, perhaps a necessary or even a sufficient condition of responsibility sharing, could be that both parties (or all parties if there are more than two[16]) abstain from exploiting their counterparts, perhaps also that there are no third parties unfairly profiting from the responsibility sharing (e.g. parties with vested interests or hidden agendas).

Exhibit 2

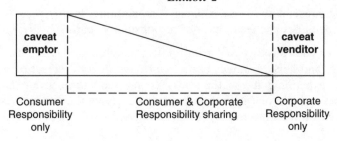

Consumer   Consumer & Corporate   Corporate
Responsibility   Responsibility sharing   Responsibility
only   only

Exhibit 3

Actor A	Actor B	
	Self-interested, amoral cost-benefit-maximizing	Potentially moral common interest maximizing
Self-interested, amoral cost-benefit-maximizing	Both A and B deny responsibility, perhaps mutually ascribe responsibility	A exploits B
Potentially moral common interest maximizing	B exploits A	A and B truly share responsibility

Such situations of conditional responsibility taking or responsibility sharing seem to be best covered by a third theory fragment, a Prisoners' dilemma perspective, cf. Exhibit 3 (and as one of the classical references cf. Rapoport, Chammah, & Orwant, 1965).

Unavoidable Responsibility Sharing

The *Parable of the Sadhu* (McCoy, 1983) is relatively well known among many business ethics teachers. Among different debriefing possibilities for this story the one with a focus on the paradoxes of responsibility sharing is perhaps the most fruitful one: The more potential helpers, the worse it perhaps is for the one needing help. One essay which fits well for being read together with the *Parable of the Sadhu* communicates the central point that the presence of others can divert attention from one's responsibility, but not diminish it (Zimmerman, 1991), or in his own words[17]:

> The mere fact that it is a *group* action (or omission) that is at issue does nothing to diminish responsibility ... It is possible that ... two or more people engage in group

action (or group omission) in such a way that all participants are fully morally responsible for the outcome of that action (or omission). Obviously, 'fully' is not used here to mean the same as 'solely'; on the contrary, it is used to mean the same as 'with no diminution' or, equivalently, 'without (even partial) excuse ... (...) As for group action, I have in mind the sort of situation where two or more people act in such a way that there is some common outcome to which they each contribute causally ... I shall understand group omission to be such that it occurs when and only when two or more people, who could engage in group action, omit to do so ... (Zimmerman, 1991, pp. 275–277).[18]

Erosive Responsibility Sharing

Zimmerman uses a kind of micro-sociology illustration for dysfunctional responsibility sharing. By comparison, the Danish business ethicist Petersen thinks rather macro-sociologically. His essay about the *Erosion of responsibility* is about unintended side effects of creating more and more responsible institutions, namely the growth of special, *role-bound* responsibilities at the expense of *universal and vague responsibility* (Petersen, 2002, cf. also once more Kaufmann, 1995, referred to above). To provide a few thought-provoking quotations:

> Important areas of our lives have become institutionalised and collectively insured. We may no longer have much responsibility left, confronted with this intricate, anonymous and amorphous system, whose internal workings and consistency we cannot wholly comprehend ... (...) Somehow it would seem that the responsibilities have been parcelled out in bits and pieces belonging to several different institutions ... (...) The more we attempt to anchor responsibilities in specific written statements and special institutions, the more we lose individual commitment to all the vaguer notions of responsibility ... The result is that although responsibilities may become very clearly and strictly defined by written rules, this makes for some very stringent and inflexible conceptions of individual responsibilities, and it may lead to rigid behaviour by rigid representatives of rigid bureaucracies ... (...) The alternative to an institutional response might be a solution in which each and everyone of us regards it as our responsibility to act in accordance with deeply held common values, with universal vague responsibilities and special vague responsibilities. Instead of an empty appeal to community there may be a need for more than rather less individualism; individualism though that would partly substitute the pseudo-solidarity that is safeguarded by systems of regulation, control and sanctions ... (Petersen, 2002, pp. 15, 29, 40)

Looking at these theory pieces taken together, responsibility sharing seems to have different aspects in a similar way as the wider term of responsibility: actor similarities, responsibility avoidance, different share size, conditions and unavoidability. One additional aspect will be addressed in the next section, which is responsibility sharing out of solidarity (as the opposite of blaming and shaming).

SHARED RESPONSIBILITY AS RISK SHARING: INSURANCE COMPANIES AND THEIR CUSTOMERS

Responsibility sharing, conceptualized with the help of the fragments presented above, can be a fruitful approach for understanding consumer ethics. As mentioned already, it can often be a good idea to distinguish between good and bad consumer ethics. In other words, by focusing on consumers as the "good guys" and consumers as the "bad guys", perhaps with situationist consumers as an important intermediate third group, where the situation determines if a given consumer behaves as a "good guy" or as a "bad guy" (cf. Brinkmann & Lentz, 2006). In this last section such thoughts will be illustrated more specifically, as responsibility sharing between insurance marketing and insurance consumer behaviour.

Instead of repeating and then further elaborating the everyday car liability insurance example mentioned above,[19] a short typological overview serves as a point of departure, where marketing and consumer ethics issues are juxtaposed. Typologies such as Exhibit 4, with or without examples entered into the cells, can be useful whenever it makes sense to distinguish marketing ethics issues by sorting them under the "four Ps" (see e.g. Smith & Quelch, 1993, p. 13).[20] In a next step, some of the theory fragments presented in the previous section will be applied to insurance company and consumer ethics.

Mutual Neutralization

Moral neutralization can be read as a more or less immature denial or "sharing" of uncomfortable responsibility, as suggested in a brief paragraph above. When it comes to insurance marketing and consumer ethics, such moral neutralization can easily turn into a vicious cycle of mutual blaming and contagious cynicism rather than constructive responsibility sharing (cf. the suggested neutralization subtype examples in Exhibit 5 below). In the case of insurance, understandable and mutual blaming can be read as a symptom of ambiguities in the insurance relationship as such, normally labelled as "moral hazard". This refers to the fact that insurance products not only cover risky behaviour, but also by their very existence contributes to risky behaviour, among the insured, and among the insurers, too.[21]

A first step away from such mutual blaming would be to look not at the counterpart only, but to accept a minimum share of responsibility for the loyal use and for the misuse of the insurance relationship, independently of what the counterpart says and does. In addition, both insurers and the

Exhibit 4

	Potential Marketing Ethics Issues	Potential Consumer Ethics Issues
Market research	Disputable research ethics; insufficient research as basis for decisions	Insufficient/uncritical information search and handling; collecting, adopting (and passing on) everyday theories about insurance products, about "taking revenge" and "successful" dishonesty included
Product	Developing and selling unnecessary, unfair or undesirable insurance products; unfair compensation for covered events and losses	Buying and misusing necessary, fair and desirable insurance products; buying and using unnecessary, unfair or undesirable insurance products
Price	Non-transparent and unfair product pricing and price discrimination	Paying too much or too little for insurance products, perhaps by giving incorrect/ incomplete price-relevant information; receiving too little or too much compensation for losses, with or without coverage
Promotion	Exploiting and reinforcing general safety desires and low product understanding among consumers, creating unrealistic expectations and giving insufficient or misleading information	Justified or unjustified blaming of insurance companies for their advertising, sales and customer treatment, blame others for one's own product misunderstanding and/or cheating
Place	Unfair "red-lining" (exclusion) of certain customer groups (and/or passing them to the competitors)	Opportunistic or false claims of customer/object addresses; unfair exploitation or boycotting of (fair and consumer-friendly) insurance companies

insured could take a self-critical look at possible elements of truth in what the counterpart claims in his or her moral neutralization.[22]

Marketing Ethics Continuum and the Consumer Sovereignty Test (CST)

If one wants to use Smith's (1995) "marketing ethics continuum" for describing, understanding and evaluating the insurance company–customer relationship, some more information is needed than what was given in Exhibit 2 above. In his text(s), Smith's favourite type is what he calls

Exhibit 5

Sykes and Matza's Original Labels and Suggested New Labels	Examples of Insurance Consumers' Neutralization	Examples of Insurance Company Neutralization
Denial of responsibility/ denial of causality	The accident was not my fault; without an accident I would not have claimed anything	We only offer insurance products – according to penal law only the cheater is responsible
Denial of injury/denial of harmful effects	Some cheating is anticipated in the premium already	If we need to let many cheaters pass this will not really hurt the honest consumers so much
Denial of the victim/victim deserves retaliation	Insurance companies exploit ignorant customers and deserve to be cheated	Insurance customers know or should know that they are held collectively responsible
Condemnation of the condemner/claiming victim responsibility	Insurance companies create temptations and ask for being cheated	A majority of the insurance consumers would cheat if they could get away with it
Appeal to higher loyalties/ claiming additional responsibilities	Cheating is not motivated by self-interest but e.g. as solidarity with friends and family	Handling of insurance fraud is good for shareholder value, for industry loyalty and for higher morality in society

consumer sovereignty. This clearly leaves most (but not 100%) of the responsibility to the corporation side, i.e. requiring at the same time more than zero consumer responsibility. Smith also introduces a three-criteria-heuristic, the *Consumer sovereignty test* (abbreviated CST), for deciding to what reasonable degree consumers really are sovereign in the idealistic-ideological sense of the word (one could have used consumer vulnerability as a label instead[23]).

For brevity, Exhibit 6 combines Smith's CST dimensions with insurance customer illustrations. Essentially, Smith's CST would suggest, idealistically and critically, that insurance companies and insurance marketers have a main (but not 100%) responsibility to increase insurance consumer sovereignty (e.g. by consumer education, by development of fair products and by fair marketing, and *not to exploit* insurance consumer vulnerability). Insurance consumers could be expected to take a critical minimum responsibility for performing their consumer role. This applies to doing some minimum amount of consumer "homework", not using trust as a responsibility

Exhibit 6. (using and extending the CST, see Smith, 1995, p. 92).

Dimensions (Smith, 1995)	Establishing Adequacy (Smith, 1995)	Insurance Relationship Dimensions	Insurance Customer-related Indicators
Consumer capability (Is the target market vulnerable in ways that limit consumer decision-making?)	Vulnerability factors – age, education, income, etc.	In addition to general consumer vulnerability, specific economic and other vulnerability in specific event/accident situations and to judge risks, i.e. over- and under-insurance	Capability of staying self-insured, i.e. coping with risks of worst-case scenarios
Information: Availability and quality (Are consumer expectations at purchase likely to be realized? Do consumers have sufficient information to judge?)	Sufficient to judge whether expectations at time of purchase will be fulfilled	Varying degrees of product information transparency and asymmetry, amount, complexity, digestability and understandability of relevant information, concerning risks and products	Capability of understanding, simplification[a] and critical evaluation of offered/available information
Choice: Opportunity to switch (Can consumers go elsewhere? Would they incur substantial costs or inconvenience in transferring their loyalty?)	Level of competition Switching costs	Insurance market qualities: real and transparent competition for the greatest possible number of consumers; fair legal rules for switching	Ability to compare, choose and switch rationally in accordance with one's self interest. Absence of irrational trust and loyalty

[a]Cf. S. Bråten's model power theory (Bråten, 1983, chapter 1, 4, 5 and 2000, chapter 9), focusing on actors' information simplification possibilities in accordance with their own needs and interests as a key criterion for successful information handling.

evasion strategy, and fulfilling a moral duty of not misusing fair insurance products nor exploiting fair insurance companies.

Conditional Responsibility Sharing

Conditional responsibility sharing is more constructive than mutual neutralization and blaming, for instance when following a prisoner's dilemma strategy of mutual trust and common interest focus as long as one is not exploited. Conditional responsibility sharing is also less idealistic (or less naïve) than taking an unconditional caveat vendor or consumer sovereignty position (or an equivalent naïve consumer trust towards companies and their marketers). If one relates this way of thinking to the insurance company–customer relationship, one can imagine four scenarios (which can be read as illustrations of the cells in Exhibit 3 above). Similar to the original prisoner's dilemma game, a co-operation and mutual responsibility sharing situation is best for all, in the long run, with a common interest in avoiding a mutual blaming and contagious cynicism situation. Defensive responsibility taking is an intermediate position, with sharing and taking relatively more responsibility, with the hope that either companies or consumers can trigger a desirable development towards mutual responsibility sharing (Exhibit 7).

INSTEAD OF A CONCLUSION

This contribution has mainly promised some conceptual clarification. Therefore, it is not natural to draw the kind of conclusion as would typically be done in an empirical paper. What it is possible to do is to formulate a few theses, as well as some suggestions for possible future empirical and practical work related to responsibility sharing in the field of insurance and insurance marketing.

Six Theses

(1) Insurance consumer and marketing ethics interdependencies can be analysed with a focus on products, pricing, promotion and place, one at a time or combined.
(2) Some mutual moral neutralization (when insurers look at the insured and vice versa) is explicable and understandable, but eventually not a sustainable alternative to moral self-criticism.

Exhibit 7

	An Amoral Insurance Company denies Responsibility	A Moral Insurance Company takes Responsibility
An amoral insurance customer denies responsibility	The worst case: Old maid-game[a]; with mutual neutralization/blaming; in the end, all parties risk the self-destruction of insurance as a societal institution	Unless the companies and/or the industry take responsibility for preventing exploitation and for self-interest protection: Insurance companies are exploited by dishonest customers (but the honest customers share the cost)
A moral insurance customer takes responsibility	Unless customers take responsibility for preventing exploitation and for self-interest protection: Naïve, trusting insurance customers are exploited by "their" insurance company and/or by the insurance industry	The ideal insurance institution: fair and necessary insurance products are marketed fairly to a target population where honest (but not naïve) customers are over-represented

[a]Cf. as an essay which uses the Norwegian-European name of the game Hernes (1981).

(3) There are good reasons for following C. Smith's arguments in favour of a consumer sovereignty position as a good compromise between idealism and realism in the case of insurance marketing.

(4) A conditional responsibility sharing position represents a good compromise between idealism and realism in the case of insurance marketing.

(5) It is important to leave a conceptual framework of responsibility sharing open for including additional theory pieces, e.g. dealing with the law/ethics interface, with responsibility as a personality variable (and perhaps an organizational level variable, too), with trust and interdependent commitment/trust.[24]

(6) Further theory development should take place in close contact with the empirical world,[25] with close co-operation with one or a few insurance companies (or industry organisations?) willing to try out how insurance customer ethics can be improved through more ethical insurance marketing.

Further Empirical Work

This paper has been developed as part of a conceptual *and* empirical pilot project about insurance consumer ethics. As mentioned above, the potential value of the concepts and distinctions introduced here requires sooner or later a translation into empirical approaches. The following next steps of the project will involve empirical work to consider issues such as:

- Mapping the perceptions of ethical challenges among insurance brokers standing "between the parties", as a question of professional and consultancy ethics;[26]
- Description, interpretation and critical-moral evaluation of insurance product marketing, mainly by conducting a quantitative and qualitative content analysis of Norwegian (or Scandinavian) advertising; and
- Complementary studies of ethical awareness among insurance marketers and insurance consumers, with a focus on product understanding and consumer sovereignty/vulnerability issues.

From Theory to Practice: Marketing Responsibility Sharing?

A recently published article discussed "... *marketing ethics* in the double meaning of the word. *Marketing* ethics could mean removing high fraud-risk products and hence cheating opportunities and temptations, re-educating insurance sales staff, recruiting honest customers, and focusing on values, caring and responsibility whenever interacting with customers. In the end, *marketing* ethics is probably the best and perhaps the only way of marketing *ethics*, as a good insurance against insurance customer dishonesty, so to speak ..." (Brinkmann & Lentz, 2006). One way of putting such an idea into practice could be to use the title of the present contribution and some of its main points as raw material for campaign ideas and campaign messages emphasizing that insurance is essentially about responsibility sharing. As an intermediate stage, focus group research among insurance employees with marketing and customer contact responsibilities and among different segments of insurance customers could be used. In practice, the following points could be used to structure a Focus Group:

- Is the insurance industry in general, and the specific company in particular, associated with CSR, good corporate citizenship (CC) and good industry ethics – if yes: why and for what and if no: why and for what? What are arguments for and against the spending of stockholder money, company resources and insurance customer money on CSR? How necessary and perhaps how risky is it to address insurance company CSR and CC as part of an imagined responsibility sharing campaign?

- How necessary and how acceptable is insurance marketing research as a basis for improving insurance marketing ethics and insurance consumer ethics, and with which research ethical limitations?
- Do you recall any specific incidents of good or bad insurance marketing or insurance consumer ethics (using the product/price/promotion/place distinction for probing, cf. Exhibit 4 above)?
- How understandable and how acceptable is moral neutralization on the insurance company and on the insurance consumer side? Should one and how could one address such neutralization in a campaign (cf. perhaps Exhibit 5 above)?
- Which insurance company and insurance marketing responsibility share is fair when it comes to insurance consumer education, fair product development and not exploiting insurance consumer vulnerability, without decreasing "insurance consumer sovereignty" (cf. Exhibit 6 above), as an unintended side effect?[27]
- Is it possible to simplify the idea of conditional responsibility sharing for marketing communication purposes, focusing on the need of mutual trust-building without being naive, and if yes, how?

NOTES

1. About service or intangible product marketing ethics cf. Rao and Singhapakdi (1997), with further references.

2. For a good presentation, see e.g. Boyne (2003). The most widely quoted, "classical" social science article about insurance and risk is probably Ewald (1991), with formulations such as: "Risk in the meaning of insurance has three great characteristics: it is calculable, it is collective, and it is capital ... (Insurance is) the compensation of effects of chance through mutuality organized according to the laws of statistics ... To the extent that one does seek to extend its benefits to the greatest number, the idea of insurance 'naturally' implies the idea of social redistribution ... It provides a general principle for the objectification of things, people and their relations. Insurance possesses several distinct combinations of technique, ... an economic and financial technique ... a moral technology ... and a technique of reparation and indemnification of damages ... The combination of these different dimensions makes insurance a *political technology* ..." (pp. 201, 205–207). Cf. also the definition by Heimer (2003, p. 288): "Insurance is a social arrangement to reduce the effects of losses by employing the resources of the group to cushion individuals ..." Cf. also as general definitions of insurance and risk as one finds them on the internet: "... promise of reimbursement in the case of loss; paid to people or companies so concerned about hazards that they have made prepayments to an

insurance company" (wordnet.princeton.edu/perl/webwn); "Insurance, in law and economics, is a form of risk management primarily used to hedge against the risk of potential financial loss. Ideally, insurance is defined as the equitable transfer of the risk of a potential loss, from one entity to another, in exchange for a reasonable fee ..." (en.wikipedia.org/wiki/Insurance); "A contract in which one party agrees to pay for another party's financial loss resulting from a specified event ..."(www. federalreserve.gov/pubs/leasing/glossary.htm) and "Risk is the potential harm that may arise from some present process or from some future event. It is often mapped to the probability of some event which is seen as undesirable ..." (en.wikipedia.org/ wiki/Risk); or "The combination of the frequency, or probability, of occurrence and the consequence of a specified hazardous event ..." (www.bees.unsw.edu.au/ohs/ definitions.html).

3. Cf., from different angles, e.g. about consumers as moral decision-makers Vitell (2003) (referring to the Hunt-Vitell decision-making model); about consumers as potentially "bad guys" cf. Vitell (2003), Fukukawa (2002), Brinkmann (2005a), Brinkmann and Lentz (2006); about consumers as potentially "good guys", with an ability to do good, to take responsibility and to behave responsibly cf. Brinkmann and Peattie (2006); all with further references. For a recent widening of the Consumer Ethics Scale for covering both bad and good behaviours see Vitell and Muncy (2005).

4. The context is a presentation and discussion of the authors' US survey dataset with responses from 123 insurance agents and 142 insurance students, addressing differences between professional and personal ethics and educational implications.

5. For further references see Cooper and Dorfman (2003) (9 out of 35 publication references are to Cooper's own works).

6. See, in addition to the source of the quotation above, as other publications of the same author and his co-authors Ericson and Doyle (2003, 2004). The 50 pp. article of Ericson and Doyle (2003) is a good summary of Ericson and co-authors' research, with a good summary of the summary on pp. 358–360. Heimer's (2003) article offers a systematic comparison and some synthesis of three main approaches.

7. Cf. three quotations from other own papers as an indication of possible questions which one could ask: ".... If there is some justice, businesses get perhaps the consumers they deserve and vice versa. Rather than criticizing business alone ... or passing on the blame to the market and to the consumers ... it seems more fruitful to consider issues such as fair trade, social and environmental sustainability on the one hand and consumer dishonesty on the other as a shared responsibility of business and consumers ..." (Brinkmann, 2004, p. 129, slightly modified). "If one assumes customer dishonesty or egoism and tries to counter such assumed egoism ... moral customers might turn egoistic instead. If the insurance companies' honesty-campaigns emphasize moral arguments, this is far less risky, but requires probably that the company has *moral credibility*. Such moralizing will probably work for most average honest customers, while the dishonest ones might read such communication as a sign of weakness and surrender and as an invitation to cheating. In other words, communication-wise, deliberate differential treatment of different customer segments seems wisest – with screening and avoiding dishonest customers ... and with treating the above-average moral and honest customers with trust and

respect ..." (Brinkmann, 2005a, pp. 191–192). "*Marketing* ethics could mean, e.g., removing high fraud-risk products and hence cheating opportunities and temptations, reeducating insurance sales staff from recruiting many to recruiting honest customers, focusing on values, caring and responsibility whenever interacting with customers. In the end, *marketing* ethics is probably the best and perhaps the only way of marketing *ethics*, as a good insurance against insurance customer dishonesty ..." (Brinkmann & Lentz, 2006).

8. Cf. also in a more ordinary sentence format: "*Responsibility* is to start with a concept which is expressed in a relational ascription norm by an evaluation of a controlled action expectation" (*ibid*). Cf. also a similar definition of Lenk, quoted in Bayertz (1995, p. 217), similarly Nunner-Winkler (1993) or as a "visualized" checklist Ulrich and Thielemann (1992, p. 18).

9. For some references and for a possibility of conceptualizing Consumer Social Responsibility as "the better half" of "Consumer Ethics", as "Political Consumerism" or "Consumer Citizenship" (cf. Brinkmann, 2004; Brinkmann & Peattie, 2006).

10. In spite of obvious differences between corporations and consumers when it comes to size and power, both corporations and consumers are actors operating in markets, as abstract legal and economic units, with a potential of doing good and causing harm. For corporations and consumers alike, the main question is how such types of responsibilities are combined and balanced wisely (this seems to be meant by "social" as a kind of "total" responsibility). The most interesting question concerns the economic affordability and sustainability of ethicalness, quite often presented in a four-cell matrix, with non-profitable versus profitable ethics as the most interesting choice (cf. Brinkmann, 2005b).

11. There is no lack of more or less general definitions where responsibility is typically explained as "an act or course of action that is demanded of one, as by position, custom, law or religion: burden, charge, commitment, duty, imperative, must, need, obligation ...'or as' the obligation to answer for actions. Often this means answering to some specified authority ..." (http://www.answers.com/topic/responsibility; the second definition of responsibility is similar to usual definitions of accountability, cf. e.g. the one of Gert (1988, pp. 214–215), or as an "ascription of such consequences which a subject has caused by its action" (Bayertz, 1995, p. 5). In my own business ethics lectures I sometimes stress responsibility as a concept that almost builds a bridge across well-known position differences between deontology (responsibility = obligation), consequentialism (responsibility *for* consequences) and virtue ethics (responsibility as a character trait). Cf. as an easily accessible source for more references http://plato.stanford.edu/entries/moral-responsibility with a recent bibliography. As a less recent selection of more or less classical and widely quoted readings see French (1991). As an anthology in German (with a bibliography) see Bayertz (1995).

12. Cf. also French (1991, pp. 3–6) about responsibility as a question of cause-effect ascriptions that cannot be justified or excused or Nunner-Winkler (1993, see also Appendix Exhibit A) who suggests that responsibility ascriptions require certain properties of *actors, actions* and of the *relationship between them*. The most important actor properties are some minimal knowledge of morality and of action effects, some ability of willed action and free will. The most important action properties are consistency with negative duties, narrow-positive and wide-positive duties. Most

interesting is her distinction referring to the relationship between actor and action (as a cause-effect question), which can produce responsibility on five different levels, ranging from any co-effect, to causal effects, to predictable, willed and un-justified-willed effects. See also *ibid* for other interesting thoughts about the "social construction" of responsibility, shared responsibility in hierarchies, diffusion of responsibility in positive and negative duty-situations.

13. In a way these labels reflect some conceptual development that again reflects societal change from traditional to modern society, from lower to higher division of labour and not least technical progress where outcome ascriptions become more and more problematic. Once negative societal effects of technology and industrialization become increasingly visible and important, by societal "self-observation", a discussion and a demand develop, focusing on "responsible" state *prevention* of such major damages (Bayertz, 1995, *ibid*). This claimed change from a classical to a modern responsibility focus is similar to the widely quoted Max Weber distinction between *Gesinnungsethik* (mindset ethics) and *Verantwortungsethik* (responsibility ethics), developed in the context of a speech about politics as profession. The underlying distinction goes between Kantian ethics (focusing on good will or intent, of behaving responsibly) and utilitarian ethics (focusing on relatively best mixes of consequences). In discussions about moral issues in the business world and elsewhere responsibility can often be used as a more neutral basic term than morality or ethics. Still, responsibility is primarily a moral term, where the moral philosophy can help with further clarification. Responsibility is an obligation, e.g. towards stakeholders with complementary rights, but responsibility also normally refers to consequences "for which" an actor is responsible. And good persons are responsible persons. Discourse ethics fits, too, obviously, e.g. by stating that corporations or individuals are responsible *towards* stakeholders, and reasonable lower and upper limits to responsibility can, at least ideally, be agreed on by a *dialogue* among all parties affected. As we read the following quotation, Weber suggests a moral obligation of analyzing and predicting *future* consequences of one's actions as well as *taking* responsibility instead of leaving it to others (Weber, 1968, pp. 57–58, authors' translation from German): "There is a deep difference between intentional-ethical and responsibility-ethical action motives, acting right and leaving the success to God or taking responsibility for the predictable consequences of one's actions ... If there are bad consequences of an action based on a good mindset, one would not hold the actor but the world responsible, or the stupidity of other individuals, or God's will having created them this way. A responsibility ethicist takes into account the average defects of human beings. He is – following Fichte – not entitled to assume their goodness and perfection. He doesn't feel like leaving the predictable consequences of one's own actions to the others". See also Müller (1992) summarizing Weber and other responsibility ethicists such as Jonas; cf. also his Weber summary in a table, p. 113.

14. That is an insurance company's expected responsibility for providing safety and full damage compensation, versus the real company's focus on specified limits to responsibility, often with reference to contract fine print.

15. In particular when it comes to insurance examples, such sharing or redistribution of responsibility can be both constructive and cynical, see the corresponding paragraph below.

16. There is also an interesting sub-question if responsibility is shared *bilaterally* or *multilaterally*, i.e. directly among two actors, among three or more actors, perhaps among actors of different kinds, such as actors and *mediating agents or organizations*, such as insurance brokers or voluntary, consumer and/or corporate non-profits such as FIVH (http://www.fivh.no/index.php), IEH (www.etiskhandel.no), ETI (http://www.ethicaltrade.org), organized as company-CSO-alliances or not (cf. Crane & Matten, 2004, pp. 346 ff., 371 ff.).

17. Zimmerman's point of departure is that "talk of two or more people sharing responsibility for an outcome is very common, (but) ... also very misleading ... because such talk seems often, perhaps always, to suggest that the responsibility of each person involved in a group action (or omission) is *diminished* simply by virtue of the fact that others are also involved and are responsible". The suggestion seems to be that there is just so much responsibility to go around – the "pie" is just so large – and the more people involved, the smaller the share for each ...

18. The three criteria mentioned in Appendix Exhibit A are then combined to a typology, where each type is illustrated and discussed quite convincingly. The conclusion is the same across all types: Causal necessity of an individual action or omission for a harmful outcome is a sufficient condition for individual moral responsibility (while the argument that an action or omission is not a sufficient condition for the outcome without the other individuals' actions or omissions is not considered a relevant excuse. Zimmerman's typology is easier understandable if it is set up as an eight-cell table (with one empty cell). The illustration cases are "a group of 10 teenagers pushing a large boulder off a plateau so that it rolls down a slope and wrecks a car at the bottom" (1), "a dozen people, with murder on their minds, each delivering one stab to the body of some victim" (2), "a group of three swimmers watching a large man drown. Each intends not to help save the unfortunate man and freely refrains from lending a hand, in the full knowledge that his contribution is required for the man to be saved" (3). If one increases the number of teenagers, murderers or swimmers ("just calling in some more friends to help") one has constructed oversupply situations that produce the same individual responsibility as the standard situations. The DeGeorge (1986) typology with a distinction of five "models" of collective responsibility ascriptions (pp. 98, cf. also Appendix Exhibit A) could be considered as an extension of situation (1) in Zimmerman's typology.

19. As a much less everyday example-in-progress cf. the 2005 US Katrina hurricane and post-Katrina flood, with all kinds of legal and moral responsibility sharing, blaming and shaming, between more or less self-interested, more or less caring and more or less honest politicians, insurance companies and their actual and potential customers. See instead and for the time being, e.g. http://www.becker-posner-blog.com/ (9 Oct 2005).

20. At the same time interdependent phenomena are artificially split, such as unjustified blaming, exploitation of illiteracy and, not least, interdependent insurance marketing and consumer behaviour.

21. See e.g. "In law and economics, moral hazard is the name given to the risk that one party to a contract can change their behaviour to the detriment of the other party once the contract has been concluded." (en.wikipedia.org/wiki/Moral_hazard); "Danger of loss arising from the nature of the insured rather than from the physical nature of the risk. This would encompass those instances where the chance of loss is

increased by an insured's carelessness, incompetence, recklessness, indifference to loss or an insured's fraudulent nature." (www.federated.ca/gloss/m.htm); "Refers to the likelihood of a person or organization willing to take on more risk as they are covered by insurance ..." (moneyterms.co.uk/glossary-i/). Cf. also Ericson et al., 2003: "... Moral risks arise in the interactive dynamics of the insurance relationship. Here, moral risk refers to the ways in which an insurance relationship fosters behaviour by any party in the relationship that immorally increases risks to others ... (...) Private insurance is socially organized to offer incentives to other parties in the insurance relationship to engage in risky behaviour with immoral consequences. Insurers themselves are often influenced in ways that encourage them to put others, including their policyholders, employees (etc., JB) ... at risk" (p. 363). The most convincing illustration is probably the risk-sharing among primary and reinsurance companies: "The originating or primary insurer lays off his bet with other insurers in order to spread the financial risk ... Reinsurers treat their insurance company partners in the same way as they treat ordinary policy holders: with suspicion ..." (p. 365). Cf. also as a similar presentation of the same reasoning Ericson and Doyle (2003).

22. Companies could for instance consider the removal of avoidable cheating temptations (such as all-risk mobile phone insurances marketed among youngsters) or practicing zero tolerance of small amount cheating. Or more principally, idealistically formulated (Ericson et al., 2003): "Once insured, the policyholder is required to be an agent of prevention responsible for governing her own risky environment and security against loss. Ideally, if every insured subject is reflexive about risks and makes rational choices to minimize them, there will be security for everyone. This security will materialize in a safer environment plus the financial benefits of lower claim costs for the insurer and lower premiums for the insured ..." (p. 372).

23. As examples of the vulnerability label see e.g. Brenkert (1998). For a comparison of sovereign versus vulnerable consumers cf. Hernes' (1978) ideal typology of powerful versus powerless consumers, listing different kinds of material and immaterial resources and handicaps (pp. 106–113):

Powerful Consumers	Powerless Consumers
Autonomous	Heteronomous
Fully informed	Lack overview
Calculating	Insecure
Stable	Unstable
Powerful	Vulnerable
Helping	Non-cooperative
Demanding	Bad at communicating demand
Equal	Unequal
Responsible	In need of help

24. Cf. for the time being Luhmann, N. (1969). *Legitimation durch Verfahren.* Neuwied: Luchterhand; Bierhoff (1995, pp. 219–220); Luhmann, N. (1979). *Trust*

and power. Chichester: Wiley; Morgan, R. M. & Hunt, S. D. (1994), The commitment-trust theory of relationship marketing. *Journal of Marketing, 58,* 20–28.

25. As good role models for such research (cf. Ericson et al., 2003; Ericson & Doyle, 2003; Ericson & Doyle, 2004), with social science-theory-based empirical work, in particular political sociology and risk society theory. Canadian Ericson et al.'s (2003) point of departure is that the (welfare) state makes itself increasingly redundant by transferring risks to private insurance companies: "As part of its efforts to minimize itself, the state actively promotes individual responsibility for risk ... The individual is now responsible for controlling her risk environment through market-based security product consumption, including the purchase of insurance" (pp. 361–362). "Responsible" insurance companies have to handle their risk business the best they can: "Faced with inadequate scientific and technical knowledge, insurers turn to knowledge of moral risk. The risks that are defined, produced, taken, and managed by the insurance industry always include moral assessment of the people and harms involved ..." (p. 362).

26. Cf. Bivins (2004), with further references and with a model on p. 59 – which is similar to Exhibit 3 above.

27. B2B-insurance marketing could in this case serve as an interesting control group.

ACKNOWLEDGMENT

This is one out of several papers which are all looking at the same research field, from similar and from different angles, empirically or conceptually. A common denominator is looking at marketing and consumer ethics as a part of business ethics, thinking holistically and in interdependencies, sharing responsibility instead of denying or passing on responsibility, understanding interdependencies rather than superficial moralizing. This contribution is a substantially revised version of notes for a presentation together with Kristi Yuthas, Portland State University, presented at the 12th Annual International Conference Promoting Business Ethics, St John's University, NYC October 2005.

REFERENCES

Bayertz, K. (Ed.) (1995). *Verantwortung – Prinzip oder problem?* Darmstadt: Wiss. Buch-gesellschaft.

Bierhoff, H. W. (1995). Verantwortungsbereitschaft, Verantwortungsabwehr und Verantwortungszuschreibung. In: K. Bayertz (Ed.), *Verantwortung-Prinzip order problem?* (pp. 217–240). Darmstadt: Wiss. Buch-gesellschaft.

Bivins, Th. H. (2004). *Mixed media: Moral distinctions in journalism, advertising, and public relations.* Mahwah, NJ: Erlbaum.

108 JOHANNES BRINKMANN

Boyne, R. (2003). *Risk*. Buckingham: Open University Press.
Bråten, S. (1983). *Dialogens vilkår i datasamfunnet*. Oslo: Universitetsforlaget.
Bråten, S. (2000). *Modellmakt og altersentrerte spedbarn*. Bergen: Sigma.
Brenkert, G. (1998). Marketing and the vulnerable. In: L. P. Hartman (Ed.), *Perspectives in business ethics* (pp. 515–526). Chicago: McGraw-Hill.
Brinkmann, J. (2004). Looking at consumer behavior in a moral perspective. *Journal of Business Ethics*, *51*, 129–141.
Brinkmann, J. (2005a). Understanding insurance customer dishonesty: Outline of a situational approach. *Journal of Business Ethics*, *61*, 183–197.
Brinkmann, J. (2005b). *Uneasy business ethics*, book project in Norwegian in progress, forthcoming.
Brinkmann, J., & Lentz, P. (2006). Understanding insurance customer dishonesty: Outline of a moral-sociological approach. *Journal of Business Ethics*, *66*, 177–195.
Brinkmann, J., & Peattie, K. (2006). *Thoughts about consumer ethics*. Working paper for journal submission (revised version of a paper presented by JB at the AMA Marketing Ethics Seminar at Notre Dame University, May 2005).
Coalition … against Insurance Fraud. (1997). *Four faces: Why some Americans do – and do not – tolerate insurance fraud*, Washington, DC (downloadable: summary: http://insurancefraud.org/four-faces.htm, paper: http://insurancefraud.org/downloads/Four%20Faces.pdf).
Cooper, R. W., & Dorfman, M. S. (2003). Business and professional ethics in transitional economies and beyond: Considerations for the insurance industries of Poland, the Czech Republic and Hungary. *Journal of Business Ethics*, *47*, 381–392.
Cooper, R. W., & Frank, G. L. (2005). The highly troubled ethical environment of the life insurance industry: Has it changed significantly from the last decade and if so, why? *Journal of Business Ethics*, *58*, 149–157.
Crane, A., & Matten, D. (2004). *Business ethics*. Oxford: Oxford University Press.
DeGeorge, R. (1986). *Business ethics* (2nd ed.). New York: Macmillan.
Dean, D. H. (2004). Perceptions of the ethicality of consumer insurance claim fraud. *Journal of Business Ethics*, *54*, 67–79.
Eastman, J. K., & Eastman, K. L. (1997). The ethics of insurance agents versus insurance students: The educational implications. *CPCU Journal*, *50*, 104–121.
Eastman, K. L., Eastman, J. K., & Eastman, A. D. (1996). The ethics of insurance professionals: Comparison of personal versus professional ethics. *Journal of Business Ethics*, *15*, 951–962.
Ericson, R. V., & Doyle, A. (Eds). (2003). The moral risks of private justice: The case of insurance fraud. In: *Risk and morality* (pp. 317–362). Toronto: Toronto University Press.
Ericson, R. V., Doyle, A., & Barry, D. (2003). *Insurance as governance*. Toronto: Toronto University Press.
Ericson, R. V., & Doyle, A. (2004). *Uncertain business*. Toronto: Toronto University Press.
Ewald, F. (1991). Insurance and risk. In: G. Burchell, C. Gordon & P. Miller (Eds), *The foucault effect: Studies in governmentality* (pp. 197–210). London: Harvester.
Ferrell, O. C., Fraedrich, J., & Ferrell, L. (2002). *Business ethics: Ethical decision making and cases* (5th ed.). Boston: Houghton Mifflin.
French, P. (Ed.) (1991). *The spectrum of responsibility*. New York: St. Martin's Press.
Fukukawa, K. (2002). Developing a framework for ethically questionable behavior in consumption. *Journal of Business Ethics*, *41*, 99–119.

Gert, B. (1988). *Morality. A new justification of the moral rules.* New York: Oxford University Press.

Gowri, A. (2004). When responsibility can't do it. *Journal of Business Ethics, 54,* 33–50.

Heimer, C. A. (2003). Insurers as moral actors. In: R. V. Ericson & A. Doyle (Eds), *Risk and morality* (pp. 284–316). Toronto: Toronto University Press.

Hernes, G. (1978). *Forhandlingsøkonomi og blandingsadministrasjon.* Bergen: Universitetsforlaget.

Hernes, G. (1981). Svarteperøkonomi. *Samtiden,* (4), 70–79.

Kaufmann, F.-X. (1995). Risiko, Verantwortung und Gesellschaftliche Komplexitat. In: K. Bayertz (Ed.), *Verantwortung - Prinzip order problem?* (pp. 72–97). Darmstadt: Wiss. Buch-gesellschaft.

Lenk, H., & Maring, M. (1993). Verantwortung-Normatives Interpretationskonstrukt.. In: L. H. Eckensberger & U. Gähde (Eds), *Ethische Norm und empirische Hypothese* (pp. 222–243). Frankfurt: Suhrkamp.

McCoy, B. (1983). The parable of the sadhu. *Harvard Business Review,* (Sept.–Oct.), 103–108, reprinted in Hoffman et al., 2001.

Müller, Ch. (1992). Verantwortungsethik. In: A. Pieper (Ed.), *Geschichte der neueren Ethik 2* (pp. 103–131). Tübingen: Francke.

Nunner-Winkler, G. (1993). Verantwortung. In: G. Enderle, K. Homann, M. Honecker, W. Kerber & H. Steinmann (Eds), *Lexikon der Wirtschaftsethik* (pp. 1185–1192). Freiburg: Herder.

Petersen, V. (2002). *Beyond rules in society and business.* Cheltenham: Elgar.

Poundstone, W. (1992). *Prisoner's dilemma.* New York: Doubleday.

Rao, C. P., & Singhapakdi, A. (1997). Marketing ethics: A comparison between services and other marketing professionals. *Journal of Services Marketing, 11,* 409–426.

Rapoport, A., Chammah, A. M., & Orwant, C. J. (1965). *Prisoner's dilemma.* Ann Arbor: University of Michigan Press.

Smith, N. C. (1995). Marketing strategies for the ethics era. *Long Range Planning, 28*(6), 126.

Smith, N. C., & Quelch, J. A. (Eds) (1993). *Ethics in marketing.* Burr Ridge, IL: Irwin.

Sykes, G. M., & Matza, D. (1957). Techniques of neutralization: A theory of delinquency. *American Sociological Review, 22,* 664–670.

Tennyson, S. (1997). Insurance experience and consumers' attitudes toward insurance fraud. *Journal of Insurance Regulation, 21*(2), 35–55.

Tennyson, S. (2002). Economic institutions and individual ethics: A study of consumer attitudes toward insurance fraud. *Journal of Economic Behavior and Organization, 32,* 247–265.

Ulrich, P., & Thielemann, U. (1992). *Ethik und Erfolg.* Bern: Haupt.

Vitell, S. J. (2003). Consumer ethics research: Review, synthesis and suggestions for the future. *Journal of Business Ethics, 43,* 33–47.

Vitell, S. J., & Grove, S. J. (1987). Marketing ethics and the techniques of neutralization. *Journal of Business Ethics, 6,* 433–438.

Vitell, S. J., & Muncy, J. (2005). The Muncy-Vitell consumer ethics scale: A modification and application. *Journal of Business Ethics, 62,* 267–275.

Weber, M. (1968). *Politik als Beruf.* Berlin: Duncker & Humblot.

Zimmerman, M. J. (1991). Sharing responsibility. In: P. French (Ed.), *The spectrum of responsibility* (pp. 275–286). New York: St. Martin's Press.

APPENDIX. EXHIBIT A

Criteria (and Author/s)	Short Description of Suggested Alternatives and/or Possible Typologies
Universal (all subjects) versus special (role-bound) responsibility (Petersen 2002/ cf. O'Neill) Relation to complementary rights: vague versus specific responsibility (ibid)	Five responsibility types • Universal-vague (often unwritten) • Universal-specific (often written) • Special-vague *and* specific • Special-specific (often written) • Special-vague (often unwritten)
Sharing of responsibility (Zimmerman, 1991)	Eight types of shared responsibility, as a combination of variable values below • Standard versus oversupplied (I, II) • Action versus omission (a, b) • Simultaneous versus sequential (1, 2)
Responsibility ascription criteria (Nunner-Winkler, 1993)	Properties of actors, actions, actor-action-relationships • Knowledge, freedom and judgment • Consistency with duties • Degrees of action result control
Size (or degree) of responsibility (Kaufmann, 1995)	Size (and perhaps market value) of responsibility as a function of • Freedom of (not externally determined) action alternatives for coping with complex tasks and challenges • Weight of risks with given probabilities and evaluations of possible consequences
Collective action responsibility (Lenk & Maring, 1995)	Three responsibility distribution problem types • Responsibility ascription for unorganized collective action

	(incl. market mechanisms and technology-related situations)
	• Individual and collective responsibility for public-collective goods and towards affected stakeholders
	• Accountability and responsibility distribution in the context of organized division of labor
Collective responsibility ascription (DeGeorge, 1986)	Five models
	• Each group member is fully responsible
	• Each group member is partially responsible
	• The group as such and all group members are fully responsible
	• The group as such is fully and all group members are partially responsible
	• The group as such is fully and only responsible (the group members are not)

Note: For further examples cf. Exhibit 1.

INSURANCE, RISK ASSESSMENT AND FAIRNESS: AN ETHICAL ANALYSIS

Daniel E. Palmer

ABSTRACT

The practice of insuring essentially involves the determination and assignment of risk to individuals. Such determinations are made almost exclusively on the basis of statistical models. As such, the determination of an individual's risk in relation to a particular form of insurance, and thus ultimately to the determination of the cost and availability of that insurance for the individual, is made in relation to her inclusion in certain statistical groups. However, a number of questions, both practical and philosophical, can be raised about the way in which an individual is assessed upon the basis of such statistical modeling. In this paper, I explore some of these issues in relation to questions of fairness. I begin by examining the basic structure of statistical risk assessment for insurance purposes. I argue that the underlying ethical concern involved with such cases involves the manner in which the attributes of the statistical groups used for insurance purposes can be said to fairly represent the individual qua individual. As such, I go on to explore the general philosophical issues involved in applying statistical models to individuals and the fairness of using such applications to make determinations about individuals for insurance purposes.

Insurance Ethics for a More Ethical World
Research in Ethical Issues in Organizations, Volume 7, 113–126
Copyright © 2007 by Elsevier Ltd.
All rights of reproduction in any form reserved
ISSN: 1529-2096/doi:10.1016/S1529-2096(06)07006-4

INTRODUCTION

Insurance companies are essentially involved in the management of risk. In order to be profitable, insurers thus have to set premiums for policies based upon an estimation of both the probability of certain adverse events along with a determination of the costs associated with those events. While determining the latter might involve practical difficulties of its own, the determination of the former gives rise to questions of a distinctly philosophical nature. One such question turns on a consideration of how individuals are rated by insurers in such processes of risk determination. To see why, we need only consider the fact that if the adverse events associated with any particular individual could be uniquely determined by insurers, then the cost of that individual's policy could be determined simply by summing the costs of those payouts together with the administrative costs of providing the policy and a given profit margin. Insurance, on this model, would simply reduce to a kind of savings plan, since there would no longer be any risk involved for either party (Light, 1991, p. 52). But, of course, this is not practically possible, and this is not how insurers determine the costs associated with individual policies. Rather, insurers must use statistical models that group individuals on the basis of certain identifiable characteristics that they share in common, and which can be correlated with certain kinds of adverse events (i.e., smokers will be viewed as being more risky than non-smokers, drivers with previous drunken driving convictions as more risky than drivers with a clean driving record, and so forth). Insurers, in essence, must discriminate between individuals not qua individuals, but qua their membership in certain categories of persons, and this, in essence, is the subject of their actuarial practices.

Anytime individuals are viewed primarily on the basis of such a type of categorization for some practical purpose, questions about the appropriateness of viewing an individual under that particular category are bound to arise. Examples of such types of questions are plentiful: as when some people raise concerns about the use of race as a category to distinguish between individuals seeking certain social positions or when others question military rules concerning the eligibility of women for combat positions (see, for example, Maitzen, 1991, p. 23). What people want to know in such situations is under what conditions it is appropriate to use particular categories for the purposes of discriminating among individuals relative to some given aim. Broadly speaking, these questions are questions of fairness then, and they seem to naturally arise whenever individuals are categorized in this way. It is not surprising then that similar questions of fairness have been raised in relationship to the categories that insurers use to discriminate among the individuals they insure (see, for instance, Beider, 1987; Daniels & Sabin, 1997; Sorrell, 1998). A number of persons have thus raised questions of such a sort in relationship to the use of categories such as race and sex in the actuarial ratings utilized in the insurance industry. I will term the general philosophical concern involved in such questions the categorization issue, and the questions of fairness that it gives rise to fairness questions. Indeed, while many ethical issues can be raised surrounding certain other practices associated with insurance, such as the selling and marketing of certain kinds of insurance, what is, I would maintain, unique about this particular kind of issue is that it is the one philosophical and ethical issue that is inherent to the nature of insurance itself.

Nonetheless, despite the fact that the categorization issue and associated questions of fairness are often raised in relation to insurance actuarial models, I do not believe that the full significance of such questions have either been fully understood or completely answered. In part, I believe this is because there are actually several different issues and concerns lurking underneath these questions of fairness. In the remainder of this paper then, I wish first to clarify several different ways in which questions of fairness have arisen in light of the categorization issue. By clarifying these distinct issues, I also hope to show what model of fairness is most properly applicable to the insurance industry and how we might conceptualize the ethical duties of insurers in relationship to the categorization issue. Finally, I will say a bit about the appropriate role of public policy in regard to these issues in the insurance industry given the previous account.

APPLYING STANDARDS OF FAIRNESS TO INSURANCE PRACTICES

Before delving into the questions of fairness with which I am concerned in this paper, I would note that I am simply assuming two things. One, I am assuming that the practice of insurance in general is a morally legitimate form of business. There might be particular forms of insurance that are necessarily unethical, perhaps such as dead peasants' insurance (see Spurgin, 2005). However, I will adopt the presupposition that by and large there is nothing inherently wrong with the insurance business. On my own view, this means both that I take it, again in general, that insurers provide legitimate services to their customers and that it is their legitimate aim to make a profit off of the provision of these services. Anyone who disagrees with either of these claims would most likely see the ethical issues involved in insurance in a radically different way, and for different reasons all together (see, for example, Light, 1991). Second, I also assume that ordinary moral norms apply to the business of insurance no more or less than they do to any other human activity. In this sense, I assume the necessity of at least a minimum level of morality that is applicable to all business practices. In this regard, I take it that despite the broader and ongoing debates that exist about the scope and extent of the moral obligations of businesses, there are certainly basic moral norms (such as honesty, respect for basic human rights, etc.) that can be properly applied to business activities. Again, someone who rejects this would take a radically different view of the categorization and fairness issues in insurance all together, in this case because there would be, for such a person, no possible ethical issue at all. I mention both of these points not only to make my own assumptions clear however, but because they both will play a role in some of the considerations that I will later raise.

Returning to the main issue though, what might it mean to say that a categorization used for insurance purposes is fair or unfair? It has some-times been taken to mean, at least by certain people in relation to certain forms of insurance, that insurance practices are unfair because they dis-criminate against certain individuals in charging them higher rates (see, for example, Light, 1991, p. 53). On this view, the fairness issue arises simply out of the use of categories to rank individuals in a way that discriminates between them (in terms of their perceived risk and the associated costs of the policies provided). Taken as a global claim however, the basis of this way of seeing the fairness issue makes little sense, since it would imply that it is simply the use of categorization all together that is unfair. On this view it is discrimination itself that is seen as intrinsically unfair (perhaps this simply stems from a linguistic confusion, since we often use the term "discrimi-nation" as a shorthand for unfair discrimination). But this cannot, at least in general, be the case, for at least two reasons. One, the claim is much to sweeping in form, since it is the very nature of insurance, as noted above, to discriminate based upon risk (Borna & Avila, 1999, pp. 355–356; Launis, 2003, p. 88). As Veikko Launis (2003) points out in this regard the "business of insurance is dependent upon accurate risk classification and differenti-ation, founded on the idea that the premiums should be more or less in proportion to the estimated risk level of policy-holders" (pp. 88–89). Thus, to argue that discrimination per se is always unfair would be to deny the fundamental point of insurance. Second, it would at least arguably often be unfair for insurers not to discriminate in some manner between those they insure, since treating policy holders equally even when they posed radically different risks would be to force some policy holders to bear the undeserved costs posed by others. This would happen, for instance, if an insurance company charged a driver with a long history of safe driving the same rate as a driver with an extensive history of accidents stemming from reckless driving habits, in essence forcing the former to subsidize the latter's reckless road habits. This, in essence, leads to the notion of actuarial fairness, the idea that persons who pose different risks ought to be charged different rates. Thus, as noted by Norman Daniels (1990), under this view insurance companies claim a moral duty "that low risk policy holders should not be punished with high premiums on behalf of the higher risk policy holders" (p. 497).

There, may, however be another kind of unfairness lurking behind the kinds of claims expressed when people say that a certain form of insurance discriminates and is thus unfair in the above manner. For perhaps what is unfair is not the discrimination itself, but the fact that persons who are discriminated against are then unable to obtain the service in question, and that is what is seen as being unfair (see, for example, Daniels, 1990; Murray, 1992). On this view, what is unfair is that certain persons, as a result of certain insurance practices, lack access to certain goods (Murray, 1992, p. 16). This seems, for instance, to be the real concern behind many criticisms concerning the kinds of categorizations used in many forms of medical or life insurance. The claim is then that what is unfair about certain insurance practices of categorization is that they exclude certain individuals from having access to some kinds of social benefits. Again, while I can certainly sympathize with the ethical concern underlying this charge, the way in which it is presented makes it utterly independent of the categorization issue at hand, and thus fails to make it clear how it relates to the issue of insurance per se. The problem is that this way of understanding the fairness issue really focuses exclusively on the fairness of people not having access to certain goods or services. And that, in itself, is a question independent of insurance practices in general. That is, if it is unfair that certain people lack access to health care, then it would be unfair if they lacked it no matter what the cause of that lack (denial by insurance companies, failure of the government to provide it, etc.). As such, the problem with this way of understanding the fairness issue is that it does not make it clear as to how this is an issue unique to the practice of insurance. Indeed, this way of understanding the problem seems often to merely suggest that if there are some goods so important that no one should lack access to them, then we should not depend upon private commercial companies to provide such services (Murray, 1992, pp. 16–17). While such a claim may, or may not, be true in relation to certain goods, it tells us nothing about what is fair or unfair in the practice of insuring itself.

Another way of understanding the fairness issue in insurance risk evaluation ties it strongly to notions of responsibility. Here, the objection is often brought that a categorization is unfair if it depends upon some trait for which an individual is not responsible, say, for example, his or her gender or ethnicity (Beider, 1987, p. 68). Fair categorizations on such a reading would be tied uniquely to traits, behavior, actions, or events for which persons are responsible and discrimination between individuals would thus be considered fair if and only if they distinguished between policyholders based upon such features. While I do not deny that issues of responsibility can affect our understanding of fairness in certain forms of insurance, I would reject the stronger claim that fairness in categorization is always dependent upon such a tracking of responsibility. First, determining a philosophical account of responsibility that could be practically applied to actuarial models is extremely challenging. For instance, the fairness of insuring drivers with rates that are based on previous drunken driving convictions would depend on this model upon knowing for certain the extent to which the individuals in question were responsible for their behavior. Given that we do not know the extent to which alcoholism is a disease and the extent to which alcoholic individuals have control over their behavior, this is a much more contentious issue than it might seem at first (Light, 1991, p. 53). Nonetheless, it seems reasonable for insurers to rate drivers with previous DUI convictions as being of greater risk than those without such records. Second, there are many traits and behaviors for which individuals are clearly not responsible, but for which it does not seem intuitively unfair for insurers to take account of in their categorization of individuals for risk assessment. For instance, a young person is clearly not responsible for being young, yet nonetheless he or she may pose objectively greater risks as a driver in virtue of being young that automobile insurers seem reasonable to take account of in their actuarial policies. Indeed, since younger and less experienced drivers are involved in more accidents than other drivers, it would once again hardly be fair to discount this fact in setting insurance rates, since doing so would unfairly shift the costs of insuring younger drivers onto older ones.

If none of the above concerns correctly capture the central issue of fairness represented in the categorization issue, then what does? I will argue that the issue turns on what Stephen Maitzen (1991) has called in a related context the issue of "statistical discrimination" (p. 23). In discussing this concept, Maitzen notes that we often use some identifiable characteristic of persons (call it "A") that is positively but imperfectly correlated with some other, perhaps underlying, characteristic B to discriminate between individuals. We use A as a surrogate or index for B, even though we would ideally discriminate on the basis of B itself (1991, p. 23). In the case of insurance then, insurers use certain traits that are correlated with adverse outcomes (again, smoking with health costs, for example). However, since the correlation is imperfect, it will be true that some individuals identified as A will not actually also have, or later display, the characteristic B. This is particularly true since there need be no causal link between the possession of characteristic A and the occurrence of B. This is made clear by the actuarial profession itself in the "Actuarial Standards of Practice," in which it is explicitly stated that "risk classification characteristics ... need not exhibit a cause-and-effect relationship" (Actuarial Standards Board, 1989).

The philosophical problem though is that it seems unfair that some individuals get treated as if they are B, even when they are not when such statistical categories are used. In the case of insurance then, the idea is that since the characterizations that insurers use to rank individuals are based upon statistical correlations and actuarial tables that are often likewise imperfect in the way in which they discriminate, it will be true that some individuals will be put into risk groups that do not reflect their "true" risk. For instance, some smokers will not incur significant additional health care costs as a result of their smoking. In this sense it does seem legitimate to speak of insurers as thus treating those persons unfairly, since the way in which they were categorized did not reflect the real risks associated with them. This, I take it, goes to the heart of the question of fairness in insurance.

STATISTICAL DISCRIMINATION AND UNFAIRNESS IN INSURANCE

This problem, I think, gets to the heart of the fairness question of the categorization issue, and we can now pose what I see as the fundamental ethical problem that it gives rise to, which is, "to what extent do insurers have an obligation to prevent the type of unfairness that results from statistical determination?" Resolving this question however is rather difficult. For one, the use of statistical models to determine risk will always result in some degree of statistical discrimination, since by their very nature they do not take account of every factor relevant to an individual's true risk. This is particularly true since such models, as noted previously, often must rely on correlations that do not necessarily indicate causal relations. But, of course, not ranking individuals at all would, as we have seen, pose equal if not far greater questions of unfairness, since it would ignore relevant differences between individuals that were truly relevant. Here I suggest we think of the problem by reference to a medical analogy. Many medical diagnostic tests also make use of imperfect indicators, and as such give rise to false positives (a person is indicated as having a condition when they do not) and false negatives (a person is indicated as not having a condition even though they really do have it). The categorization issue of fairness, I believe can be thought of similarly. The various traits used by insurance companies to determine individual risk also give rise to false positives (they indicate that insuring a person will involve more costs than will in fact be the case) and false negatives (they indicated that insuring a person will involve fewer costs than they actually will). And, of course in both cases, those that give rise to false positives and those that give rise to false negatives, persons will end up being treated unfairly (since they were rated as posing more, or less, risk than they actually do). So, the question becomes, "to what extent do insurance companies have an ethical obligation to prevent false positives and false negatives in the categories that they use in their actuarial ratings?" This, I think, is the most philosophically significant and ethically important question raised by the categorization issue. However, I would suggest that it is also the most puzzling one, since, as indicated above, there is no option that will give the optimal result, that no one is treated unfairly in the relevant sense.

COPING WITH UNFAIRNESS, THE ETHICS OF STATISTICAL DISCRIMINATION

How then should insurers respond to issues of statistical discrimination and the potential unfairness it gives rise to in an ethically responsible manner? My cue comes from the insurance industry itself, and the principle that already guides its thinking about issues of categorization. For instance, Richard Epstein (1985) notes that in determining what categories to use in ranking risks "market processes select the most homogeneous subgroup on which it is possible to obtain aggregate statistics at a reasonable cost" (p. 313) In this sense, Epstein is thus simply iterating that insurers and others who make use of statistical discrimination already are well cognizant of the issue of false positives and false negatives, and have a general strategy, based in market principles, for dealing with this issue. His response is that they are justified in using those categories that are most accurate in determining individual risk that can be obtained at a justifiable cost. Of course, for Epstein the cost in question is merely the monetary cost of determining the most appropriate category. My suggestion is that an ethical approach to setting insurance raises through statistical categories will include ethical costs as part of the costs of their analysis. As I see it there are three general points that are essential to this ethical cost benefit analysis as it applies to the insurance industry, each of which I will briefly outline below.

First, I think there is a general duty of care on the part of insurers to take account of the likelihood of such false positives and false negatives when determining the categorization of individuals in their actuarial practices. This is simply because as we have seen above false categorizations that result from statistical discrimination are unfair. As such, the costs of the potential unfairness to the individuals who might be affected are a legitimate consideration for insurers to take account of in their actuarial practices. Another way of making this same point is to point out that as even Epstein (1985) notes there is always multiple categories that can be used to rank individuals in terms of their statistical risk (p. 313; see also Light, 1991, p. 53). Any particular individual will thus "fit" into multiple categories depending upon how we choose to categorize her. That choice will depend in part on the costs of opting for one category over the other. Again, the economic costs of using one categorization over another may be an important factor, but given the potential for statistical discrimination, another kind of cost will be the harms that are caused to individuals when they are put into a category that is in some way misrepresentative of them qua individual. In some cases this harm may be merely paying higher premiums than they ought to, but in other cases there might also be more significant harms, such as the failure to obtain needed health care or to have access to the financial security necessary to protect their families. But, in any case, it is part of a general duty of care toward others for insurers to consider the costs of the unearned harms that are brought about through statistical discrimination.

Second, I would argue that the extent of this duty of care to avoid false positives is dependent upon the nature of the costs that are involved. That is, the ethical duty of care as I see it requires that insurers be particularly sensitive to unfairness caused by statistical discrimination when that unfairness carries with it a greater potential to significantly harm individuals affected by such unfairness. That is, in some cases, for instance in the case of medical insurance, individuals who are affected by statistical discrimination unfairly stand to loose a great deal as a result of this discrimination, mainly their access to basic health care. Since health is a fundamental good that underlies the pursuit of nearly all other goods, anything that potentially affects an individual's access to health care poses a significant harm to that individual. As such, I would argue that health insurers have a greater burden to avoid statistical discrimination then, say, liability insurers. The basic idea here is that there should be a proportionality between the moral risks associated with statistical discrimination and the duty of insurers to avoid utilizing categories that pose greater potential for such discrimination. The higher the moral costs, the greater the duty to find categories that minimize such discrimination.

As an example, there has been a great deal of controversy over the potential use of genetic information by insurers in setting policies (see for instance, Brockett & Tankersley, 1997; Capron, 2000; Hedgecoe, 1996; Kass, 1992; Murray, 1992). To my mind, what is particularly problematic with the use of such information is that the link between certain genetic factors and specific diseases and illnesses is often overestimated (Brockett & Tankersley, 1997, p. 1671). As such, there is great potential for insurance providers to rely on genetic test that provide very imperfect indicators in screening insurance applicants. Such practices thus potentially give rise to significant number of false positives, and in doing so potentially prevent significant numbers of persons from having access to health insurance unfairly. Since a lack of affordable insurance can in turn significantly affect a person's health, such statistical discrimination poses a significant moral harm in many cases. Since health insurers have other ways of effectively spreading risk available, they should avoid using genetic screenings for the basis of categorization as a general means of determining health risks except in those cases where there is a direct causal link between a specific genetic component and the development of a specific disease or condition and there is no other way of accounting for the potential costs of such a disease or condition actuarially.

Third, earlier in this paper I rejected the idea that fairness in insurance is always directly connected to responsibility. Nonetheless, I think there is a sense in which the underlying idea behind that view can play a role in the ethical analysis of statistical discrimination. At heart, the weaker claim that I would support is that insurers need to be particularly careful in using statistical categorization when the defining characteristics used are not ones which individuals can, by their own efforts, modify. The reasoning here is that false positives are much more problematic if they are not subject to correction by the individuals themselves then if they are not, since in the former case an individual can do nothing to respond to the unfairness in question. On the other hand, individuals are at least responsive to categorizations of the latter sort, and thus they have the opportunity to modify the manner in which they are categorized. In this sense, it is important that insurers take on a greater burden in avoiding unfairness that results from statistical discrimination when individuals have no potential to modify the manner in which they are categorized.

For example, I would argue that what is particularly problematic about using racial categorizations, for insurance ratings, even if there is some statistical support for them, is that an individual who is unfairly discriminated against using such categories has no potential to alter the manner in which he or she is categorized, since he or she has no control over his or her racial identity. Since it is likely that racial categories will almost always be imperfect indicators for other characteristics of interest to insurers, they should be weary of using them if there is any alternative categories available that would provide similar outcomes. Further, since there is a long history of such categories being used in a harmful manner, the affects of reifying these categories within society is particularly problematic. On the other hand, while it may be true, for instance, that an automobile insurer who categorized drivers in terms of driving experience might similarly unfairly discriminate against some individuals, the individuals in question have the potential, through establishing a clean driving record, to alter the manner in which they are categorized. As such, the latter practice, while not perfect, is far less ethically problematic than the former. Though the connection with responsibility that I am arguing for here is much weaker than that earlier discussed, it does incorporate the notion that at least in some contexts, an individual's control over his or her characterization should "count." While incorporating the three elements of the duty of care that I have outlined above into the actuarial practices of insurers will not completely eliminate statistical discrimination and the unfairness in can give rise to, it will significantly diminish the moral costs associated with the worst forms of such unfairness, and do so within a framework of analysis that is already standard in insurance practice.

ADVERSE SELECTION AND THE NEED FOR PUBLIC POLICY

Of course, within the arena of competitive markets there is an additional concern for companies that choose to adhere to ethical principles. The concern is that companies that chose to act ethically will put themselves at a advantage with those companies that refuse to act ethically. commentators have noted, this problem is particularly per- insurance industry, where the problem is typically formulated in terms ∪. e consequences of adverse selection (see, for example, Brockett & Tankersley, 1997, p. 1664 and Capron, 2000, p. 269). Adverse selection occurs when information is available that allows lower risk individuals to opt out of a particular insurance pool, leaving only higher-risk individuals within that pool. This, in turn, drives up premiums within that pool. In a competitive market, adverse selection can be particularly problematic. If companies make use of different categorizations in their ratings, their premiums will reflect this. Companies that make use of more restrictive categories may be able to offer lower premiums by refusing more persons who are potentially of greater risk and attracting those with the lowest risk. This in turn will force companies who refuse to make use of such categories to take on a greater proportion of high risk individuals, driving up both their expenses and their premiums and causing them to be at a competitive disadvantage. And this is true even when, as I have maintained is often the case, the categories used are only imperfect indicators of individuals' real risk. In this sense, a company that seeks to avoid false positives in its ratings for ethical reasons will typically expose themselves to more risk than companies that use more restrictive categories with higher rates of false positives. That is, from a purely competitive advantage, avoiding false positives will typically be costlier in economic terms for insurers than encouraging them in setting one's actuarial rates (whereas the opposite is true of false negatives). The effects of adverse selection can be seen in the demise of community rating in health insurance in the United States: as more insurers began to make use of expansive forms of risk rating they began to drain potentially lower risk subscribers away from the pools of the companies that used community ratings, eventually forcing those companies to adopt similar rating practices (Kass, 1992, p. 6).

The same problems are likely to attach to companies that adopt ethical standards in their rating practices. Avoiding the ethical costs of unfairness in statistical discrimination will often lead to greater financial costs in an unregulated financial market. Thus, if ethical standards are to flourish in the insurance industry, there is a necessary, if limited, role for public oversight and regulation. The goal of this oversight should be directed toward not only discouraging the grossest forms of unethical practices, such as fraud, within the insurance industry, but to fostering a climate in which higher ethical standards can profitably be adopted by insurance companies without undue competitive hardship. In this sense, public oversight of the categorization systems used in the actuarial ratings used by insurance companies is justified precisely in order to ensure that companies that act with ethical due care toward their customers are not unfairly punished in the market. It is not my purpose here to discuss the specific role that public regulation should take in any particular market. The nature and extent of regulation within the insurance industry is already extremely complex, and even a cursory examination of this arena would be far beyond the scope of this paper. I merely wish to point here to the underlying philosophical justification for public regulation given the nature of the product itself. The specific form such regulation will take will vary according to the particular form of insurance in question and the empirical context of the market in which that insurance is sold.

I would note however that just as the unfairness of statistical discrimination will depend in part upon the nature of the harms that results to individuals and to society as a result of that discrimination, so too the extent of regulation that is justified over actuarial ratings will be dependent upon the kinds of harms that their potential misuse can cause. In this respect, I would argue that some forms of insurance, particularly health insurance, are in need of much more stringent regulation than others, say for example travel insurance. As the sorts of harms that can result from the categorization problem are much more serious in the former case than in the latter case, public involvement takes on a special urgency in overseeing the former that it does not in the latter. In this regard, I would agree with those ethicists who have argued that the potential misuse of genetic tests in setting insurance ratings calls for special attention by state and federal regulator agencies (see, for instance, Kass, 1992, p. 11).

CONCLUSION

In this paper I have examined what I have argued is the central philosophical and ethical problem of insurance, the issue of fairness as it relates to the categorization problem. I have argued that the real problem of fairness in insurance hinges upon issues of statistical discrimination inherent in the use of the actuarial risk classification of individuals for insurance purposes. While I have argued that the type of unfairness that statistical discrimination can give rise to cannot be wholly eliminated, I have maintained that insurers should be aware of its potential to adversely affect individuals. In conjunction with such awareness, I have argued that insurers can develop an ethical framework for minimizing the worst harms that can result from statistical discrimination that fits well with current assumptions and practices regarding risk assessment. I have also argued that public policy regarding insurance practices should be geared toward providing regulations that ensure a level playing field in those cases where adverse selection could unfairly disadvantage insurers who acted to minimize the unfair affects of statistical discrimination in their categorization models. My aim has thus been to offer a general framework of ethical analysis that both academics interested in business ethics and those working in the insurance and regulation industry can flesh out more fully in relation to specific forms of insurance.

REFERENCES

Actuarial Standards Board. (1989). Actuarial Standard of Practice, No. 12: Concerning Risk Classification, http://www.actuarialstandardsboard.or/pdf/asops012_014.pdf

Beider, R. (1987). Sex discrimination in insurance. *Journal of Applied Philosophy*, *4*(1), 65–75.

Borna, S., & Avila, S. (1999). Genetic information: Consumers' right to privacy versus insurance companies' right to know a public opinion survey. *Journal of Business Ethics*, *19*, 355–362.

Brockett, P., & Tankersley, E. (1997). The genetics revolution, economics, ethics and insurance. *Journal of Business Ethics*, *16*, 1661–1676.

Capron, A. (2000). Genetics and insurance: Accessing and using private information. *Social Philosophy & Policy*, *17*(2), 235–275.

Daniels, N. (1990). Insurability and the HIV epidemic: Ethical issues in underwriting. *The Millbank Quarterly*, *68*(4), 497–525.

Daniels, N., & Sabin, J. (1997). Limits to health care: Fair procedures, democratic deliberation, and the legitimacy problem for insurers. *Philosophy and Public Affairs*, *26*(4), 303–350.

Epstein, R. (1985). *Takings: Private property and the power of eminent domain*. Cambridge, MA: Harvard University Press.

Hedgecoe, A. (1996). Genetic catch-22: Testing, risk and private health insurance. *Business & Professional Ethics Journal*, *15*(2), 69–86.

Kass, N. (1992). Insurance for the insurers: The use of genetic tests. *Hastings Center Report*, *22*(6), 6–11.

Launis, V. (2003). Solidarity, genetic discrimination, and insurance: A defense of weak genetic exceptionalism. *Social Theory and Practice*, *29*(1), 87–111.

Light, D. (1991). The ethics of corporate health insurance. *Business & Professional Ethics Journal*, *10*(2), 49–62.

Maitzen, S. (1991). The ethics of statistical discrimination. *Social Theory and Practice*, *17*(1), 23–45.

Murray, T. (1992). Genetics and the moral mission of health insurance. *Hastings Center Report*, *22*(6), 12–17.

Sorrell, T. (Ed.) (1998). *Health care, ethics and insurance*. New York: Routledge.

Spurgin, E. (2005). The problem with 'dead peasants' insurance. In: J. DesJardins & J. McCall (Eds), *Contemporary issues in business ethics*, (5th ed.) (pp. 213–221). Belmont, CA: Wadsworth.

REASONABLE RESTRICTIONS ON UNDERWRITING

Joseph Heath

ABSTRACT

Few issues in business ethics are as polarizing as the practice of risk classification and underwriting in the insurance industry. Theorists who approach the issue from a background in economics often start from the assumption that policy-holders should be charged a rate that reflects the expected loss that they bring to the insurance scheme. Yet theorists who approach the question from a background in philosophy or civil rights law often begin with a presumption against so-called "actuarially fair" premiums and in favor of "community rating," in which everyone is charged the same price. This paper begins by examining and rejecting the three primary arguments that have been given to show that actuarially fair premiums are unjust. It then considers the two primary arguments that have been offered by those who wish to defend the practice of risk classification. These arguments overshoot their target, by requiring a "freedom to underwrite" that is much greater than the level of freedom enjoyed in most other commercial transactions. The paper concludes by presenting a defense of a more limited right to underwrite, one that grants the legitimacy of the central principle of risk classification, but permits specific deviations from that ideal when other important social goods are at stake.

Insurance Ethics for a More Ethical World
Research in Ethical Issues in Organizations, Volume 7, 127–159
Copyright © 2007 by Elsevier Ltd.
ISSN: 1529-2096/doi:10.1016/S1529-2096(06)07007-6

There are very few issues in business ethics that are as polarizing as the practice of risk classification and underwriting in the insurance industry. Not everyone who seeks indemnification against a particular loss faces the same probability of suffering that loss, or faces a loss of equal magnitude. Thus insurers typically try to ascertain both the magnitude and probability of the loss for which a prospective policy-holder seeks indemnity, in order to determine an appropriate premium level. The ideal is to charge each policy-holder the so-called "actuarially fair" premium, which represents the anticipated cost of compensating that individual for the loss, multiplied by the probability that the loss will occur during the term of the policy. In reality, insurers are often unable to determine the risks that each individual faces. Thus they use a system of more-or-less broad classification, in order to determine which "risk pool" or class an individual falls into. This is used to determine a base premium, which is then "topped up" to cover transaction costs, commissions, and possibly – but not necessarily – profit.

Theorists who approach these insurance practices from a background in economics or business often start from the assumption that the actuarially fair premium represents the most "equitable" (Bossert & Fleurbaey, 2002) or "just" arrangement, such that any deviation from actuarial fairness requires justification.[1] Rates are considered "unfair" if "the insured is overcharged for the loss exposure in comparison with another similar loss exposure" (Outreville, 1998, p. 149), but there is no question that individuals who present *different* loss exposures should be charged different premiums. On the other hand, theorists who approach the question from a background in philosophy or civil rights law often begin with a presumption *against* actuarially fair premiums and in favor of so-called "community rating," in which everyone, no matter what their background risk profile, has access to the same insurance policy at the same price (Daniels, 1991; Austin, 1983). Deviations from this baseline are then regarded as standing in need of justification. As a result, the entire practice of underwriting is presented as morally suspect. Tom Baker (2003), for instance, describes the idea of actuarial fairness as "a watered-down form of liberalism that privileges individual interests over the common good and that privileges, above all, the interests of insurance institutions organized on its terms" (p. 277).

Critics of risk-classification (or more tendentiously, "statistical discrimination") have derived considerable support from a series of Supreme Court decision in the United States that disallowed categorization according to sex in defined-benefit pension schemes. The insurance industry also suffered a series of public-relations disasters associated with its underwriting practices, particularly in the United States where the absence of comprehensive public health insurance has made conditions of access to private health insurance a highly charged moral and political issue. This became especially apparent in the early stages of the AIDS epidemic, when insurers began refusing coverage not just to individuals who had contracted the HIV virus, but also those with a record of having been tested for it (on the grounds that only people who engaged in high-risk behavior would elect to test themselves). A similar furor erupted in the 1990s when it was discovered that over half of American insurers routinely denied health, life and disability coverage to battered women, on the grounds that victims of domestic abuse had an adverse claims history. These episodes resulted in legislation in several American states imposing restrictions on the "freedom to underwrite" of insurers, preventing insurers from requesting certain types of information from prospective policyholders, or else directly prohibiting them from charging different premiums to member of different groups (Hellman, 1997; Austin, 1983).

The result has been the development of considerable inconsistency in public policy. Certain forms of risk classification are prohibited for certain types of insurance, but not others. No general legal principles have been developed to govern the practice either, in part because the ideal of actuarial fairness is rejected by many as inherently discriminatory or unjust. My goal in this paper will be to critically evaluate the latter claim. I begin by examining three different arguments that have been given, purporting to show that the practice of charging actuarially fair premiums is inherently unjust. I will try to show that each of these arguments is informed, in one way or another, by an essential misunderstanding of the mechanism through which insurance serves as a source of cooperative benefit. I go on to consider the two primary arguments that have been offered by those who wish to defend the practice of risk classification. These arguments, I will argue, overshoot their target, by demanding a "freedom to underwrite" that is much greater than the level of freedom enjoyed in most other commercial transactions. Thus, I conclude by presenting an outline and defense of a somewhat more limited "right to underwrite," one that grants the legitimacy of the central principle of risk classification, but permits specific deviations from that ideal when other important social goods are at stake. This in turn allows us to develop relatively precise criteria for determining what constitutes a reasonable restriction on underwriting.

I

The world is full of risk. Knowing the probability of various events is extremely useful when it comes to engaging in practical deliberation.

Unfortunately, what matters to most of us when we make our plans is not the background probability of an event, but the actual frequency with which it occurs. We know that a fair coin has a 50 percent probability of landing heads, but we also know that flipping it 10 times is quite unlikely to produce exactly 5 heads and 5 tails. As a result, we need to be concerned not just with the mean, but also with the variance – how far individual outcomes can be expected to deviate from the mean, and how often. However, it is also well known that as the number of tosses increases, the frequency will tend to converge with the probability (a phenomenon often referred to as "the law of large numbers"). In other words, increasing the number of trials induces *statistical stability* (Hacking, 2002, pp. 190–192); it decreases the variance in the distribution. This increase in stability is the central mechanism through which insurance schemes are able to produce welfare benefits for their members.

To see how a group of individuals can benefit from the law of large numbers, it is important to remember that individuals are often risk averse. Consider a farmer who under normal conditions is able to produce 10 tons of grain – enough to feed his entire family well throughout the winter. However, his land is also subject to a highly localized blight, which sometimes wipes out the entire crop. Suppose that the chances of this blight striking his field in a given year are 20 percent. Although the expected annual output of his field is therefore 8 tons, he would gladly swap a guaranteed revenue of 8 tons for the gamble that he faces between 10 tons or nothing. That way, his family would have a bit less to eat, but they would never risk starvation.

On his own, this is something that he cannot achieve. Suppose, however, that there are 100 small farmers who find themselves in identical circumstances, all facing the danger of this highly localized blight. They might agree to a "risk-pooling" arrangement, under which farmers who lose their crop in a given year are compensated by those who do not. Under this arrangement, the objective risk of blight does not diminish: 20 of the 100 farmers can, on average, expect to lose their crops. However, with the risk-pooling arrangement, each farmer can expect a revenue that will be, with 95 percent probability, between 7.2 and 8.8 tons (see Moss, 2002, pp. 28–31). Because the farmers are risk averse, this gamble has greater *subjective utility* than the gamble that gives each individual farmer an 80 percent chance of getting 10 tons and a 20 percent chance of nothing (even though the two gambles have the same mathematical value).

Thus what insurance offers is a form of superior "risk management," but not necessarily "risk abatement." It does not eliminate the loss but just redistributes it. Of course, the insurance arrangement has the agreeable consequence of preventing anyone in the community from starving. But it is important to keep in mind that this is not why people buy the insurance. Insurance is not charity. They buy insurance in order to reduce their own uncertainty. If some farmers happened to like the gamble, and thought that it was worth risking starvation in order to get a shot at the full 10 tons of grain, then they would have no incentive to join the insurance scheme.

It is important to note as well that the risk-pooling arrangement is neither a gain from trade nor a straightforward economy of scale, but rather a *sui generis* source of collective benefit. Theorists sometimes mistakenly assimilate the gains that come from *trading* risks with those that come from *pooling* risks (e.g. see Barr, 1998, pp. 111–112; Easterbrook & Fischel, 1991, p. 53). In the former case, two individuals with different levels of risk aversion can generate efficiency gains by exchanging a risk – specifically, the one who is most risk averse can pay the other, in return for a promise of indemnity in the case of an outcome that it is too far from the mean. Here, the welfare gain is possible only because one person is less risk averse than the other. In the case of insurance, however, people with the same level of risk aversion and risk exposure can still benefit from the "law of large numbers" mechanism, by agreeing to hold the risk in common. This is the typical arrangement within a mutual society, which was the dominant model of (non-commercial) insurance in the 20th century (Hansmann, 1992). Here there are no investors or stockholders, the company is owned by the policy-holders, and all of the money paid out in claims is simply levied from the policy-holders in the form of premiums.

The mutual society also provides the best model for examining the merits of actuarially fair premiums. Because there are no investors, the controversial issue of "profit" is taken off the table. Premium levels are determined by "the insurance company," but the company in this case is simply a group of managers appointed to act as agents of existing policy-holders. In this case, it is not difficult to determine how premiums are determined. Take the example of 100 small farmers above. One can start by imagining a meeting at which all the potential policy-holders get together in order to determine the terms of the insurance arrangement. (This is not so fanciful, since many early mutual societies did originate in this way, as witnessed by the fact that publicans were often the founders and record-keepers for early "friendly societies" [Neave, 1991, p. 51].) Together the farmers can be confident of producing close to 800 tons of grain, while losing 200 tons to the blight. Each farmer who joins the pool can therefore receive a guarantee of 8 tons of grain, in return for a commitment to contribute all that he is able to grow to the pool (either 10 tons, or 0 tons, depending upon how things work out).

This is equivalent to keeping one's own crop, and paying a premium of 2 tons into the insurance pool. (When 80 farmers contribute 2 tons each, it generates the 160 tons needed to indemnify the 20 farmers who lose their crops.) Thus what each farmer pays in the way of a premium is equal to the expected loss that he brings to the pool, viz. a 20 percent probability of drawing 8 tons while contributing nothing.[2]

Of course, the assumption so far is that each farmer is identically situated – having the same amount of land, the same level of productivity, and experiencing the same probability of suffering from the blight. But what if one of the farmers happened to have a plot of land that was twice the size of anyone else's? If he sought to insure his entire crop (i.e. sought a guarantee of 16 tons), it stands to reason that his premium should be higher. Indeed, the natural thing would be to charge him a premium that was twice as high, in reflection of the fact that the magnitude of the loss that he may impose upon the other members of the insurance pool is twice as large. But similarly, if a farmer had a plot of land that for some reason was twice as likely to be struck by the blight, then it would also be natural to charge him a higher premium. Indeed, the natural thing would be to charge him a premium that was twice as high. A 40 percent probability of drawing 8 tons while contributing nothing represents the same expected loss as a 20 percent probability of drawing 16 tons while contributing nothing.

Thus the reasoning that leads to higher premiums for people seeking indemnity for losses of greater magnitude directly parallels the reasoning that leads to higher premiums for people who present a greater risk of loss. Those who expect to take more out of the pool should be required to put more in. This is the principle that underlies the idea of actuarial fairness, which simply stipulates that the premium paid by an individual should be equal to that individual's expected loss (magnitude multiplied by the probability).

This proposal appears simple, and one can certainly imagine it serving as a basis for agreement in an initial meeting at which individuals get together to form an insurance pool. There are a number of "real world" complications that arise, however, when it comes to determining just what the probability of a given loss is for a given individual. Many philosophers in fact think there is no "fact of the matter" as to whether a particular event, taken all by itself, can be said to occur with some probability. Either it happens or it does not. Probabilities belong only to classes of events, as a function of the frequency with which they occur, or as a function of our ability to predict them, based upon the frequency with which they occur (Hacking, 1975). Thus the only way to determine the probability of an individual's loss is to pick out some sort of frequency to which it belongs.

With respect to certain events, the individual's own history may provide a sufficient record (so that the insurer is able to use so-called "experience rating" to determine that individual's premium). More often, the individual's own history is inadequate, and so insurers seek to establish a "class rate," by finding a larger group to which that individual belongs (Outreville, 1998, pp. 150–151) and seeing what the loss frequency is within that group. Thus a person who has just learned how to drive has no safety record, and so no basis for estimating his or her chances of having an accident. An insurer may notice, however, that young men have an accident rate that is significantly higher than that of young women, or that single men have a much higher accident rate than married men (Dahlby, 1983). Thus the insurer might respond by classifying individual policy-holders into such groups and using the frequency of losses among members of the group as a way of determining the expected loss that the individual brings to the insurance scheme.

This is where things get controversial. Class rating may seem like a form of guilt by association. Just because *other* young men are terrible drivers does not mean that *this* particular young man is going to be one. But of course, this is not a very helpful observation. If we knew how things were going to turn out in the end, then there would be no need for insurance. All that we have to go on in designing insurance contracts is the ex ante perspective. The way to think about the fairness of premium schemes is to imagine all of the policy-holders getting together in an initial meeting, in order to create the insurance pool. In principle, they are not obliged to do business with anyone, and so are not obliged to admit into the pool anyone that they do not want. Furthermore, the terms under which individuals are to be admitted are entirely up for negotiation. Under such conditions, if the best available information indicates that young men pose a particularly elevated risk, then these young men are going to have to offer more in the way of premiums in order to secure admittance.

Of course, there are a number of important "second best"[3] problems that arise when it comes to implementing actuarially fair premium schemes. In most cases, insurers will not have all the information that is needed to determine the expected loss that an individual brings to an insurance pool, and therefore cannot actually calculate the actuarially fair premium. They are left having to approximate that premium, using the best information available. Yet one cannot assume that refining the partition of the insurance pool using new information will necessarily bring the premiums that all individuals pay closer to the actuarially fair level. Thus there is room for significant injustice to arise out of attempts to implement an actuarially fair premium scheme in a world of imperfect (and asymmetric) information (Abraham, 1986, p. 86; Promislow, 1987, p. 216). For example, when insurers decided to deny health and disability insurance to battered women, most did not distinguish between those who continued to live with their abusive partner and those who had ended the relationship (Hellman, 1997, p. 361). Members of the latter group may well have been disadvantaged by the fact that information injurious to their risk rating was easily available (police reports, hospital records, etc.), while potentially exculpatory information (present living arrangements) was either unavailable or unverifiable.

Yet these sorts of "second best" problems are not where critics of actuarial fairness have focused their energies.[4] The most important arguments have all been directed against the principle itself. Critics argue that actuarially fair premiums are inherently unjust, and thus not even what insurers should be aiming for. The discussion that follows will therefore focus upon these sorts of principled objections, setting aside all "second best" considerations. This is not to suggest that problems arising at the level of the "second best" are not serious – in many cases they are enormously so. The discussion will be restricted to the principle of actuarial fairness simply because the arguments about "second best" problems cannot really begin before it is established what a "first best" solution looks like, and this question is still subject to enormous controversy.

II

The most damning criticism of risk classification and "class rating" is the claim that it represents plain old-fashioned discrimination. It penalizes certain individuals, not for their individual characteristics, but merely because of their membership in a group. This is, in effect, what the United States Supreme Court decided in *City of Los Angeles Department of Water and Power v. Manhart* (435 U.S. 702 [1978]), with respect to the use of sex-segregated actuarial tables in the determination of contribution levels to a defined-benefit pension plan. These types of pensions are essentially insurance products (with the payroll contributions being the premiums). Like life annuities, they generate a stream of fixed payments until the death of the beneficiary, thus providing insurance against the risk of outliving one's retirement savings. (Otherwise put, they represent an arrangement under which multiple individuals pool their retirement savings in order to reduce uncertainty.) Since women on average live longer than men, the expected value of a typical pension of this type is of greater value to women than to men at the time of retirement. Thus the employer in this case created a system of differential contribution levels for its employees, with women paying a higher premium than men. The Supreme Court ruled that this was a violation of Title VII of the Civil Rights Act of 1964, which prohibits discrimination against "any individual because of his race, color, religion, sex, or national origin" by employers.[5]

In order to reconstruct the court's reasoning, it is helpful to introduce a couple of distinctions, implicit in the judgment, but drawn out more explicitly in an influential gloss on that judgment by Brilmayer, Hekeler, Laycock, and Sullivan (1980). In civil rights law, there is an important distinction between permissible and impermissible grounds for discrimination, and between disparate treatment and disparate impact. It is permissible for employers to treat employees differently, according to some characteristic that they possess, provided that they are able to demonstrate a "business necessity" for so doing. For example, it has been deemed permissible for employers to require that candidates pass a weight-lifting test in order to be considered for certain heavy manufacturing jobs (*Bowe v. Colgate-Palmolive Co.*, 416 F.2d 711 [7th Cir.1969]). This of course will have a disparate *impact* upon women, since women are on average able to lift less than men. But this does not count as disparate *treatment* of women, because the effect is indirect, and is a consequence of a system of discrimination based upon permissible grounds. If, however, the employer were to refuse to consider women for such jobs on the grounds that they are less likely to pass the weight-lifting test, this would constitute impermissible discrimination. The mere fact that some characteristic is statistically correlated with a characteristic that serves as permissible grounds for discrimination does not make it permissible for the employer to use the former as grounds for discrimination as well. In other words, the characteristic "being permissible grounds for discrimination" is not preserved through probabilistic inference. This is as it should be, since an arrangement under which women were excluded from certain manufacturing jobs on the grounds that women in general are less likely to be able to lift heavy weights is clearly unfair to those women who *are* able to lift such weights, and thus do possess the relevant job qualification (however unlikely this may be ex ante).

According to the Supreme Court's reasoning in *Manhart*, charging women more for their pensions on the grounds that they are less likely to die young is like excluding women from certain classes of employment on the grounds that they are less likely to be able to lift heavy weights. According to Brilmayer et al. (1980):

> American women as a group currently live longer than American men as a group, just as
> they are able to lift less weight as a group. But some women will die earlier than some
> men, just as some will be able to lift more weight. An employer who pays annuities on
> the basis of integrated tables in effect distinguishes among his employees on the per-
> missible basis of longevity, for those individuals who live the longest will collect the most
> periodic payments and thus the largest total sum. Of course, the employer's practice may
> have disparate impact on men, for as a group they may not live to collect as many
> periodic payments as women. If he tries to avoid this disparate impact by using seg-
> regated tables – making larger periodic payments to all men as a group – he distinguishes
> on the basis of sex. This would be disparate treatment, for individual men and women of
> equal longevity would be treated differently: both periodic benefits and total benefits will
> be greater for a man than for a woman of equal longevity (pp. 510–511).

Central to this argument is the idea that "longevity" in this case constitutes
the permissible basis for discrimination. Thus equality requires that all employees receive the same ex post net benefit from the pension scheme *unless*
they differ with respect to longevity (just as all job applications for a position in heavy manufacturing must be considered equally unless they differ
with respect to weight-lifting ability). Naturally, using longevity as grounds
for discrimination has disparate impact on men, just as a weight-lifting test
has disparate impact on women. This is permissible. However, the employer
is *not* entitled to use sex as a predictor of longevity, in order to determine
pension benefits, because the former is merely statistically correlated with
the latter. According to the Court's ruling, even though women are more
likely to receive more periodic payments after retirement, "there is no assurance that any individual woman working for the Department will actually fit the generalization on which the Department's policy is based.
Many of those individuals will not live as long as the average man. While
they were working, those individuals received smaller paychecks because of
their sex, but they will receive no compensating advantage when they retire"
(*Manhart*, 435 U.S. 702, 708 [1978]). Thus sex-segregated actuarial tables
violate equality, by creating a situation in which a man who lives to the same
age as a woman would pay less for the pension benefits received.

This argument is ingenious, and at first glance also seems compelling.[6]
And even though it is limited in scope from a legal point of view (to relations
between employers and employees, and with respect to only the enumerated
categories of discrimination), the moral implications of the argument are
much broader. If sound, the argument shows that actuarially fair premiums
in general violate the principle of equality. It suggests, for instance, that
automobile insurance companies that charge drivers of red cars higher premiums than drivers of beige cars (of the same make and model) violate

equality. In this case "having an accident" constitutes permissible grounds for discrimination. Yet risk-rating in accordance with color means that people who drive beige cars and do have accidents pay less for the same benefit received as drivers of red cars who have accidents. Why should we reward people just for driving beige cars?

Yet the analogy that the argument depends upon is clearly strained. First of all, one can see the sense in which individuals are "rewarded" for their weight-lifting ability by being given access to an employment opportunity, but it is odd to think of a defined benefit pension scheme as "rewarding" individuals for longevity (as thus of longevity as a "permissible grounds for discrimination"). What is the point of discriminating on this basis? It is difficult to avoid the impression that the purpose of the pension scheme is being misdescribed. Second, there is the fact that, in the case of weight-lifting, it is the *negative* correlation between being female and the property that is being rewarded that motivates the discrimination against women. Yet in the case of pensions, there is a *positive* correlation between being female and the property that is being rewarded. So if the goal was actually to use sex as a predictor of longevity, and people were being paid *more* for living longer, then that should have led to an arrangement under which women were charged *lower* premiums than men. Here we can see the most serious problem with the framework that the Court used to describe the issue: it is unable to make any sense of the idea that sex is being used as a *predictor* of longevity. This in turn generates a serious misunderstanding of the purpose of segregated actuarial tables.

The employer in *Manhart* unfortunately muddied the waters by suggesting that the rationale for the sex-segregated tables was fairness to its male employees *as a class*. Instead of having each individual who lives a given number of years receive a net benefit of equal magnitude, they suggested that the goal was to have men as a class receive net benefits that were of equal (average) value to those received by women as a class. But this is clearly a terrible argument. It suggests, as the Court rightly saw, that proponents of sex-segregated actuarial tables did not want to use sex as a predictor of longevity, but rather wanted to *add* sex to longevity on the list of legitimate bases for discrimination. Under such an arrangement, each individual would get the same net benefit as each other individual, unless they differed in longevity *or sex*. But what could possibly motivate adding sex to the list of discriminators, since it obviously results in unequal treatment of individuals? The suggestion that it was being done in order to achieve fairness to classes – so that, in the aggregate, men receive the same average net benefit as women – is a strange rationale. Under such an arrangement, women would be forced to contribute more to the pension scheme, not because they were expected to live longer (this is the rewarded property!), but *merely* because they were women. This is plain old-fashioned discrimination. The Court quite rightly observed that the goal of civil rights legislation is to protect individuals from this sort of treatment, and that the language of the statute explicitly prohibits it.

The problem with the judgment lies in the framing of the question. It starts with the way that the principle of equality is applied (both by the Court, and in the more perspicuous argument of Brilmayer et al. [1980]). The conflict is not one between equality for individuals versus equality for classes. The relevant contrast is between equality ex ante and equality ex post. Consider the situation in which one uses a randomizing device, like a coin toss, in order to allocate an indivisible good between two individuals. A proposed distribution that gives each individual a 50 percent probability of getting the indivisible good creates a situation that is equal ex ante, but of course, the distribution that results from the coin toss (i.e. ex post) seems quite unequal, since one person gets the entire good and the other gets nothing. What makes this final distribution acceptable is the fact that the expected value of the lottery ex ante was exactly (or roughly, depending upon the *equalisandum*) the same for both individuals. The Supreme Court's approach in *Manhart*, on the other hand, would have us saying that the distribution is actually equal ex post, except that "winning a coin toss" represents a permissible ground for discrimination.

Numerous critics of *Manhart* have pointed out that the analogy between weight-lifting (or height) and longevity is faulty, because in the case of weight-lifting one can simply do a test to see how much a person can lift, and so there is no reason to rely upon the statistical correlation between sex and weight-lifting ability. In the case of longevity, on the other hand, there is no way of checking to see when a person will die (Kimball, 1979, p. 118). Indeed, if it were possible to do so, there would be no reason for insurance in the first place – each person could simply save exactly as much as he or she required for retirement (Kimball, 1979, p. 133). Yet these critics have failed to artic-ulate the full force of this objection. What the element of uncertainty means, in the case of insurance, is that the principle of equality must be applied ex ante. Since there is no way to guarantee that the *ultimate benefit* of entering into an insurance scheme will be the same for all individuals (if there were, people could just save), we must ensure that the *expected benefit* be the same for all.[7] This is precisely what the actuarially fair premium represents – each individual pays a premium sufficient to cover the *expected loss* that her par-ticipation in the insurance scheme brings. Thus actuarially fair premiums are not motivated by a commitment to equality for classes rather than for in-dividuals, but rather by a commitment to ex ante equality for individuals.

Thus, contrary to the Court's ruling, the point of risk classification and underwriting is not to ensure that each risk class receives an equal benefit, but rather to ensure that each individual receive an equal expected benefit. The strange idea that "longevity" constitutes permissible grounds for discrimination in pension schemes should be rejected (as should the idea that "having an accident" constitutes permissible grounds for discrimination in automobile insurance). Both ideas are a consequence of the mistaken attempt to apply the principle of equality ex post rather than ex ante.

Of course, there are a number of complicated "second best" issues that arise with respect to the use of crude partitioning devices, like sex, to estimate the expected loss that an individual brings to an insurance arrangement. These are not at issue here. What is noteworthy about the reasoning of *Manhart* is that it attacks the basic principle of actuarial fairness, claiming that such premium schemes violate equality even under optimal conditions. The discussion here is intended to show that this argument is based upon a misapplication of the principle of equality. There may still be cogent arguments to be made against the use of sex-segregated actuarial tables for defined-benefit pension schemes. It is, however, a mistake to think that the use of such tables is a case of plain old-fashioned discrimination.

III

The second major argument against risk classification and underwriting is based upon the moral intuition that it is unfair to penalize individuals for circumstances that are outside of their control, or for things that are not their fault (Daniels, 1991; Hellman, 1997; Abraham, 1986, pp. 89–92). According to this view, it is acceptable for insurers to penalize a driver with a history of moving violations by charging him a higher premium – after all, he has the option of improving his driving habits – but it is unacceptable to penalize a young man with higher premiums merely because young men in general have bad driving habits. Similarly, it is thought reasonable to penalize smokers by charging them higher premiums for home insurance, but not people who live in high-crime neighborhoods. And, of course, since people have no control over their sex, race, age, or for the most part, health status, insurers should be prohibited from charging differential premiums on the basis of such characteristics.

Thus Norman Daniels (1991), in an influential article on health insurance, claims that the argument for actuarially fair premiums rests upon a "controversial premise," viz. "that individuals should be free to pursue the economic advantage that derives from any of their individual traits, including their proneness to disease and disability" (p. 504). (The idea that individuals should not be penalized for their circumstances, in an insurance context, is equivalent to the idea that individuals should not be advantaged by their circumstances, since it is the *relative* premium level that determines what counts as a penalty or an advantage.) Thus Daniels (1991) imputes the following argument to proponents of actuarial fairness:

1. Individual differences – any individual differences – constitute some of an individual's personal assets.
2. People should be free, indeed are entitled, to gain advantages from any of their personal assets.
3. Social arrangements will be just only if they respect such liberties and entitlements.
4. Specifically, individuals are entitled to have markets, including medical insurance markets, structured in such a way that they can pursue the advantages to be derived from their personal assets (p. 505).

Daniels goes on to point out that this argument constitutes a direct statement of the basic premises underlying Robert Nozick's (1974) libertarianism, which is a highly controversial political philosophy. Many others, including John Rawls (1971) and Ronald Dworkin (2000), believe that the outcome of the "natural lottery" is an effect of brute luck, not desert, and so individuals have no moral entitlement to benefit from their natural endowment. According to G.A. Cohen's (1989) influential formulation of this thesis "a large part of the fundamental egalitarian aim is to extinguish the influence of brute luck on distribution" (p. 931). Anyone who shares this intuition should be unmoved by the argument for actuarial fairness, Daniels claims. Indeed, this is reflected to some degree in current employment legislation, he argues, where "we believe that justice requires us to sever consideration of race, sex, or handicaps from deliberations about hiring, firing, and reimbursement for services performed, although in practice we fall far short of what justice demands .... Thus we reject, in its most general form, the view that all individual differences can be a moral basis for advantage or disadvantage"(Daniel, 1991, p. 506).

This is, however, a very odd reading of current anti-discrimination law. Daniels is essentially claiming that actuarially fair premiums are unjust because they conflict with luck-egalitarianism, which is the most widely shared liberal conception of justice. The *prima facie* difficulty with this argument is that it appears to hold insurers to a higher standard of ethical conduct than any other business enterprise. Individuals routinely benefit from their natural endowments (intelligence, beauty, creativity, etc.) or from brute luck (plentiful rain, an early frost, a change in interest rates, etc.) in market transactions, and we think nothing of it. The idea that individuals should only be penalized for their choices and not their circumstances may be part of some luck-egalitarian ideal, but it is not part of what Christopher McMahon (1981) has called "implicit morality of the market."

The reasons for this are not hard to find. The task of carrying out the luck-egalitarian project of indemnifying individuals against the effects of bad brute luck will in many cases require pure redistributive transfers – i.e. win-lose transformations. Thus any business arrangement (including an insurance scheme) organized along luck-egalitarian principles could leave individuals worse off than if they had never chosen to participate (or bought insurance) at all. Such an arrangement might not even offer them the *prospect* of being better off. Thus in the absence of altruistic preferences, such an arrangement cannot emerge as a result of private contracting. Private contracting is only feasible when there is at least an ex ante Pareto-improvement. Why would individuals sign up to pay for someone else's misfortune? This is good samaritanism. There may be a moral case to be made for such behavior, but to propose such principles as a basis for the legal regulation of the marketplace is essentially to argue that there should not be a marketplace.

Thus what Daniels has actually produced is not really an argument for restrictions on underwriting by private insurance companies, but rather a general egalitarian argument for social insurance in the health care sector. He observes that "the design of health-care systems throughout most of the world rests on a rejection of the view that individuals should have the opportunity to gain economic advantage from difference in their heath risks" (1991, p. 507). But this is precisely why the health care systems that he refers to are operated in the public sector. The fact that there is a strong case to be made for the state to deliver a particular type of service, in accordance with certain principles of distributive justice, does not mean that there is an equally strong case to be made for the state to compel the private sector to deliver that service under the same terms. Most welfare states also offer defined-benefit pension plans that are financed in accordance with principles that impose non-actuarially fair premiums (often aimed at producing a more progressive distribution of retirement income). But this does not mean that the state would be justified in imposing progressive payment schedules on private pension plans.

Daniels (1991) acknowledges that his argument may simply militate in favor of public insurance (p. 518). However, he also wants to suggest that the basic luck-egalitarian principles, which require "community rating" in private health insurance, are not entirely foreign to the marketplace, and that many other enterprises are subject to similar restrictions. This is why he claims an analogy between restrictions on underwriting and anti-discrimination law in other areas of private contracting, and why he argues that anti-discrimination law is based upon a rejection of "the view that all individual differences can be a moral basis for advantage or disadvantage" (1991, p. 506). But in order to see the problem with this claim, one need look no further than the *Manhart* judgment. The court had no trouble with the idea that height, or weight-lifting ability, or longevity, could count as permissible grounds for discrimination or advantage, even though individuals have very little control over these characteristics. Even sex has been ruled a permissible grounds for discrimination if the employer can show that being of one sex or the other is itself actually necessary for performance of the job. Thus anti-discrimination law does not follow a luck-egalitarian logic. What the law restricts employers from doing is using criteria that are not *relevant* to job performance as a basis for discriminating against individuals. And this is clearly not what insurance companies are doing, when they practice risk classification and underwriting.

Daniels actually sums up the problem with his own view when he writes that the argument for actuarial fairness and the practice of denying coverage to high-risk individuals, "is persuasive only if the important function of health insurance is risk management. Because health insurance has a different social function – protecting equality of opportunity by guaranteeing access to an appropriate array of medical services – then there is a clear mismatch between standard underwriting practices and the social function of health insurance" (1991, p. 514). This may be true, but one could just as easily argue that current pricing practices in the grocery industry are acceptable only so long as one thinks that the function of that industry is to sell food to people – however, since the true social function of the grocery industry is to protect equality of opportunity by guaranteeing adequate nutrition for all citizens, there is a clear mismatch between the practices of the industry and its social function. As one can see, this is not an argument for changing pricing practices in the grocery industry, it is an argument for socializing the grocery industry.

When the argument is formulated with respect to groceries, the problems with it become immediately apparent, in a way that they do not when it is formulated with respect to insurance. This is because of a widespread misunderstanding of how the insurance industry works, which leads many people to think that the industry does have a "social function" that extends beyond mere risk management. In particular, it is widely thought that the goal of insurance is not merely socialize *risk*, but rather to socialize the actual *losses* against which individuals seek indemnity. Even very knowledgeable commentators are prone to confusion on this score. Carol A. Heimer (2003), for example, writes that "at its most basic, insurance is a social arrangement to reduce the effects of losses by employing the resources of the group to cushion individuals. The key task of insurers is to organize the insurance pools, turn them into groups with a common fate, and act as agents of these groups" (p. 288). Deborah Hellman (1997) argues that legal restrictions on underwriting are desirable, on the grounds that they represent "a first step toward treating the misfortunes of poor health and disability as communal responsibilities" (p. 359).

But the goal of private insurance is not to pool *losses*. That would require altruism as an economic incentive on the part of a large number of the participants in the insurance pool. Why would one person want to take on someone else's loss? The fact that socialization of losses generates a group benefit does not mean that it generates a benefit for each individual. The reason people sign up for insurance is because of risk aversion, and because they seek to reduce subjective uncertainty. The reduction in uncertainty is *achieved* through a socialization of losses, but the latter is instrumental to the former, it is not the objective of the arrangement. Thus participants in an insurance scheme will not accept any sort of socialization of losses, only ones that are conducive to the management of certain risks, and on terms under which the welfare benefits stemming from the reduction in subjective uncertainty outweighs the cost of having to indemnify others for their losses.

Of course, there are cases in which there is a powerful argument to be made for socialization of certain losses. An epidemic disease such as AIDS or SARS provides a powerful example. Daniels himself describes the creation of mandatory insurance for high-risk drivers to be a case where "our social interest in guaranteeing a public good ... is allowed to overrule otherwise sound (and actuarially fair) underwriting practices" (1991, p. 510). I believe that health insurance represents a similar case, in which a particular public policy objective trumps the argument for industry practices. It is, however, misguided to transform this into an argument against risk classification in the private insurance industry. Insofar as there is a strong case to be made for socializing losses, rather than just socializing risks, then there is a strong case to be made for the involvement of the public sector.

What then should we say about our intuition that, when people are charged high premiums as a consequence of events or circumstances that are not their fault – such as being abused by their husbands (Hellman, 1997) – that they are being treated unjustly? The first thing to note is that insurance arrangements in general tend to wreak havoc with our intuitions about responsibility and desert. Much of this has to do with a simple tension between our moral reasoning, which is firmly governed by the language of free will, and the perspective that one must adopt when making statistical generalizations. Indeed, François Éwald (1986) has argued that the development of social insurance in the 19th century required a fundamental break with the central concepts of rights and responsibility that determined the structure of 19th century "liberal" capitalism. Central to this development was the discovery that the rate of industrial accidents was highly predictable, regardless of who was responsible. Since sometimes a worker would be at fault, and sometimes the owner, the most socially efficient arrangement was simply to have both groups set aside a certain amount of money to indemnify the victims under a "no fault" arrangement. Yet even if this is better for everyone involved, it does mean that we can no longer expect the operations of the insurance system to track our intuitions about responsibility. (One can see the same thing with no-fault automobile insurance. Under such arrangements, some people will clearly get benefits that, from a strict view of personal responsibility, they are not entitled to. Does that make the arrangement unacceptable?) Similarly, the way that the insurance industry handles fraud offends the moral intuitions of some people, because it is governed more by a concern over loss-ratio security than by the binary opposition of guilt and innocence. As a result, the insurance industry tolerates a lot of behavior that the criminal justice system would regard as felonious (Ericson, Doyle, & Barry, 2003, pp. 340–346).

Second of all, our intuition that it is somehow more legitimate for an insurance company to penalize individuals for the consequences of choices they have made, rather than the circumstances they find themselves in, is perfectly cogent, but it does not count against the principle of actuarial fairness. When dealing with a person who voluntarily runs a risk, or chooses to act in a way that increases the risk of a particular loss, there are strong moral hazard arguments in favor of insurance schemes that penalize or deter such behavior (e.g. increasing premiums). Naturally, in the case of circumstances that are outside the individual's control, there is no moral hazard argument for increasing premiums. But this does not mean that there are no other arguments for charging higher-risk individuals higher-premiums. Most obviously, there is an adverse selection argument (discussed in Section VI), and this argument applies regardless of whether one is dealing with the individual's choices or circumstances.

Thus the luck-egalitarian argument against actuarial fairness fails. It is based upon the plausible intuition that it is permissible, from the standpoint of justice, to penalize individuals when the high risks that they bring to an insurance scheme are the product of their own voluntary choices – since it at least gives them the option, in cases where they find the insurance too expensive, of changing their own behavior. Yet this does not make it impermissible for insurers to charge individuals higher premiums merely *because* they are high risk.

IV

Finally, it is often suggested in the debates over actuarial fairness that the problem with risk classification and underwriting is that it leaves high-risk individuals unable to afford insurance (Daniels, 1991; Ericson et al., 2003). This is often felt to be unjust, because it leaves certain individuals excluded from a beneficial social arrangement that the rest of the population is able to enjoy. Yet though this argument occurs with enormous frequency, it is based on a confusion. Naturally, insurance *costs less* for high-risk individuals when they are pooled with a group of low-risk individuals in a "community rating" scheme. That is because they are using the insurance scheme, not just to secure the benefits of reduced uncertainty, but also to externalize some of the costs associated with their losses onto other members of the insurance pool. The problem with this arrangement is that it can easily make insurance unaffordable for the low risks – since the inclusion of high-risk individuals within the insurance pool can drive premiums to a level where low risks are better off "self-insuring" (e.g. putting their own money into a rainy-day fund, or else just tolerating the uncertainty). It is precisely this exclusion of *low-risk individuals* from the insurance market that constitutes the classic efficiency loss associated with adverse selection (Akerloff, 1970).

One might be inclined to think that segregating the insurance scheme, so that higher-risk individuals pay a higher premium than low-risk individuals, simply creates the opposite problem, excluding high-risk individuals from the market. But the two situations are not parallel. With pooling, the reason that low-risk individuals drop out is that the premium level becomes so high that it is no longer worth their while to buy insurance (because the premium significantly exceeds the "actuarially fair" rate). But with a segregated pool, it will still be worthwhile for high-risk individuals to buy insurance. Their premiums are high in reflection of the fact that the loss exposure they bring to the insurance scheme is high, but it will still be better for them (assuming risk aversion) to buy insurance than to face the loss without indemnity.

Nevertheless, some commentators do speak as though there were an asymmetry in the position of low- and high-risk individuals, such that insurers are less willing to deal with the latter, even when they have the ability to pay. This appears to be based on another misunderstanding of how most insurance markets function. There are in fact two models of insurance (Hacking, 2003, p. 28). The first is the mutual society described in the first section of this paper. Under such an arrangement, a group of individuals with identical preferences and levels of risk aversion can nevertheless benefit by agreeing to pool their losses and gains. The benefits in this case stem from the reduction of uncertainty thanks to the law of large numbers. The second model, which Hacking refers to as the "Lloyd's of London" model, essentially involves a trade between a risk-averse and a risk-tolerant individual. Lloyd's rich "names" bet on outcomes, much as gamblers bet on horses. The names make money by getting lucky, betting that losses do not occur – collecting the premium but not having to pay out a claim. High-risk individuals, in this case, are like racehorses with terrible odds. There needs to be a huge potential payoff in order to persuade anyone to bet on them, and once the odds get bad enough, they cannot attract any bettors.

The Lloyd's model of insurance is particular well-suited for dealing with risks for which there is little or no actuarial knowledge (e.g. uncommon, low-risk, events). Thus high-risk individuals may be unable to secure insurance from companies operating on the Lloyd's model. But this is not the case with the mutual society model, which is the one that predominates in the standard categories of health, life, home, and automobile insurance. This model is structurally neutral with respect to high- and low-risk individuals, since both groups can benefit equally from forming their own insurance pools. Thus there is no reason, in principle, that risk classification should leave high risks any less able to purchase insurance than low risks in the standard run of cases. Generally speaking, if people can afford a loss, then they can afford the insurance to cover that loss. Of course, if they cannot afford the loss, then they may not be able to afford the insurance either. But there is no independent issue of whether they can afford the insurance, and thus no special question of justice that arises with respect to the cost of insurance.

Of course, there is considerable evidence to show that high-risk individuals are less likely to purchase insurance when they are put into a high-risk pool and charged a higher premium (e.g. with automobile insurance, see MacAvoy [1977, p. 38]). The important point is that these people drop out of the insurance market, not because the insurance policy no longer has value to them (as is the case with low-risk individuals who drop out of a community-rated pool), but for some other reason, such as an inability to pay. The way that individuals discount the future is also likely to become a more significant factor as premiums increases, leading many to forego insurance because of a hypertrophied valuation of the present cost of the premium versus the future benefit of the potential indemnification. These, however, are "second-best" problems, which do not speak against the principle of actuarial fairness.

Consider a person who is, by genetic predisposition, almost guaranteed to get a particular form of cancer, and is thus facing the prospect of a significant financial loss for private medical care. Since there is very little uncertainty in this outcome, what this person needs to do is start saving in order to cover the cost of future cancer treatment. Of course, insofar as there is some uncertainty and this individual is able to find other people who are similarly situated, there is no reason that they cannot get together to pool their savings, and thereby achieve the efficiency gains of an insurance arrangement. Setting aside transaction costs, this insurance is guaranteed to cost less than the cancer treatment, simply because the savings realized by the individuals who happen not to require that treatment are distributed out to all members of the insurance pool. Naturally, some people may not be able to afford the treatment, in which case they may not be able to afford the insurance. But that is not the fault of the other participants in the insurance scheme, it is a problem of bad brute luck, or perhaps injustice in the distribution of income. The important point is that the anticipated loss is what the high-risk individual is unable to afford, not the insurance to cover that loss.

Thus what many people are articulating, when they worry that risk classification will leave high-risks unable to purchase insurance, is not an objection to the practice of risk classification, but rather a desire to see the losses to which high-risk individuals are exposed socialized (and an attempt to use private insurance as a way of achieving this objectives). For example, what they object to is not that some people cannot afford health insurance, but that some people cannot afford cancer treatment. Yet rather than arguing that the latter costs should be directly socialized, by having the state pay for cancer treatment for everyone, they seek to socialize it indirectly (and partially), by externalizing a large segment of the cost onto other policy-holders in the high-risk individuals' insurance plan by imposing restrictions on underwriting (MacAvoy, 1977, p. 39). Thus the concern that risk classification will leave some individuals unable to afford insurance is often just a misleading way of arguing that individuals should not have to bear the burden of certain losses.

There is nothing intrinsic to the nature of being high risk that makes a person any less able to participate in an insurance plan than being low risk. Wherever there is uncertainty, people can benefit from risk-pooling arrangements. Problems arise only when there is an information asymmetry that makes the insurer, or other policy-holders, unable to distinguish between low and high risks. Thus it is simply false in many cases to claim that actuarially fair premiums leave high-risks unable to purchase insurance. In fact, insurers are sometimes eager to insure high-risks, because such accounts generate a larger flow of premiums, and therefore potentially larger investment returns. Ironically, it is often restrictions on underwriting that leave high-risk individuals unable to buy insurance. While insurers can be legally prevented from setting higher rates for certain classes of individuals, they are seldom obliged to sell a policy to anyone who comes along (except in special cases, such as automobile insurance or health insurance in certain jurisdictions). Thus they are often better off not selling policies at all to high-risk individuals (Pauly, 1984). Restrictions on underwriting can therefore motivate "cream-skimming" on the part of insurers, which in turn may leave high-risk individuals unable to buy insurance, even if they are willing and able to pay an actuarially fair premium.

V

Surveying these arguments against actuarial fairness, it is sometimes difficult to avoid the impression that critics have failed to appreciate the full consequences that the rejection of this principle would entail. Most of the cases that have attracted controversy involve members of groups who are already stigmatized or subject to unjust discrimination being denied insurance or charged higher premiums by insurance companies. Furthermore, given that disadvantaged individuals tend to be exposed to higher levels of risk (by virtue of living in high-crime neighborhoods, driving less safe vehicles, eating a poorer diet, working in less safe conditions, suffering more ill health, etc.), community rating tends to be progressive with respect to income and social class (Abraham, 1986, p. 76). But if one is to abandon the principle of actuarial fairness, one must do so across the board. And there are many cases in which doing so will not have progressive consequences. With respect to men and women, for instance, while women are the primary beneficiaries of the use of community rating for annuities, men stand to derive an equally large benefit from the use of community rating for life insurance. Similarly, men benefit considerably from the use of community rating in automobile insurance. To select just one example, during a period of intense debate over the use of sex-segregated actuarial tables in the calculation of automobile insurance premiums in Canada, it was calculated that community rating would see the average premium of a single woman between the ages of 21 and 22 rise by over 61.3 percent, while the average premium of a man in the same category would drop by 11.6 percent (Dahlby, 1983, p. 130). The result would be a significant redistribution of wealth from female to male drivers.

While the unfairness of this arrangement seems palpable, one must to be very careful when seeking to articulate the complaint. The natural inclination is to say "Why should women be forced to subsidize the terrible driving habits of young men?" Yet to formulate the argument in this way is to buy into precisely the sort of "fairness to groups" argument that the justices of the United States Supreme Court so effectively dissected in *Manhart*. After all, there is no requirement the women as a group come out the same as men as a group. In order to demonstrate unfairness, it is necessary to show that individual women are treated unfairly by the community rating arrangement. This is the challenge confronting those who would like to show that deviations from actuarial fairness are unjust.

The first thing to note is that, in an idealized "mutual society" insurance arrangement of the sort considered here, premiums are always actuarially fair in the aggregate. This is a simple function of the fact that total claims paid out are equal to total premiums taken in. Now, as we saw in the first section, the most obvious argument for actuarial fairness in premiums is the principle that those who expect to take more out of the pool should be expected to put more in. In cases where each individual's premium is equal to the expected loss that he brings to the pool, each individual derives a pure welfare benefit from participating in the insurance arrangement – the mathematical value of participation is equal to the mathematical value of the gamble that he faces without insurance, it is just that the former has higher subjective utility because it is less risky. In cases where an individual's premium deviates from the actuarially fair level, it means that this person derives not just a welfare benefit from participating in the insurance arrangement, but also a monetary benefit, since the mathematical value of participating in the insurance pool now exceeds the value of the uninsured gamble (Bossert & Fleurbaey, 2002, p. 114). Furthermore, since premiums are actuarially fair in the aggregate, the fact that one policy-holder derives a monetary benefit from participating in the insurance scheme means that some other policy-holder must suffer a monetary loss. As a result, when premiums deviate from the actuarially fair level there will be cross-subsidization within the insurance pool, or an implicit transfer of wealth between policy-holders. Another way of putting it is to say that when an insurance company fails to charge actuarially fair premiums, it allows high-risk policy-holders to externalize some of the costs they face onto other policy-holders. Thus the insurance pool, which is intended to be a source of mutual benefit in the form of welfare gains, is used as way of effecting implicit redistributive transfers between individuals (Kimball, 1979, p. 106).

This sort of cost-externalization is widely regarded as contrary to the basic principles of justice, even by theorists whose work is often appealed to in defense of the principle of community rating. Dworkin (2000), for instance, states that one of the central virtues of his "resource egalitarian" auction is that it forces individuals to take into consideration the full cost that their choices impose upon others (p. 70; see also Gauthier, 1986, p. 225). When a high-risk individual joins an insurance pool governed by a community rated premium, it generates a negative externality for all the other participants. It is like the person who orders an expensive drink or appetizer when dining in a large party at a restaurant, knowing that the bill is going to be divided up evenly between everyone. When the cost of each diner's meal is shared collectively, it allows those with more expensive tastes to externalize the cost of their actions onto others (which in turn erodes the value of the communal eating arrangement). Thus there is an argument to be made for "internalizing" the externality, by giving each diner an individual bill.[8] The same moral intuition, when applied to the case of insurance, suggests that individuals should be charged an actuarially fair premium.

This argument is, in my view, sufficient to establish a general presumption in favor of actuarially fair premiums, from the standpoint of justice. This is, however, just a presumption. It has not been shown that deviations from actuarial fairness are necessarily unjust. This is because the high-risk individual who joins an insurance scheme does not merely generate a negative externality. She also creates a slight positive externality for all other participants in the insurance pool, via the "large numbers" effect, by virtue of having increased the size of the pool. Thus she is not a pure free-rider. Her inclusion in the pool generates a welfare benefit for all the other policy-holders, even if it also imposes a slight monetary loss upon them. Furthermore, there will be a region in which the welfare benefit generated by expansion of the pool outweighs the welfare loss occasioned by the monetary disadvantage imposed upon the other policy-holders. As a result, it can be in the interest of everyone in the pool to accept new members, even when these new members are charged less than the actuarially fair premium. (Just as it can be in the interest of firms to hire more workers, even when doing so depresses average output. It is only when the marginal gains in net output reach zero that the firm should stop hiring.)

There is no question that when premium schemes offer a monetary advantage to some individuals and a disadvantage to others, it results in some people getting a better deal out of their insurance purchase than others. The question is whether this itself is unjust. According to some conceptions of justice, especially strictly egalitarian ones, it may turn out to be so. But there is no question that variations in the level of welfare benefit derived from commercial transactions are tolerated by the "implicit morality of the market." In the absence of price discrimination, for instance, consumers who are further in from the margin derive a larger welfare benefit from their purchases than those who are closer to the margin. A person who would have been willing to pay $20,000 for a flat-screen television may be able to buy it for $5000, because the latter sum represents the most that other more price-sensitive consumers are willing to pay. Even with insurance, highly risk-averse individuals derive more benefit from their policies than less risk-averse individuals, and yet we do not take this to be an affront to justice.

This is not an accidental feature of the market. One of the fundamental features of capitalism is the repudiation of the notion of a "just price" – or of a principled division of the gain from trade – in favor of a competitive determination of price levels. The value of the efficiency gains associated with the establishment of market-clearing prices is taken to outweigh the value of a more egalitarian determination of price levels. The core criterion used to evaluate market transactions is therefore the Pareto-principle, or the requirement that exchanges be mutually beneficial. The desire to achieve market-clearing prices, however, requires a willingness to tolerate transactions in which these mutual benefits are unequally divided. Thus the fact that some people get more out of their insurance purchases than others is not a special injustice, but rather an ordinary feature of commercial transactions in a capitalist economy. The insistence that any deviation from actuarial fairness is unjust, on the other hand, is essentially an insurance-specific version of just price theory.

As a result, the argument for actuarial fairness in premium levels does create a presumption in favor of the justice of such schemes, but it does not show that deviations from actuarial fairness are necessarily unjust. It therefore does not preclude restrictions on underwriting, especially when it can be shown that some *other* important social good is promoted through such restrictions. Governments do this routinely. As long as the insurance scheme remains mutually beneficial for all parties, there is nothing wrong with restrictions on underwriting that for some good reason (i.e. non-capriciously) give some people access to the scheme on preferential terms. The argument for actuarial fairness only precludes restrictions on underwriting that eliminate this benefit for some people (i.e. make it more attractive for low-risks to self-insure). Thus the demand for an unrestricted "freedom to underwrite" is a demand for a degree of freedom for insurers that no other type of business enjoys in a modern market economy.

VI

This brings us finally to the centerpiece of the insurance industry's defense of its underwriting practices: the adverse selection argument. There are both moral and non-moral versions of this argument. According to the non-moral version, it does not really matter whether it is just or unjust to charge actuarially fair premiums, it is necessary for insurers to do so if they wish to remain solvent. This is because community rating gives low-risk individuals an incentive to defect from the insurance scheme. Thus if the insurer charges a premium that represents the average loss in a pool that includes both high- and low-risk individuals, claims will wind up exceeding total premiums collected, simply because low-risk individuals will drop out of the pool (or high-risk individuals will join in great numbers). This is the adverse selection problem (Akerloff, 1970; Rasmusen, 1986, pp. 230–235). In some cases, these low-risk individuals will defect to another insurer offering a lower premium and a pool with fewer high-risk individuals. But in other cases, the low-risks will drop out of the insurance market altogether. (Moral versions of the adverse selection argument then point to this deadweight loss as a case of injustice perpetrated against these low-risk individuals.)

There is, however, an ambiguity in the adverse selection argument, which can be clarified using the game-theoretic distinction between a Nash equilibrium and the core of a game. A particular insurance arrangement is in equilibrium if no individual participant has an incentive to drop out and "go it alone." The *feasible set*, therefore, represents the set of possible cooperative arrangements that offer individuals expected payoffs higher than those that could be obtained through the non-cooperative strategy of self-insurance. Depending upon how risk-averse individuals are, this set can be fairly large. The *core* of a game, on the other hand, represents an arrangement from which no individual *or coalition of individuals* has an incentive to defect (Ordeshook, 1986). The core will tend to be much smaller (indeed, sometimes it will be non-existent), because not only must the arrangement offer benefits that are superior to what the individual could achieve through self-insurance, it must also be superior to what any subset of insured individuals could achieve by defecting and forming their own insurance pool.

Consider the example of three-person cooperative project, in which the gains from cooperation significantly exceed the returns to individual strategic action. There are various ways in which this "cooperative surplus" could be divided up between the players. In principle, any individual should be willing to accept even a tiny fraction of the cooperative surplus, with the lion's share going to the other two players, so long as the tiny fraction received leaves that individual with a better outcome than she could achieve through defection (i.e. dropping out of the cooperative scheme altogether). Thus highly inequitable divisions of the cooperative surplus will still be within the feasible set, as long as every player gets at least something (Gauthier, 1986, p. 178). Such divisions may not be in the core, however, because the player who is most disadvantaged may be in a position to make a "divide and conquer" offer to one of the other players, promising to exclude the third player from the cooperative agreement altogether in return for larger payoffs for them both. Obviously this is only possible if the cooperative project is subject to decreasing returns to scale (Gauthier, 1993, p. 46), but this tends to be the case with insurance. Thus interactions with a risk-pooling structure will tend to have cores, simply because the "large numbers" effect diminishes as the pool grows larger.

An insurance arrangement that deviates significantly from the principle of actuarial fairness in premiums is unlikely to be in the core of the relevant game, simply because the low-risk individuals (assuming they are sufficiently numerous) could all defect and form their own insurance pool. It is sometimes argued, on this basis, that adverse selection problems will begin to show up the moment that premiums take individuals outside the core (Daniels, 1991, p. 513). This is, however, dubious as an empirical contention. The defection of a *coalition* is a form of collective action and is thus much more difficult to organize than the defection of an individual. It would be difficult to find any workplace, for instance, in which the division of labor and reward was genuinely in the core of the underlying interaction. The most talented group of employees could almost always benefit by defecting from the firm and setting up their own shop. This does happen, but just as often it does not. Thus it is not adequate, when considering insurance schemes, to suggest that the *mere* fact that a premium scheme takes policy-holders outside of the core will necessarily generate an adverse selection problem. There are too many other complicating factors. The only thing that can be said with confidence is that a premium scheme that takes some policy-holders outside of the *feasible set* (i.e. makes self-insurance a more attractive strategy) is likely to generate an adverse selection problem, because defection in this case does not involve collective action, individuals simply cancel their policies.

Thus the adverse selection argument does not provide a powerful justification for the principle of actuarial fairness. If premiums had to be in the core, then there would be a strong case to be made on adverse selection grounds for actuarial fairness. But if premiums only need to be within the feasible set, then the adverse selection argument only shows that they must not depart too radically from that principle. There is, however, likely to be considerable zone of tolerance for deviations. In this context, it is worth recalling that many flat-rate "friendly societies" – which essentially eschewed any actuarial basis for the calculation of premium levels – survived well into the 20th century (Emery, 1996). Furthermore, it was seldom bottom-up pressure from policy-holders that led to greater risk-classification and differentiated premiums, but rather the aggressive lobbying efforts of actuaries, which date back to the beginning of the 19th century (see Ansell, 1835; Baker, 2003). Although there are certain important exceptions, risk classification has seldom been a defensive response to bottom up adverse selection problems, and has more often been used as a competitive tactic by insurers against one another. In other words, rather than policy-holders using private information to purchase insurance at prices below the actuarially fair level, thereby creating losses for insurers, historically it has been more common to see insurers instituting risk classification schemes as a way of creating low-premium pools, which could then be used to entice clients away from rival insurers (Baker, 2003). It is worth recalling that in order for adverse selection to cause a serious problem, absent these competitive tactics, policy-holders must be at least roughly aware of the expected loss that they bring to an insurance pool. Yet individuals are seldom in such a position, simply because they have neither the interest nor the ability to analyze the relevant data. With automobile insurance, for instance, an insurer typically knows a lot more about the accident risk posed by a particular driver than the driver ever will. Thus in practice adverse selection has often turned out not to be the powerful force that economic theory predicts it to be.

As a result, a premium scheme that *merely* takes a group of policy-holders outside the core is unlikely to provoke defection. Under real-world conditions, not only are there significant transaction costs and collective action problems associated with such a defection, but individuals themselves usually lack to information needed to determine whether defection would be advantageous (i.e. whether they are in the core or not). Thus the real danger is not "classical" adverse selection, but rather the prospect that rival insurers, sensing an opportunity, will try to identify and recruit low-risk individuals from the community-rated pool, in part by informing them that they are implicitly subsidizing other participants in their existing insurance pool. In other words, the major problems with community-rated premiums are the various forms of cream-skimming that they encourage.

But because the most important problems arise out of the competitive behavior of insurers, and not strategic behavior on the part of policy-holders, the argument fails to provide a very powerful defense of the idea that risk classification is somehow "necessary" to ensure the financial solvency of insurers. Naturally, if one company is engaging in aggressive risk classification and underwriting, then rival firms may be forced to respond in kind in order to remain solvent. But so long as legal restrictions on underwriting apply equally to all firms in an industry, then this is not a concern. For example, in jurisdictions where sex-segregated automobile insurance policies are not permitted, it is possible in principle for a group of female drivers to defect from existing insurance schemes and form their own pool, with much lower premiums. But since the restrictions on underwriting make it impossible to exclude men from this new pool, or to charge them higher premiums, any such move would be quickly undermined by the number of male drivers who would be attracted to the lower premiums as well.

Thus the argument from adverse selection fails to show that an unrestricted freedom to underwrite is a business necessity. There are simply too many ways in which legal restrictions on underwriting can counteract the tendency, and ensure that insurers who refrain from engaging in a particular type of risk classification are not put at a competitive disadvantage by virtue of that fact. Of course, serious problems can arise from the incentives that are inadvertently created for insurers to find ways around the law. The biggest concern, mentioned above, is that insurers will simply drop entire classes of clients or red-line residential districts in order to avoid attracting high-risk clients (whom they do not have a right to charge extra). There is also the possibility that insurers will avoid certain clients, or charge them extra, in circuitous and indirect ways that are difficult to regulate. For example, although it is generally regarded as discriminatory to refuse individuals insurance coverage on the basis of their sexual orientation, it was suggested at one point that health insurers were refusing to provide coverage to male hairdressers (Aaron & Bosworth, 1994, p. 269). Needless to say, this sort of behavior not only reproduces the injustice that the original legislation was intended to prohibit, but compounds it in various ways.

Thus restrictions on underwriting must be carefully weighed, and not undertaken lightly, as they do have a strong tendency to generate perverse effects. The argument from adverse selection is important in that it draws attention to the strategic context in which insurance decisions are made. One cannot simply legislate changes in premium levels or underwriting practice without taking into consideration the changes that this will cause in the purchasing decisions made by policy-holders, along with the competitive tactics used by insurers. On the other hand, it is far too simplistic to say that any deviation from actuarial fairness is *bound* to generate such perverse consequences. There is far too much friction in the real-world marketplace for that to be the case. Thus the argument from adverse selection adds very little to the basic argument from justice when it comes to supporting the practice of risk classification. Restrictions on underwriting certainly have redistributive effects, but so long as the outcome remains within the feasible set of policy-holders, these redistributions fall within the range that market institutions normally permit. Furthermore, such restrictions need not create significant adverse selection problems, unless they are so extreme as to drive low-risk individuals from the market entirely.

VII

The argument so far has been focused entirely upon the *principle* of actuarial fairness in premiums. The conclusion has been that actuarial fairness represents a just ideal, but that restrictions on underwriting which move the premium scheme away from actuarial fairness are permissible when doing so is needed in order to achieve some important social good, and when doing so will not create significant Pareto-inefficiencies as a result of low-risk individuals dropping out of the insurance market. Thus I defend a somewhat more limited "right to underwrite" than those who insist upon actuarial fairness, or require that premiums be kept within the core. Neither of these is necessary in order to ensure that the insurance scheme remain advantageous for all parties involved. Furthermore, mutual advantage is all that is required in order for the transaction to be satisfy "the implicit morality of the market." Thus while it remains permissible for firms to charge actuarially fair premiums, it is not necessary, and there is nothing in principle wrong with statutory restrictions on underwriting that take certain policy-holders outside the core. It is wrong, however, for restrictions on underwriting to take any policy-holder outside his or her feasible set.

NOTES

1. In their paper "Equitable Insurance Premium Schemes," Bossert and Fleurbaey (2002) write: "The basic assumption underlying our analysis is that the most equitable insurance premium scheme is one where the premium paid by each agent is equal to the expected value of the payout of the insurer to this agent" (p. 114). This assumption is not defended, it is taken as the point of departure.

2. For a more formal calculation of the "pure premium," see Outreville (1998, p. 156).

3. The term comes from the celebrated paper by Lipsey and Lancaster (1956), which showed that if it was impossible to satisfy one of the conditions needed for a competitive market economy to achieve Pareto efficiency, then strict adherence to the remaining conditions would almost certainly make the outcome less, rather than more, efficient.

4. For a sober discussion of the basic "second best" problems that arise, and some principles to guide insurers, see Abraham (1986, pp. 64–100).

5. It is worth noting that Title VII discrimination is not the only form of discrimination that underwriting practices might run afoul of. The more obvious suggestion might be that the practice of charging different policyholders different premiums was a form of price discrimination. This is prohibited in the United States by the Robinson–Patman Price Discrimination Act of 1936, which makes it unlawful "to discriminate in price between different purchasers of commodities of like grade and quality." This is not a powerful argument, however, because it is not difficult to make the case that insurers are selling a different product to clients in different risk-classes – since the actuarial value of each policy is different, depending upon the risk profile of the individual and the magnitude of the loss. Furthermore, it should be noted that there is considerable tolerance for price discrimination in the market. The Robinson–Patman Act only targets forms of price-discrimination that have anti-competitive consequences. Practices such as price-skimming – when new goods are introduced at inflated prices, and then dropped over time – are considered quite normal, even though they amount to forms of price discrimination. They are usually regarded as morally unproblematic, simply because those who wind up paying the higher prices are generally those who derive the largest welfare benefit from the purchase. This is also clearly true in case of insurance, since high-risk individuals get more value out of the policies that they purchase.

6. It is far more persuasive than the arguments of Austin (1983), who merely points to the fact that risk classification will have disparate impact as a way of showing that the practice involves unjust discrimination.

7. Kimball (1979) overstates the case somewhat, arguing that what employees receive in return for their contributions is simply risk-protection, i.e. the welfare benefits associated with the insurance scheme, and so it does not matter what benefits, if any, they ultimately receive. This involves a rather excessive disregard for the benefits. Insurance allows individuals to exchange one gamble for another, less risky one. It is, however, the (at least rough) mathematical equivalence of the two gambles that makes the individual willing to enter into the exchange. Thus the person who acquires an annuity is not just purchasing risk-protection, he is also purchasing an income stream that must be approximately equal to that achievable through savings (i.e. self-insurance).

8. This analogy is due to Promislow (1987, p. 217). He uses it to dramatize some of the "second-best" problems that may arise with risk-classification under conditions of imperfect information. Consider a situation in which a waiter, while refusing to give individual bills, offers to split the bill into two: one for diners on the north side of the table, another for diners on the south. Assuming that diners should pay their own way, under what conditions would this and would this not be a more just arrangement?

REFERENCES

Aaron, H. J., & Bosworth, B. P. (1994). *Economic issues in reform of health care financing.* Brookings Papers on Economic Activity. Washington, DC: Brookings Insititute.

Abraham, K. S. (1986). *Distributing risk.* New Haven: Yale University Press.

Akerlof, G. (1970). The market for "Lemons": Quality uncertainty and the market mechanism. *Quarterly Journal of Economics, 84,* 488–500.

Ansell, C. (1835). *A treatise on friendly societies.* London: Baldwin and Cradock.

Austin, R. (1983). The insurance classification controversy. *University of Pennsylvania Law Review, 131,* 517–583.

Baker, T. (2003). Adverse selection and risk classification. In: R. V. Ericson & A. Doyle (Eds), *Risk and morality.* Toronto: University of Toronto Press.

Barr, N. (1998). *The economics of the welfare state* (3rd ed.). Oxford: Oxford Univesity Press.

Bossert, W., & Fleurbaey, M. (2002). Equitable insurance premium schemes. *Social Choice and Welfare, 19,* 113–125.

Brilmayer, L., Hekeler, R., Laycock, D., & Sullivan, T. (1980). Sex discrimination in employer-sponsored insurance plans: A legal and demographic analysis. *University of Chicago Law Review, 47,* 505–560.

Cohen, G. A. (1989). On the currency of egalitarian justice. *Ethics, 99,* 906–944.

Dahlby, B. G. (1983). Adverse selection and statistical discrimination: An analysis of Canadian automobile insurance. *Journal of Public Economics, 20,* 121–130.

Daniels, N. (1991). Insurability and the HIV epidemic: Ethical issues in underwriting. *The Milbank Quarterly, 68,* 497–525.

Dworkin, R. (2000). *Sovereign virtue.* Cambridge, MA: Harvard University Press.

Easterbrook, F. H., & Fischel, D. R. (1991). *The economic structure of corporate law.* Cambridge, MA: Harvard University Press.

Emery, J. C. H. (1996). Risky business? Non-actuarial pricing practices and the financial viability of fraternal sickness insurers. *Explorations in Economic History, 33,* 195–226.

Ericson, R. V., Doyle, A., & Barry, D. (2003). *Insurance as governance.* Toronto: University of Toronto Press.

Éwald, F. (1986). *L'État providence.* Paris: Grasset.

Gauthier, D. (1986). *Morals by agreement.* Oxford: Clarendon.

Gauthier, D. (1993). Fairness and cores: A comment on laden. *Philosophy and Public Affairs, 22,* 44–47.

Hacking, I. (1975). *The emergence of probability.* Cambridge: Cambridge University Press.

Hacking, I. (2002). *An introduction to probability and inductive logic.* Cambridge: Cambridge University Press.

Hacking, I. (2003). Risk and dirt. In: R.V. Ericson & A. Doyle (Eds), *Risk and morality.* Toronto: University of Toronto Press.

Hansmann, H. (1992). *The ownership of enterprise.* Cambridge, MA: Harvard University Press.

Heimer, C. A. (2003). Insurers as moral actors. In: R. V. Ericson & A. Doyle (Eds), *Risk and morality.* Toronto: University of Toronto Press.

Hellman, D. S. (1997). Is actuarially fair insurance pricing actually fair? A case study in insuring battered women. *Harvard Civil Rights-Civil Liberties Law Review, 32,* 355–411.

Kimball, S. L. (1979). Reverse sex discrimination: *Manhart. American Bar Foundation Research Journal, 4,* 83–139.

Lipsey, R. G., & Lancaster, K. (1956). The general theory of the second best. *Review of Economic Studies, 24,* 11–32.

MacAvoy, P. W. (1977). *Federal-state regulation of the pricing and marketing of insurance.* Washington, DC: American Enterprise Institute for Public Policy Research.

McMahon, C. (1981). Morality and the invisible hand. *Philosophy and Public Affairs, 10,* 247–277.

Moss, D. A. (2002). *When all else fails.* Cambridge, MA: Harvard University Press.

Neave, D. (1991). *Mutual aid in the Victorian countryside.* Hull: Hull University Press.

Nozick, R. (1974). *Anarchy, state and utopia.* New York: Basic Books.

Ordeshook, P. C. (1986). *Game theory and political theory.* Cambridge: Cambridge University Press.

Outreville, J. F. (1998). *Theory and practice of insurance.* Dordrecht: Kluwer.

Pauly, M. V. (1984). Is cream-skimming a problem for the competitive medical market? *Journal of Health Economics, 3,* 87–95.

Promislow, S. D. (1987). Measurement of equity. *Proceedings of the Society of Actuaries, 30,* 215–237.

Rasmusen, E. (1986). *Games and information* (2nd ed.). Cambridge, MA: Blackwell.

Rawls, J. (1971). *A theory of justice.* Cambridge, MA: Harvard University Press.

HEALTH INSURANCE: ECONOMIC AND ETHICAL ISSUES

Alfonso R. Oddo

ABSTRACT

Health care spending in the U.S. continues to outpace inflation and wage growth, which is likely to keep the burden of rising health care costs in the spotlight. As health care costs increase, health insurers face the challenges of providing quality health care at a reasonable cost. Some health care providers and insurers use economic measures such as return on investment to assess the effectiveness of health care. How does one measure the value of health? What are some of the advantages and disadvantages of using economic measures to evaluate health care?

This paper looks health care costs and who pays for them. What portion of health care costs is borne by employers? What portion by employees? Who does or should pay for health care of people who are uninsured? What is the role of insurance? If people do not have health care insurance, does it matter whether the reason they are uninsured is because they cannot afford it or because they choose not to be insured?

Selvam (2002) belives that the number one ethical dilemma in the U.S. is how to address the almost 40 million Americans who lack health care coverage. With rising hospital costs, even the hardest-working and most prudent persons are at risk. Many workers do not have health insurance and even if they are covered, they may not get what they need. What are some of the ethical issues facing patients, health care providers and

Insurance Ethics for a More Ethical World
Research in Ethical Issues in Organizations, Volume 7, 161–168
ISSN: 1529-2096/doi:10.1016/S1529-2096(06)07008-8

insurers? What role should government have in assuring that all people receive quality health care?

MEDICAID

A survey conducted by the Health Foundation of Greater Cincinnati asked participants about who should receive Medicaid coverage; what they would eliminate from the budget in order to pay for Medicaid; and what they themselves would pay to keep Medicaid coverage for eligible Ohioans who otherwise would not have health insurance. Of the people surveyed, 86% had some type of health insurance and 14% were uninsured. More than 15% of the people with insurance were covered by Ohio Medicaid. When asked what they would most like to see Ohio lawmakers choose to pay for Medicaid, 61% of Ohioans surveyed said increase cigarette or alcohol taxes (Health Foundation, 2005).

THE UNINSURED

About 80% of uninsured Americans say they are in good, very good or excellent health. The percentage of uninsured Americans who are happy with their health ranges from 72% in Texas to 90% in Hawaii, according to a statistical portrait of the uninsured compiled by researchers at the State Health Access Data Assistance Center at the University of Minnesota.

America's Health Insurance Plans, Washington, the leading insurance industry trade group, and the National Association of Health Underwriters, Arlington, VA, have been emphasizing the diversity of uninsured Americans and the need for solutions to meet the needs of specific types of uninsured individuals. "The myth is that the uninsured are all poor and in poor health," according to the University of Minnesota health access data center. "But many are working and healthy, and there are a large number who are potentially insurable," even in states that allow medical underwriting in the individual market (Bell, 2005).

The report does not look at the income or net worth of uninsured Americans, but the report does include statistics dealing with uninsured workers. The percentage of working adults who are uninsured is under 10% only in Delaware, Minnesota and the District of Columbia, according to the report. In 7 states, more than 20% of working adults are uninsured. In Texas, the state with highest percentage of uninsured working adults, about 27% of workers say they are uninsured. Even in states where many uninsured residents have health problems, most uninsured individuals believe they are insurable.

HOSPITALS

Class action suits accuse hospitals of profiting from the uninsured. At risk are the limited resources hospitals have to fulfill their mission of providing care for the uninsured and all patients in the community. Nearly 40 lawsuits are underway, targeting not-for-profit hospitals in 21 states. The hospitals are accused of violating their tax-exempt status by seeking collection for unpaid debts and charging uninsured patients higher rates than insured patients. The plaintiffs argue that they are the third-party beneficiaries of hospitals' tax exemption and have a constitutional right to the charity that hospitals are obligated to provide. They seek seizure of hospital endowments so they can guarantee free medical care.

Hospitals have no motive to swindle the American public. In fact, they have a moral, legal, and ethical obligation to care for people regardless of their ability to pay. Hospitals did not create the problem of uninsured Americans. This is a societal issue that should not be settled in the courts. In this instance, litigation is being pursued by those who have not taken a societal view.

There is no constitutional right to free medical care in our country. Until our nation decides to provide universal health care, hospital emergency rooms will continue to be the option of first and last resort for our indigent and uninsured. Last year, not-for-profit hospitals across the country provided $23 billion in free care. Every Massachusetts hospital contributes to the state's $500 million "free care" pool, and when an injured or sick patient arrives at an emergency room, in need of care but unable to pay, the hospital covers the costs by drawing from the pool.

Yet the uninsured population far exceeds the amount refunded by the state, leaving hospitals with millions of dollars in losses. It is projected that there will be $722 million of free care provided by Massachusetts hospitals this year and that number will spike to $783 million in 2005. To cover it, hospitals turn to surpluses, if any, in their endowments. These endowments are, in most cases, the only cushion hospitals have (Bender, 2004).

To defend themselves, hospitals will have to tap their endowments to the detriment of all involved, including the very people who these lawsuits are allegedly designed to help. Aside from fundamental legal flaws, the litigation of not-for-profits is embarrassing in its absurdity. Our nation's health care delivery system is in dire financial straits and hospitals are straining under ever-rising costs. The best performing hospitals are operating on the thinnest of margins, and the rest have negative cash flow.

Tens of thousands of uninsured people in Massachusetts and across the country are victims of our inability to find meaningful solutions to our national health care crisis. It is a crisis that deserves thoughtful, collaborative solutions. Absent that, hospitals bear the brunt of the problem. As a society, we should be doing everything possible to help not-for-profit institutions fulfill their mission.

ECONOMICS

One of the factors driving up health care costs for business is the problem of uncompensated care. The cost of caring for those who are unable or sometimes simply unwilling to pay for their health care is frequently shifted to those patients who do pay. And because those paying patients are usually covered by employer-based health insurance, it is frequently the employers who absorb the cost.

Some say that someone who can afford it, such as employers and health insurance companies, must pay for the care because it would be unthinkable to let an individual be denied health care simply because they do not have the money. It may be time to reevaluate our medical ethics in light of the changing face of medical economics and embrace an idea of patient autonomy that includes patient responsibility, even if that means that the patient suffers adverse consequences from voluntarily deciding to underinsure.

Morreim (1992) believes that "The changing economics of medicine have fundamentally, permanently altered the relationship between physician and patient." Traditionally, that relationship has been dyadic, but no longer. In the vastly more complex present and future, the physician's obligations to the patient can no longer be a single-minded, unequivocal commitment, but rather must now reflect a balancing. Patients' interests must be weighted against the legitimate competing claims of other patients, of payers, of society as a whole and sometimes even of the physician himself.

Although the notion is not new that physicians should exercise a broader perspective when determining how to allocate scarce medical resources, Morreim's recommendation for achieving that goal will go against the grain of many ethicists, health care providers and politicians. Morreim approaches her subject from the viewpoint of economics, incorporating how people actually behave economically, rather than how we would like them to behave or how they ought to behave.

In an effort to contain costs, some insurance companies and health care providers have created systems where physicians benefit financially from cost-conscious care. Doctors do not owe it to their patients to commandeer others' money and property just because a given patient has need of it. They are not obligated to hoard, poach, cheat, lie or game the system in order to obtain resources to which the patient is neither legally nor ethically entitled. And they are not ethically authorized to undertake those tactics even where they believe a patient is being denied a resource to which he is morally entitled.

Morreim wants to make the patient an economic player in health care decisions, and let the patient bear the impact of those economic decisions. The trend in medical ethics is away from paternalism and toward autonomy. Yet this has not been the trend in medical economics. If we believe in patient autonomy, we must also believe in patient responsibility, because autonomy without responsibility is not autonomy.

"If someone who has chosen a minimal health plan (e.g., to save money for skiing trips) subsequently needs the costly care that he rejected earlier, we may feel compassion for him. We may even wish charitably to help him, but we have not wronged him if we refuse, because his choice was made knowingly and rationally." And if a patient finds himself uninsured or underinsured based on a previous rational decision, "he either must pay for the care himself or go without."

"The reality may seem harsh, yet it is the only way in which to make, and adhere to, an economically and medically rational health care system." It is also the only way to honor fully the patient's previous autonomous decision regarding how much health care to purchase. Autonomous people must be responsible people, even if they make the wrong decision. Autonomy does not guarantee that an individual will make the right decision, only that the individual will be the one making the decision.

RETURN ON INVESTMENT

Employers that are most aggressive about holding down rising health care costs are applying an unprecedented level of business discipline to the task. Aggressive employers are applying business decision-making practices because health care costs are skyrocketing while corporate earnings are plummeting (Ceniceros, 2002). Those two developments have made employee health care a companywide business concern rather than merely a benefits department function.

So, in a shift from the past, more benefits and human resources managers who are aggressive about reducing their costs are now calculating their return on investment when making health care purchasing decisions. The practice involves determining how much a given program or measure will cost and comparing that amount to the savings it is likely to produce over time. Along with developing an increased sense of urgency, aggressive benefits managers also are undertaking a combination of actions, because no single measure is adequate to address rising costs.

Some, for example, are purchasing disease management programs from vendors other than their health plans, and others are looking at "clinical risk adjustment" when purchasing health care products such as disease or patient management programs. Clinical risk adjustment looks at the clinical quality and outcomes resulting from specific programs.

Consumerism engages employees in cost cutting by giving them greater responsibility for determining how their coverage plans are designed and how their health care dollars are spent. An integral aspect of consumerism is providing employees with the data they need to make informed purchasing decisions. The term "self-service" is often used to describe health plans with a consumerism aspect.

Employers like consumerism because it increases employee sensitivity to the price of health care. The models also allow employers to become less involved in coverage decisions while giving employees greater control over their care. Consumerism may have some pitfalls. For example, employers fear that employees may forgo necessary treatment to save money.

Additionally, while consumerism rests on increasing employee participation in health care purchasing, but many employees have limited time or interest in getting involved in their health care. Even though employers are uncertain about the appropriate level of employee involvement, they continue to implement consumerist measures because they consider it a good idea to get employees involved in purchasing their own health care.

CONVERGENCE

The United States has been the only country in the industrialized world relying primarily on optional employer-based health insurance. Access to care is not a legal right in the United States as it is in Europe, Canada and most other industrialized nations. However, a safety welfare net system exists for the poor and elderly.

In the rest of the world, access to health care is a right for all citizens paid for either by social insurance funds with member and employer contributions or from tax funding. Most of these systems allow for private medical insurance either by opting out of state-sponsored schemes or as additional health insurance schemes that provide additional benefits or reimbursement.

However, in the coming decade, these two different health-financing systems will start converging, according to a report by Pricewaterhouse-Coopers. The United States will look a bit more like Europe and Canada. In turn, Europe and Canada's systems will embrace more aspects of the United States system (PricewaterhouseCoopers, 1999).

In the United States, more costs and decisions about health will shift toward government purchasers and consumers. Rising costs, changes in the workplace and the age of workers themselves are contributing to this shift. Baby boomers start turning 65 in 2010, moving more Americans into a government-funded system. The shift toward government as the primary payer is already under way. In 1997, government programs in the United States accounted for 46.4% of health spending, up from 40.5% in 1990. In addition, the United States government has been taking a stronger role in the regulation of private health care, with recent examples being the mandated 48-hour maternity stay, mental health coverage requirements and the much-debated Patient Bill of Rights. This is a sea change from regulation of private insurance, which previously rested with state governments.

During the past five years, most employers have moved their retirement programs from defined benefit to defined contribution. Through these programs, employees take responsibility for their investments. I think an awful lot of people think the defined contribution program is the way to go, says Edward Miller, M.D., CEO of Johns Hopkins. Moving to defined contribution in pension plans has been very successful.

Moving to a defined contribution program may allow employers to better control their cost obligations of providing health care benefits. Health benefits are becoming more of a dissatisfaction of employees, says one employer who spoke of the hassles of negotiating coverage denials with insurers on behalf of workers.

There is a better than 50% chance that we will see a defined contribution system in Medicare by the year 2010, says Dr. William Roper, who formerly headed the agency that administered Medicare in the United States. Margaret O. Kane, president of the National Committee on Quality Assurance in the United States, agrees: Medicare will definitely be vouchered by

2010. The rest of the system could go either way. But, the role of employers as the base of private health coverage will erode significantly.

CONCLUSIONS AND IMPLICATIONS

With health care costs increasing, many Americans are bearing more of the financial responsibility for health care as more employers are reducing the portion of the cost that they cover. And for those people who cannot or choose not to pay more for health care, their health care coverage is reduced or eliminated. However, if the U.S. government assumes a larger role in providing health care, we may see improved health care coverage similar to the systems in Europe and Canada.

REFERENCES

Bell, A. (2005). Majority of uninsured may be insurable. *National Underwriter Life & Health*, *109*(17), 8.
Bender, E. L. (2004). *Blaming hospitals*. Boston, MA: Boston Globe, Sept. 6, p. A15.
Ceniceros, R. (2002). Aggressive managers eye health care ROI. *Business Insurance*, *36*(25), 14.
Health Foundation of Greater Cincinnati. (2005). Survey finds Ohio residents in favor of tax increases to support medicaid. *Hospital Business Week*, June 5, p. 12.
Morreim, E. H. (1992). *Balancing act: The new medical ethics of medicine's new economics*. Norwell, MA: Kluwer Academic Publishers.
PricewaterhouseCoopers. (1999). *Health cast 2010: Smaller world, bigger expectations*. New York, NY: PricewaterhouseCoopers.
Selvam, A. (2002). What will be the field's top ethical issue in five years? *Hospitals & Health Networks*, *76*(3), 32–33.

A MEDICAL DILEMMA: HOW SHOULD PHYSICIANS RESPOND TO PATIENTS' QUESTIONS ABOUT PAY?

Chalmer E. Labig and Kenneth Zantow

ABSTRACT

Managed care organizations use physician incentives to control costs and ensure their financial viability. While the efficacy of incentives may be questioned, substantial challenges exist for physicians who must balance the well-being of their patients and the focus of their professional training with organizational financial concerns. Many physicians experience difficulty in discussing incentive pay with patients (Pearson & Hyams, 2002), even though patients want to know (Pereira & Pearson, 2001) and tend to trust physicians more who are forthright about the issue (Levinson, Kao, Kuby, & Thisted, 2005). Of interest here are patients' perceptions of the ethicalness of commonly used physician pay incentives. The results of our findings suggest that patients may view these incentives from a different perspective than health policy experts and physician executives. Specifically, our findings indicate that patients perceive incentives based upon patient satisfaction and clinical efficiency more ethically than incentives based upon revenue generation. These views are significantly related to

Insurance Ethics for a More Ethical World
Research in Ethical Issues in Organizations, Volume 7, 169–185
Copyright © 2007 by Elsevier Ltd.
ISSN: 1529-2096/doi:10.1016/S1529-2096(06)07009-X

*physician visits. We offer suggestions for future research in light of recent
pay disclosure regulations.*

Changes in the health care industry during the past 20 years have created
new types of physician organizations, such as group practices that are
owned by hospitals, for-profit companies, or one or more of the physicians
who are affiliated with the practice. These organizations employ physicians
in a more traditional employer–employee relationship. In the past, physicians worked primarily for themselves in what we think of as private practice. While efforts to control costs and ensure the financial viability of these
organizations lay primarily with the physicians, their professional training
focuses on patient's health as their primary concern, creating potential
conflicts of interest (Stell, 2004; Callahan, 2004). Incentives within physician
pay systems in these organizations are being used to reinforce behaviors that
maximize specific desired outcomes, including financial as well as health
outcomes.

Pay systems have a complex impact on employees and organizations. The
ability of incentives to produce performance has certainly been questioned
(Beer & Katz, 2003; Kohn, 1993). Incentives, which may produce the desired
behaviors in physicians, have proven problematic in other industries (see for
example, Seller Beware, 2004). Recent research suggests that among executives, incentives are not related to performance and can have many negative effects such as the elimination of desirable behaviors that are not
rewarded (Beer & Katz, 2003; Kerr, 1975). Some evidence indicates that
incentives tend to replace intrinsic motivation with extrinsic motivators
(e.g., Frey, 1994). Yet financial incentives can be effective at producing
desired behaviors when properly designed and implemented (Gupta &
Shaw, 1998).

In addition to the effects of incentive pay on physician behavior, early
evidence suggests that incentive pay may also affect the physician–patient
relationship. Unfortunately, very little research has examined the impact of
physician incentive pay on patients. Research in this nascent area suggests
that: (1) physicians tend to "talk around" patient questions about how they
are paid rather than the answer forthrightly (Pearson & Hyams, 2002); (2)
patients distrust physicians who deny that money influences their decision-
making; and (3), physicians who solicit the feelings and perspectives of their
patients are more trusted by them (Levinson, Kao, Kuby, & Thisted, 2005).
Although the majority of patients are generally unaware of how their physicians are paid, there is evidence that patients are interested in knowing and

are more uncomfortable with capitation arrangements than with fee-for-service or salary with withholds (Pereira & Pearson, 2001). Regulation requiring disclosure of payment terms may also adversely affect the patient–physician relations depending on how the patient evaluates various pay schemes.

Patient perceptions of physician behavior, in the context of patient satisfaction surveys, have become an important part of the health care landscape (Reiboldt, 1999). The value of these perceptual satisfaction measures are the subject of criticism (Haas, 1999), but are also highly regarded by some health care organizations (Weber, 2004). The patients' perspective is therefore important to health care regulators, managers, and physicians. Feelings of distrust of the physician based upon the types of incentives used, an ethicality bias, could jeopardize both the impact of regulations requiring disclosure, the value of the satisfaction measures, and potentially, the relationship of the physician and patient. At the most basic level, perception of incentives as unethical can have repercussions for any business, including placing them at a competitive disadvantage in the marketplace.

The present study examines patients' perceptions of the ethicalness of various commonly used pay incentives and bases of pay for physicians within an ambulatory treatment context. This is an exploratory study with two primary objectives: examine the relative ethicalness of physician incentives as determined by patients, and determine whether these views relate to the patient use of physician services. We expect to find that patients perceive pay incentives and other practices that reinforce quality of care or patient satisfaction as more ethical than pay incentives or other practices that reinforce control of costs or enhancement of revenue. The remainder of the paper is organized as follows. First, we outline the most common bases of physician pay, the use of incentives, and how these are limited by regulations. Next, we examine the perceived ethicality of these incentives from a patients' perspective and derive hypotheses examining the relationship of different incentive types to patient use. We then describe the results of our hypotheses tested on a sample of health care consumers.

BASES FOR PHYSICIAN INCENTIVES

Physician incentives vary according to the type of organization with which the physicians are associated. The two extremes of managed care organizations (MCOs) are health maintenance organizations (HMOs) and preferred provider organizations (PPOs). The nature of each of these types of organizations results in different pay variables and incentives. The following section describes these organizations and the nature of the incentives.

Health Maintenance Organizations

An HMO, contracting with employers to provide health care to their employees, charges employers a specific amount per employee per month to cover the cost of their employees' health care expenses. In turn, HMOs usually pay what is referred to as capitation rates to their primary-care physicians (PCPs). Physicians then receive a fixed amount per month for each employee who selects them as their PCP. Each member of the HMO (employees of contracting employers) must choose one of the HMO's PCPs.

The PCPs receive the same payments regardless of how many times the covered employees visit their offices. The PCP also determines which, if any, specialty-care physicians (SCPs) the employees (their HMO patients) need to see. The compensation structure in this system involves two common methods that provide a certain amount of financial risk for a PCP: withholds and capitated pools for non-primary care services.

A withhold is simply a percentage of the primary-care capitation that is held back every month and used to pay for cost overruns in the HMO's referral or institutional services. Whatever money is leftover at year's end is distributed to those PCPs whose costs and related charges are under the amount collected from employers for their employee's health coverage. Capitated pools for referrals to SCPs and institutional services (like hospitals) are also created, and monies remaining in them at the year's end are available for distribution to PCPs whose patients' costs are less than their related capitated rates. Consequently, HMOs, and PCPs employed by or under contract with them, have an incentive to provide as little care as necessary and thus run the risk of under-utilization to achieve financial success (Reiboldt, 1999). One of the most common problems for PCPs with capitation is the chance that their patients will be sicker than usual. HMOs often employ stop-loss protection against expensive cases to protect against this situation (Kongstvedt, 2001).

In this system, several incentives are relevant. PCPs will be interested in increasing the number of patients who select them in order to increase the potential capitation pool both individually and of the group. Controlling costs are also common incentives both internally, through managing office expenses, and by limiting referrals to SCPs. An added incentive accrues in having patients who are as healthy as possible. Often HMO pay-incentive plans distribute the positive balances remaining in the risk pools using a variety of measures such as member satisfaction and quality of care. In addition, the risk pools may be individual-based or group-based. Usually only those PCPs with positive individual balances receive monies left in the pools at year's end.

Preferred Provider Organizations and Indemnity Insurance

A complete picture of today's types of health insurance is very complicated. This section discusses PPO and traditional indemnity plans and the incentives that tend to be used in these plans. PPOs negotiate discounts from providers and offer employers health insurance at lower cost than if employers used traditional health insurance in which non-discounted charges are paid for services. (PCPs in a PPO are often called network physicians in that they are a part of the PPO's broad network of providers.) Their employees can see network physicians for lower cost than those out of network. Congruently then, PPOs tend to pay their PCPs on a discounted fee-for-service basis. Capitation is not practical as a payment basis for PPOs because PCPs can refer to other physicians out of network or their patients can choose to seek out-of-network PCPs, and thus either have those expenses not be charged against them or avoid work (Kongstvedt, 2001).

Indemnity insurance plans like the traditional Blue Cross/Blue Shield plans also pay on a fee-for-service basis tied to what is considered usual, customary, or reasonable charges. There exist commercially available databases that report actual charges around the country. However, fees are not necessarily consistent across medical specialties, so resource-based relative value scales (RBRVSs) have been developed to determine fees on a common basis across the various procedures. Under RBRVSs, each procedure (CPT or current procedural terminology) has a relative value associated with it based on the effort the physician must put forth to do it. However, the use of RBRVSs is not without its detractors who believe that inconsistencies are a fact of life with such scales (Lantos, 2003).

Under conditions of fee-for-service, the more procedures physicians perform, the more they earn. Thus, there may be a problem of over-utilization, with physicians performing more procedures than are really necessary for effective treatment. Another set of problems is referred to as upcoding and unbundling. This is a method of coding procedures as those paying more than the procedure actually carried out, or coding and charging individually for actions previously combined in order to gain a larger reimbursement. Withholds, commonly used in capitated pay plans to cover medical cost overruns, can be applied to fee-for-service pay plans; but it is difficult to do on an individual physician basis without PCP gatekeepers (Kongstvedt, 2001).

Global fees are a hybrid of capitation and fee-for-service in that they transfer a moderate level of risk to the provider physician (Johnson, 2005). Many, if not most, individual plans are a blend of the HMO and PPO plans. For example, point of service (POS) plans allow patients to decide on each incidence of medical problem whether to use an in-house PCP or go out of network. Many are such a blend of types that already potentially problematic ways of paying physicians become even more inadequate when they are designed to insure the appropriate levels of medical care for patients.

Patient satisfaction measures are used as one of the bases of incentives in capitated environments as well as fee-for-service ones (Reiboldt, 1999). These measures can focus on a wide range of factors such as access to care, doctor–patient communication, specialty care, and overall ratings of care. Many measures of patient satisfaction have been constructed and evaluated. Although they are frequently criticized as invalid (Haas, 1999), patient satisfaction measures continue to be an important part of physician incentive systems. For example, in the very lucrative incentive system in one of the country's largest independent practice associations, the patient satisfaction factor is second in importance and strength to only quality indicators (Weber, 2004).

Quality-of-care measures of performance have been resisted by physicians for several reasons (Zismer, 1999). They feel that process can be confused with quality as adherence to processing protocols is usually the way quality is measured, epidemiological outcomes are a reasonable measure but may be a minor contributor to overall quality, and actual clinical outcomes can result from many factors outside the control of physicians including patient compliance. Despite these reactions, many physician practices began introducing quality factors into their compensation plans during the mid-1990s (Porn, 2004). The collection of Health Plan Employer Data and Information Set (HEDIS) data by the National Committee for Quality Assurance (NCQA) has facilitated the use of "quality" information in compensation plans. Recently the National Quality Forum's Ambulatory Measure Project is attempting to establish evidence-based quality measures in seven areas of care: asthma/respiratory conditions, depression/behavioral health, bone diseases, heart disease, hypertension, prenatal care, as well as immunization and screening (Porter, 2005). The American Academy of Family Physicians (AAFP) has taken a lead in endorsing such standards, but whether they should be used in physicians' compensation plans is quite another matter.

As for physicians, issues of fiduciary responsibility (McCullough, 2002), power, autonomy (Forsberg, Axelsson, & Arnetz, 2001), and loss of or change in professionalism (Kitchener, 2002) all represent conflicts of interest that physicians feel as they are faced with incentives that reward aspects of their practices other than tending to their patients' health. A recent study specifically examined physicians' attitudes about the ethicalness of personal financial incentives designed to encourage physicians to be more restrained in their use of medical resources for individual patients (Sulmasy, Bloche, Mitchell, & Hadley, 2000). In this study, over three-fourths of physicians surveyed found these incentives most unethical (Sulmasy et al., 2000). Sixty-nine percent of the physicians believed that not telling their patients about such incentives is most unethical. This study also illustrates an interesting dynamic of those physicians who are working within one of these incentive systems. Physicians who reported that the overall personal financial incentives in their practices encouraged them to reduce services were significantly more likely to have ethical objections to such incentives than those who reported no such encouragement. Under these incentives, the physicians also tended to believe that their own patients' trust in them had diminished and that their undivided loyalty to patients had been diminished.

In summing up the state of physician incentive pay, especially for PCPs, capitation plans theoretically encourage PCPs to seek out new patients thereby increasing their capitated revenue, and decrease their patients' expenses through careful selection of procedures in order to gain year-end payment of withholds. Fee-for-service plans, which also encourage attracting new patients but can encourage lack of concern for health care resources, are controlled by the use of withholds where possible. Under PPOs and Indemnity Insurance plans, relevant incentives reward an increased number of procedures, patient satisfaction, and quality of care. The search for other bases of incentives has continued with a current increased emphasis on patient satisfaction and quality measures (Porn, 2004). The use of incentives is naturally a concern of physicians and, as we will see in the next section, it has prompted much regulation by those concerned with potential physician actions.

REGULATION OF PHYSICIAN PAY INCENTIVES

Physician pay incentives have become the focus of much regulatory interest. Regulations have been generated at the state and national level that restrict pay practices in order to protect patients' interests and the interests of physicians. These include: limits on receipt of payments from referrals, limits on withholds, stop-loss protection for physicians, mandatory disclosure of incentives to patients, and surveys of patients' satisfaction with HMOs (Johnson, 2005).

In the last few years, Congress passed and amended the Ethics in Patient Referrals Act of 1989. These laws, commonly referred to as the Stark laws, forbid physicians from referring clients to ancillary facilities in which they have a financial interest and forbid them from receiving payments from hospitals and other health care providers based on the number of patients they refer to these facilities.

In order to protect PCPs and limit the degree of risk to which their income is subjected, the Centers for Medicare and Medicaid Services (CMS) set a 25% limit on withholds. CMS also placed limits on income that can be paid in bonuses to 25% of potential payments. In a similar vein, physicians and their groups can be held responsible for only 10% of the referral costs that exceed the per-patient limits. Although these limits only apply to medical costs applicable to Medicare and Medicaid, they emphasize the concern on the part of policy makers that excessively large incentives could influence physicians' treatment decisions contrary to the best interests of their patients (Johnson, 2005).

CMS requires the disclosure of information to patients about any physician pay-incentive plan, including whether referral services are covered in the plan and the type of incentive arrangement such as withhold, bonus, or capitation. Such general information is required for all plans an insurer may offer, and not the specifics about how a patient's individual physician is compensated related to the care provided him/her. In addition, managed care companies must conduct customer satisfaction surveys of both current and past enrollees who received Medicare or Medicaid. The results of these surveys must be reported to regulators.

While the Stark regulations seek to limit over-utilization of medical services by prohibiting referrals to facilities in which the referring physicians have a financial interest, all other regulations seek to limit under-utilization in managed care settings. Thus, there appears to be more concern about under-utilization of medical services than over-utilization. This may reflect the assumption that too little treatment is potentially far more harmful than too much or unnecessary treatment. The former is perceived as life threatening while the latter is only wasteful of patients' time and our limited health care resources.

REACTIONS TO PHYSICIAN PAY INCENTIVES

A review of the literature produced very few studies of patient reactions to physician pay issues. The existent literature suggests that patients have interest in physician pay and concern about the nature of incentives. Kao, Zaslavsky, Green, Koplan, and Cleary (2001) found that about half of the adults surveyed wanted more information about how their physicians were paid. More significantly for the purposes of this paper, the study also found that about 76% of patients thought that a bonus paid for ordering fewer tests than average would affect their quality of care.

Studies examining withholds and capitation give additional insight. Pereira and Pearson (2001) investigated patient's reactions to withholds and capitation. They describe withholds as money held back from either salaried or fee-for-service paid physicians equal to 10% of fees or salary and returned to them at year's end based on achievement of certain goals related to quality of care, member satisfaction, and financial performance. Capitation is described as putting doctors' income at some risk but they get most of whatever money is left over after the cost of care is subtracted from the monies collected to provide care (Pereira & Pearson, 2001). Their findings suggest that patients are more uncomfortable with capitation than withholds. Sixteen percent were uncomfortable with salaried with withholds, and 25% were uncomfortable with fee-for-service with withholds while 53% of respondents were uncomfortable with capitation. Although their study was not designed to understand the reasons for the differences in patients' reactions to capitation versus withholds for physicians, they suggested that their subjects may have perceived a link between quantity of care and the income their PCPs receive (Pereira & Pearson, 2001). This view is supported by the Kao et al. (2001) study where about 53% of the respondents thought that a withhold would affect care.

The perception by patients that physician incentives might determine how a physician treats the patient is at the center of our present study. Incentives that seek either directly, by rewarding the limiting of referrals or withholding treatment, or indirectly, by increasing the number of patients that a doctor sees in a given day, to limit patient care and maximize financial outcomes for the physician and their employer are in conflict with patient expectations. We have chosen to address this issue from the point of perceived ethics due in large part to the ethical conflict experienced by physicians when faced with the choices that these types of incentives provide (McCullough, 2002; Forsberg et al., 2001; Kitchener, 2002; Sulmasy et al., 2000). Like the physicians, patients are expected to view incentives that are oriented to controlling costs or enhancing revenues as less ethical than incentives that reward the primary purpose of physicians, patient care. We are also interested in examining how the perception of physician pay incentives is related to physician use.

METHODS

Sample and Procedure

This study employed a cross-sectional survey research design. The participants were a student sample of patients in the mid-western region of the U.S. A total of 101 participants completed questionnaires. Approximately 47% were male and 53% female. Seventy percent were between 21 and 30 years old, 19% between 31 and 40, 8% between 41 and 50, 3% were 20 years or less, and 1 student (1%) was between 51 and 60. About 72% were undergraduates and 28% were in graduate school. The students were asked about their experience with traditional health care plans (where you can see any doctor of your choice), HMOs, and PPOs. Ninety-eight percent had experience with some form of health care plan. Twenty-three percent only had experience with a traditional health care plan, 25% only with PPO, and only 8% with an HMO. Some subjects had experienced both traditional and PPO (8%), traditional and HMO (7%), and PPO and HMO (19%). About 8% had experienced all three types of health care plans. Approximately 88% had visited the doctor within the last year; with 63% reporting they had been two or more times.

Measures

A short questionnaire was prepared that addressed current health care pay incentives for physicians, the subjects' demographic information, and their health care coverage history. For the purpose of this study, 14 items were developed representing commonly used physician incentives as described to the authors by an expert practitioner, Robert Bohlmann, Principal of the Medical Group Management Association Consulting Group. The items addressed: revenue enhancement, cost control, patient satisfaction, and quality of care. For each of the incentives the subjects were directed to respond using a five-point scale (1 = very unethical, 2 = somewhat unethical, 3 = neither ethical nor unethical, 4 = somewhat ethical, 5 = very ethical) to the various items. All of the items for the scales were prefaced by the phrase: "Indicate your perception of the ethics of each of following bases for physician incentive pay."

Because the items were developed for this study, we conducted a principal components factor analysis with oblimin rotation in SPSS 12. The oblimin rotation was used since these incentives are not assumed to be orthogonal. A

Table 1. Results of Rotated Principal Components Factor Analysis.

Variable	Clinical Efficiency	Patient Satisfaction	Revenue Generation
Use of clinical performance measures for office visits such as cancer screening, influenza vaccination, etc.	*.88*	.26	.41
Following practice standards for symptoms presented by each patient in terms of what tests to order and treatments to be offered	*.85*	.37	.24
Application of quality of antibiotic use measures which have been field tested in hospitals such as those for lower respiratory tract infection guidelines	*.83*	.36	.33
Treating patients at lower cost than average	*.73*	.07	.31
Average scores on patient surveys measuring their satisfaction with the physician	.35	*.86*	.06
Scores on surveys mailed to patients	.15	*.84*	−.11
Ratings of "mystery" patients who are paid to visit and evaluate physicians	.29	*.83*	−.08
Results of follow-up calls to patients from the doctor's nurse about the last office visit	.33	*.72*	.13
Monetary value of patient services personally performed	.28	−.12	*.89*
Average number of patients encountered per day	.32	−.08	*.79*
Amount of profit margin	.35	.01	*.76*
Amount of effort put forth during a given time period as measured by complexity of what is done during each office visit	.18	.20	*.73*
Number of new patients seen each month	.37	−.17	*.68*
Eigenvalue	4.64	3.05	1.29
Percentage of variance	33.16	21.78	9.21
Cumulative percentage of variance	33.16	54.94	64.15

Note: Italized numbers indicate factor loadings

rotated three-factor solution resulted using 13 items (Table 1). One item, minimizing office maintenance and utility expenses, was deleted due to factor loadings less than .50 (Nunnally, 1967).

Clinical Efficiency. The first factor is comprised of items that describe efficiency in the clinical setting. This scale consists of four items: following practice standards for symptoms presented by each patient in terms of what tests to order and treatments to be offered; use of clinical performance measures for office visits such as cancer screening, influenza vaccination, etc.; application of quality of antibiotic use measures that have been field tested in hospitals such as those for lower respiratory tract infection guidelines; and treating patients at lower cost than average (alpha = .836).

Patient Satisfaction. This factor is comprised of four items used to measure patient satisfaction: average scores on patient surveys measuring their satisfaction with the physician; ratings of "mystery" patients who are paid to visit and evaluate physicians; scores on surveys mailed to patients; and results of follow-up calls to patients from the doctor's nurse about the last office visit (alpha = .832).

Revenue Generation. The third scale consists of items that describe physicians' efforts to generate revenue. The four items used to measure revenue generation are: number of new patients seen each month; average number of patients encountered per day; monetary value of patient services personally performed; and amount of effort put forth during a given time period as measured by complexity of what is done during each office visit (alpha = .819).

ANALYSIS AND RESULTS

The means, standard deviations, and correlations of scales representing the factors are reported in Table 2. Paired samples t-tests were conducted to determine whether the means of the scales were different as predicted, with Revenue Generation being perceived as less ethical than either Patient Satisfaction or Clinical Efficiency. The first t-test was to determine whether the difference in means of Patient Satisfaction and Revenue Generation scales was significant. The results indicated that the means are different ($t = -3.21$, df $= 100$, $p < .01$) such that Patient Satisfaction is seen as significantly more ethical than Revenue Generation. The second t-test examined the means of Patient Satisfaction and Clinical Efficiency. The means appear similar, and a paired t-test did not find that the two means were statistically significantly different. The third t-test examined whether the mean of the Clinical Efficiency is significantly higher than that of Revenue Generation. A paired t-test indicated that this difference was statistically significant ($t = -5.35$, df $= 100$, $p < .01$). The comparison of the means demonstrates that patients viewed incentives based upon Patient

Table 2.   Correlation Matrix with Means and Standard Deviations.

	Mean	S. D.	1	2	3	4	5	6
1 Physician visits last 5 years	10.14	13.4	1					
2 Age	2.35	.71	.054	1				
3 Gender	.53	.50	.210	.125	1			
4 Revenue Generation	3.05	.90	−.008	−.026	.026	1		
5 Patient Satisfaction	3.49	.97	−.255*	.050	−.027	−.046	1	
6 Clinical Efficiency	3.58	.83	.245*	.154	.030	.353**	.389**	1

Note: Missing data reduced sample to 85.
*Correlation is significant at the 0.05 level (2-tailed).
**Correlation is significant at the 0.01 level.

Satisfaction and Clinical Efficiency as more ethical than those based upon Revenue Generation, supporting our expectations.

We were also interested in the relationship of these views of the ethicalness of physician incentives with the number of times that patients see physicians. A hierarchical regression analysis (Cohen & Cohen, 1983) was used to examine this relationship. In this method, variables are entered as blocks so as to provide an estimate of the incremental explanatory power of the block, as well as the individual regression coefficients. In the first series of analyses, the first block consisted of the control variables and the second block the scales. The results of this analysis predicting the number of physician visits during the past 5 years was significant overall ($R^2 = .287$, $p < .01$); and each of the scales was significant, as indicated in Table 3. Patient perceptions of the ethicalness of physician incentives are related to health care use.

DISCUSSION

This exploratory study of patients' perceptions of the ethicalness of various commonly used pay incentives provides health care regulators, health care managers, and physicians with some additional insight into the patient–physician relationship. Specifically, the findings of this study illustrate that patients view the ways that physicians are rewarded differentially in terms of their ethicalness. Commonly used physician incentives were perceived by patients in this study to fall into three categories, Patient Satisfaction, Clinical Efficiency, and Revenue Generation. Scales developed in these categories indicated that incentives that address patient care by reinforcing Patient

Table 3. Hierarchical Regression Analyses – Perceptions of Ethical Nature of Dimensions of Physician Incentives Predicting Number of Visits to Physicians over Previous 5 Years[a].

Block	R^2	R^2_{Block}	df	β
Control variables	.045	.045	2, 82	
Age				.720
Gender				5.56
Incentive scales	.287**	.242**	5, 79	
Revenue Generation				−3.632**
Patient Satisfaction				−6.456**
Clinical Efficiency				8.596**

[a]Dependent variable = Visits to doctor in last 5 years. $N = 85$.
*$p < .05$.
**$p < .01$.

Satisfaction and Clinical Efficiency are seen as more ethical than incentives that address the financial needs of the organization. These findings are consistent in many ways with the research on physicians that indicates that an ethical dilemma exists for them if the organization attempts to influence them to make patient care decisions based in part on organizational financial reasons.

The highly important physician–patient relationship may then be influenced by this ethicality bias that patients seem to have about physician pay. Like other biases, perceived ethicality may influence the evaluation of physician and health care organization performance. While this is not directly addressed in this study, we do find that patient views of the ethics of the three physician incentive scales are related to physician use. Further research is warranted on the relationship of patient views of physician incentives and the patient evaluation of physician performance and patient satisfaction. The cross-sectional nature of this study prohibits the establishment of causality, so it is equally possible that the view of physician incentives by patients is influenced by physician visits or if views of the ethicality of incentives predict physician use. Each of these possibilities has potential impact on our health care system under current regulations. It is unknown whether this ethicality bias might also influence the patient–physician relationship in other ways, but the trust between a patient and his/her physician is important for many reasons, the least of which may be the patient's state of health. The need to protect patient–physician relations should be a major concern of regulators interested in long-term cost-effective health care.

Certainly, patients' perspectives are important to the health care industry as disclosure of how a physician is paid is implemented. More research is needed to understand patients' perspectives about physician pay incentives. The present regulations demanding that health care plans inform enrollees about how they compensate their physicians and other providers is not based on knowledge of how patients process and react to such information. Our findings suggest that patients view incentives based on Patient Satisfaction and Clinical Efficiency as undifferentiated from an ethical perspective. This may indicate that efforts, which are often viewed as limiting physicians' autonomy, could be viewed positively by patients. Common perceptions that managed care results in worse care than non-managed care may be inaccurate or based on general misperceptions and political rhetoric. It appears from the data in this study that patients may understand the need for control of health care processes from a clinical efficiency perspective. In addition, it is unknown whether such current disclosure information promotes greater understanding or misunderstanding of attempts to insure quality patient care at affordable costs.

The professional standing of physicians may be impeded by this lack of knowledge because of inappropriate communication of physician pay information. At the most basic level, perception of incentives as unethical may have negative repercussions for any business, including placing them at a competitive disadvantage in the marketplace. More importantly, the results of this study may reflect misunderstood patients' views about our current health care delivery system. Little is understood about the reactions of the general public to many aspects of our overwhelmingly complicated health care system. There can be little doubt that patients feel drowned in a sea of paperwork in trying to get their medical bills paid by insurers. In evaluating the ethics of compensation bases for physicians, they may not be sensitive to efforts within the health care organization to increase revenue.

This study has many limitations stemming from a cross-sectional design, the size of the sample, and its convenience nature, the fact that our sample consisted of students, and the use of newly created items assessing how incentives are viewed. It does contribute to the discussion among health care professionals vis-à-vis the use of incentives as pay for physicians, including whether new incentives are needed (Hyman & Silver, 2001). This study also presents a unique view into how compensation systems, particularly incentives, are perceived by consumers. Perception of the ethics of pay incentives is a little studied area. This area of inquiry can provide insight into how occupations in general are ethically evaluated and, to the extent that consumers make decisions based upon the ethical nature of a service provider, may suggest incentive strategies that would provide a competitive advantage.

REFERENCES

Beer, M., & Katz, N. (2003). Do incentives work: The perceptions of a worldwide sample of senior executives. *Human Resource Planning*, *26*(3), 30–44.

Callahan, D. (2004). *The cheating culture*. Orlando, FL: Harcourt, Inc.

Cohen, J., & Cohen, P. (1983). *Applied multiple regression/correlation analysis for the behavioral sciences*. Hillsdale, NJ: Erlbaum Dombeck.

Forsberg, E., Axelsson, R., & Arnetz, B. (2001). Effects of performance-based reimbursement on the professional autonomy and power of physicians and the quality of care. *The International Journal of Health Planning and Management*, *16*(4), 297–310.

Frey, B. S. (1994). How intrinsic motivation is crowded out and in. *Rationality and Society*, *6*(3), 334–352.

Gupta, N., & Shaw, J. (1998). Let the evidence speak: Financial incentives are effective!!. *Compensation and Benefits Review*, *30*(2), 26–31.

Haas, M. (1999). A critique of patient satisfaction. *Health Information Management*, *29*(1), 9–13.

Hyman, D. A., & Silver, C. (2001). Just what the patient ordered: The case for result-based compensation arrangements. *Journal of Law, Medicine & Ethics*, *29*(2), 170–173.

Johnson, B. A. (2005). Medical practice and compensation plans. In: L. F. Wolper (Ed.), *Physician practice management* (pp. 543–568). Sudbury, MA: Jones and Bartlett Publishers.

Kao, A. C., Zaslavsky, A. M., Green, D. C., Koplan, J. P., & Cleary, P. D. (2001). Physician incentives and disclosure of payment methods to patients. *Journal of General Internal Medicine*, *16*, 181–188.

Kerr, S. (1975). On the folly of rewarding A while hoping for B. *Academy of Management Journal*, *18*, 769–783.

Kitchener, M. (2002). Mobilizing the logic of managerialism in professional fields: The case of academic health centre mergers. *Organization Studies*, *23*(3), 391–420.

Kohn, A. (1993). Why incentive plans cannot work. *Harvard Business Review*, *71*(5), 54–63.

Kongstvedt, P. R. (2001). Compensation of primary care physicians in managed health care. In: P. R. Kongstvedt (Ed.), *Essentials of managed health care*, (4th Ed.). Gaithersburg, MD: Aspen Publication.

Lantos, J. (2003). RVUs blues. *Hastings Center Report*, *33*(3), 37–45.

Levinson, W., Kao, A., Kuby, A., & Thisted, R. A. (2005). The effect of physician disclosure of financial incentives on trust. *Archives of Internal Medicine*, *165*, 625–630.

McCullough, L. B. (2002). Power, integrity, and trust in the managed practice of medicine: Lessons from the history of medical ethics. *Social Philosophy and Policy*, *19*(2), 180–211.

Nunnally, J. (1967). *Psychometric theory*. New York: McGraw-Hill.

Pearson, S. D., & Hyams, T. (2002). Talking about money: How primary care physicians respond to a patient's question about financial incentives. *Journal of General Internal Medicine*, *17*, 75–78.

Pereira, A. G., & Pearson, S. D. (2001). Patient attitudes toward physician financial incentives. *Archives of Internal Medicine, 161*(10), 1313–1317.

Porn, L. (2004). Physician compensation. In: B. A. Keagy & M. S. Thomas (Eds), *Essentials of physician practice management* (pp. 291–310). San Francisco, CA: Jossey-Bass.

Porter, S. (2005). AAFP, other stakeholders endorse starter set of performance measures, AAFP News Now 5/4/2005 (www.aafp.org/x34179.xml).

Reiboldt, J. M. (1999). *Physician compensation systems.* Norcross, GA: Coker Publishing.

Seller Beware. (2004). *Economist, 370*(8358), 65.

Stell, L. K. (2004). Two cheers for physicians' conflicts of interest. *The Mount Sinai Journal of Medicine, 71*(4), 236–242.

Sulmasy, D. P., Bloche, M. G., Mitchell, J. M., & Hadley, J. (2000). Physician's ethical beliefs about cost-control arrangements. *Archives of Internal Medicine, 160*(5), 649–657.

Weber, D. O. (2004). Pay-for-performance programs pressure and please physicians. *The Physician Executive, 30*(3), 6–11.

Zismer, D. K. (1999). Compensation challenges in specialist groups: A guide for the uninitiated. *Physician Performance and Payment Report, 1*(1), 9–11.

AN EYE FOR AN EYE: INVESTIGATING THE IMPACT OF CONSUMER PERCEPTION OF CORPORATE UNFAIRNESS ON ABERRANT CONSUMER BEHAVIOR

Kyoko Fukukawa, Christine Ennew, and Steve Diacon

ABSTRACT

This paper examines why ordinary people engage in aberrant consumer behavior (ACB), and pays particular attention to the extent to which consumer perceptions of corporate 'unfairness' lead to a response in kind. The study examines five ethical scenarios including insurance claim exaggeration and software piracy, using data from 344 UK consumers. Ajzen's theory of planned behavior (TPB) provides an initial analytical framework. The study also adopts an additional variable, perceived unfairness, referring to the extent to which an actor is motivated to redress an imbalance perceived as unfair.

In comparison to TPB, the study reveals different components of ACB. Furthermore, analysis of variance indicates that consumer perceptions of unfairness by insurance companies provide a significant reason for claim

Insurance Ethics for a More Ethical World
Research in Ethical Issues in Organizations, Volume 7, 187–221
Copyright © 2007 by Elsevier Ltd.
All rights of reproduction in any form reserved
ISSN: 1529-2096/doi:10.1016/S1529-2096(06)07010-6

exaggeration. This suggests that ACB is one form of market response to unfair corporate performance. Thus it is argued that an examination of ACB will not only help to understand which ethical aspects of corporate performance might be perceived as unfair, but also to evaluate the extent to which it contributes to a negative perception of particular industries and corporations. The closing discussion considers how a consumer negative response to corporate performance might relate to pricing, product attributes and customer relationships.

INTRODUCTION

The current study examines why ordinary people engage in aberrant consumer behavior (ACB). Fullerton and Punj (1993) define ACB as 'behavior in exchange settings which violates the generally accepted norms of conduct in such situations and which is therefore held in disrepute by marketers and by most consumers' (p. 570). Retail fraud, insurance fraud and software piracy are well known examples of the behavior in question. Krasnovsky and Lane (1998, p. 228) suggest that aberrant behavior such as shoplifting reaches its 'peak' during adolescence; the implication being that ordinary adult consumers are said to have gone through moral development, so leading them to deem consumer aberrance such as shoplifting as unacceptable (Babin & Griffin, 1995, p. 668). Nevertheless, Fullerton and Punj (1993) argue that in fact 'misbehavers are representative of consumers overall, not a group apart' (p. 570); and company losses relating to ACB perhaps bear this out. Indeed, with an estimated cost to industries running over several billions of pounds annually in the UK alone, a fuller understanding of ACB is surely paramount to practitioners who engage in policy making and marketing strategies.

Borna and Stearns (1998) have argued that, to some degree, a consumer's unreasonable expectation and behavior toward markets can be alleviated, even with existing knowledge of business and economics, by various forms of intervention, including government intervention (e.g. cracking down on counterfeiting businesses and tightening trading regulations). More broadly Fullerton and Punj (2004) describe the various intervention strategies as falling into two main categories namely education and enforced deterrence. As is borne out by the literature reviewed here, these two categories of intervention generally refer in a rather static way to the influence (or content) of consumer beliefs and personality traits. What is less observed is a more dynamic, complex process, i.e. how individual beliefs and dispositions, social influence, situational specifics and institutional contexts each have their significance and weighting as factors in the ethical decision-making process. The current study examines whether consumers are willing or prepared to engage in norm-breaking behavior as consequences of a perceived unfair relationship with firms. The empirical study uses different ethical scenarios to examine how consumers respond to a particular ethical situation. Following analysis of the findings, the study addresses the importance of drawing firms' attention to the relationship between consumers and businesses in terms of fairness, in order to identify practical implications of ACB in the marketplace.

LITERATURE REVIEW

ACB has proved to be difficult to research in some respects, not least due to the sensitive nature of the topic, but also because of its very diversity. For example, the range of contexts can include shoplifting, retail borrowing, insurance fraud, counterfeiting and software piracy, each of which are discussed in turn below.

Shoplifting as retail fraud, in the form of the illegal acquisition of goods, is recognized to be a serious crime (Babin & Griffin, 1995). The British Retail Consortium (2004) reports that customer theft in 2003 cost the sector £410 million. As mentioned above, shoplifting is often considered chiefly an adolescent behavior, thus this type of research mainly focuses on a narrow set of generational groupings (see, Babin & Griffin, 1995; Cox, Cox, & Moschis, 1990) and is concerned with factors such as peer group influences (Babin & Griffin, 1995; Cox et al., 1990). The current study, however, focuses on another form of shoplifting, so-called 'disposition of goods'. The disposition of goods can be considered to include both intentional and unintentional fraud, but for the purposes of this study refers particularly to cases of consumers 'returning deliberately damaged merchandise after the product was conventionally acquired and consumed' (Strutton, Vitell, & Pelton, 1994, p. 254). So, for example, one of the scenarios adopted refers to the returning of a stained suit in order to obtain a refund, despite having previously used the item. The concept of 'retail borrowing' shares similar characteristics with shoplifting in the form of disposition, but more specifically is defined as 'the purchase of an item with the [*prior*] intent to return the same item for a refund once the item has been used, with satisfaction, for a specific purpose' (Piron & Young, 2001, p. 121). Overall, examining situations of both the fraudulent acquisition and the disposition of goods,

Strutton et al. (1994) argue that the ordinary (adult) consumer on occasions will deem shoplifting as an inappropriate behavior, but at other times may be able to justify their behavior.

Insurance fraud is another common form of ACB, and its annual estimated loss to the UK insurance industry is a considerable £1–2 billion (Day, 2005) and in the US an even more sizable $30 billion.[1] Based on such statistics it might well be assumed that a large number of consumers appear to find insurance fraud (i.e. inventing a fictitious claim and exaggerating a claim) an acceptable form of behavior. It has been shown, for example, that such dishonest behavior is frequently supported by a generalized view of 'everyone is doing it', 'no victim crime' and 'it is a way of getting money back from insurance companies' (Litton, 1998). Such ways of justifying engagement in insurance fraud appear to coincide with the reasoning behind shoplifting as practiced by ordinary adult consumers noted above. However, of further significance to this study in particular is that acceptability and tolerance toward consumer insurance fraud increases particularly in a situation in which individuals have negative perceptions toward insurance companies (Tennyson, 1997). Cummins and Tenneyson (1996), for example, found that this accepting attitude toward fraudulent activities positively influences the frequency of liability claims with respect to automobile insurance.

The estimated losses to the economy from *counterfeit goods* – some $79 million worth worldwide in just one month, as reported in October 2004[2] – has led to a large body of empirical study. Concerned here specifically with the consumption (rather than the organized 'business') of counterfeited goods, the major elements of research relate to attitude and intention to buy or acquire such goods, as well as the influencing factors. Behavior with respect to this form of consumption is likely to be motivated by product traits (e.g. Cordell, Wongtada, & Kieschnick, 1996), price (e.g. Albers-Miller, 1999), peer influence (e.g. Albers-Miller, 1999) and a perception of fairness of business practice (Tom, Garibaldi, Zeng, & Pilcher, 1998). As will become evident, the latter motivation of perceived (un)fairness is certainly borne out by the current study. Additionally, consumer behavior related to counterfeit goods is found to be moderated by a higher degree of risk perception (i.e. getting caught and product faulty, Chakraborty, Allred, Sukhdial, & Bristol, 1997) and lawfulness attitude (Cordell et al., 1996). The country of origin of counterfeit goods is also said to influence purchasing decisions (Chakraborty et al., 1997) and studies have shown that consumers who have previously purchased counterfeited goods have a more favorable attitude toward buying counterfeits (Tom et al., 1998). The current study makes an example of a specific form of counterfeiting, namely software piracy. In this case the level of perceived risk is relatively low, due largely to the behavior itself being a rather informal, private activity. In other words interaction between customers and business is limited, so potentially leading to the undermining of the exchange setting.

Software piracy is a relatively new form of consumer aberrant behavior. However, its practice has grown rapidly among 'ordinary people' and become a worldwide phenomenon – the financial significance of which cannot be ignored. According to the British Software Alliance (BSA), piracy in the UK alone costs the industry £1.6 billion annually. The International Data Corporation (IDC) estimate that at a global level businesses and consumers will spend over $300 billion on PC software over the next five years. However, they also predict that over the same period almost $200 billion worth of software will be pirated. In light of these figures it is argued that lowering piracy by just 10% over 4 years 'would add more than one million new jobs and $400 billion in economic growth worldwide' (Second Annual BSA and IDC global Software Piracy Study, Business Software Alliance, 2005, p. 4). Attitude toward software piracy can differ among different social groups (Taylor & Shim, 1993) and levels of activity can vary between national cultures (Husted, 2000). However, it has disseminated quickly as a common consumer practice and has been found to be one of the most acceptable forms of aberrant behavior (Vitell & Davis, 1990 cited in Taylor & Shim, 1993). While those consumers who consider software piracy to be a form of an unethical behavior are inclined to indicate an intention *not* to practice the behavior in question (Wagner & Sanders, 2001), the fact that the behavior is indeed widespread leads to the presumption that a large number of consumers may not even perceive software piracy to be an ethical issue at all. What is clearer is that acquisition of pirated software may be motivated by economic gain in relation to the high cost of the original authorized product, the perception of low impact on others (e.g. Grass & Wood, 1996), a high level of peer influence (Al-Jabri & Abdul-Gader, 1997), as well as low risk perception or high opportunity to engage in the behavior in question (Chang, 1998). Many of these factors are indeed borne out by the current study.

The proceeding review suggests various factors that are considered to influence the decision-making process of ACB. Those commonly referred to include economic gain, positive attitude, social and peer influence, risk perception (cf. an existence of opportunity), the degree of consequences to others and also the perception of fairness of business. With the exception of perceived unfairness, Fullerton and Punj (1993) suggest each of these factors can be categorized under the first of two broad headings: 'consumer traits and predisposition'. A significant question arises as to whether such factors can then be considered generic in any way or are indeed situation specific. It is a problem that cannot necessarily be resolved by referring to the literatures discussed above since all are concerned with factors specific to single contexts. The issue of perceived unfairness is not highlighted by these factors. Instead, it is necessary to refer to what Fullerton and Punj (1993) place under a second broad heading of the 'characteristics of exchange settings and marketing institutions'. This area of interest has received relatively less research interest, apart from limited studies again relating only to single contexts (e.g. Tom et al., 1998).

The current study aims to integrate concerns that come under both these two headings, in order to examine the varying impact and combination of factors as they relate to different ethical scenarios. There are two significant aspects to note: firstly, it can be understood that by using a range of scenarios (as will be detailed in the Method below) the study contextualizes characteristics of different exchange settings with respect to ethical situations. In this respect a useful precedent is set by the Muncy and Vitell (1992) study, which contextualized the characteristics of exchange settings across 27 different scenarios and found that consumer ethical belief does indeed differ depending on the specificity of each context (for more on this type of research a useful and extensive review can be found in Vitell, 2003). Secondly, using perceived unfairness, the study captures the underlining theme of the characteristics of marketing institutions in order to explore a particular aspect of consumer motivation and sense of opportunity to engage in ACB. Numerous institutional characteristics may offer possible explanations for aberrant consumer practices as directed toward businesses; ranging, for example, from perceptions of whole industries to the issues relating to the size and reputation of firms, as well as more specific customer-business relations.

Types of industries as a whole can present the consumer with certain concerns of an ethical nature. As a result consumers' ethical expectations toward a single firm may in fact be an expectation held in common toward all firms within the same sector. For instance, Roman and Ruiz (2005, p. 441) argue that consumers have a lower ethical expectation of salespeople's behavior when they have a more negative perception of that particular industry. Equally, there may be a need to consider the *reputation of a firm*, reflecting the fact that consumers take account of how a firm is performing in the marketplace. This is consistent with common anecdotal descriptions of 'fat cat' businesses; multinational companies, for example, are often perceived as being overbearing profit makers and their associated marketing activities and business practices are criticized as 'unfair' and 'abusive' (cf. Cox et al., 1965 cited in Hunt & Chonko, 1984). As a response to such an undesirable situation – and even to gain competitive advantage – multinational companies have long been attempting to improve their image and communicate 'good practice' to consumers by getting involved with social concerns such as health projects, educational and recreational needs and other such civic-based concerns (Porter & Kramer, 2002). In a similar vein, the *size of firms* in relation to ethical situations may also influence consumers' perception toward firms. For instance, consumers may be less concerned about financial losses suffered by big firms than those of small local businesses. That may be because consumers expect that big firms are making enough profit to absorb losses and/or because consumers may become acquaintances or even friends with people running small firms and so feel it inappropriate to engage in exploitative behavior. An argument can be made to the effect that as part of one's 'traits and predisposition' a consumer may be predisposed to bear a negative attitude toward 'big business' in general (Fullerton & Punj, 1993, p. 572). This again highlights the importance of the current study's approach to consider how factors compound and differ across scenarios, rather than to simply consider specific factors in a static, targeted fashion.

In some instances the effects of combinations between factors can be secondary to the effects of a single distinct influencing factor. However, in other situations the effects of factor interaction can form the dominant influence. In this respect, as Fullerton and Punj (1993, p. 573) note, the *customer–business relationship*, i.e. consumer interactions with businesses and indeed their employees, presents a more complex interaction of factors which may determine how consumers behave. As the relationship marketing literature suggests (e.g. Morgan & Hunt, 1994; Gronroos, 1997), if businesses are concerned with establishing and developing successful exchanges with consumers, ethical dimensions in the relationship require their thorough attention. It is a point echoed by Mitchell and Chan (2002), following their investigation into UK consumers' attitude and behaviors toward a wide range of ACB.

Above all, as Fullerton and Punj (1993, p. 570) point out, 'the challenge for researchers is to identify those factors or interactions of factors which are likely to lead some consumers to misbehave some of the time' (the very same point is acknowledged in Babin & Griffin, 1995, p. 668). The current study draws upon a similar interest in seeking to identify the common factors noted above, as well as the characteristics of ethical contexts (i.e. exchange setting) and of firms and industries (i.e. marketing institutions). More specifically, the study aims to examine whether consumer perceptions toward institutions, as well as behavioral beliefs, significantly influence ACB across different ethical contexts. Furthermore, the study also explores how the role and strength of these factors varies depending on the specificity of the ethical context. It is believed that an examination of such specificity helps explain and interrogate why ordinary people choose to misbehave 'some of the time'.

DEVELOPING AN EMPIRICAL FRAMEWORK

As discussed in the foregoing review, several factors have been either discussed and/or examined by the previous studies in various contexts. Considering the factors that commonly emerged in the proceeding discussion, the theory of planned behavior (TPB, Ajzen, 1991) appears to capture these common factors and was thought to be an appropriate initial theoretical framework to guide the current study. It is worth noting that the model not only captures the various influencing factors of ACB, but also posits that these factors influence intention to perform, which approximate the actual occurrence of the behavior in question. TPB has been applied directly to investigate various consumer ethical behaviors[3] and some such studies have also been significant for the development of ethical decision-making models in specific contexts of consumption.[4]

However, while TPB provides an initial framework for the current study, the model was enhanced based on previous relevant research as discussed in the literature review and as informed by previous empirical investigation that combines qualitative and quantitative analysis (Fukukawa, 2002). In this earlier investigation, a list of factors believed to influence the decision-making of ACB was generated based on an extensive literature review and the findings of in-depth interviews and focus groups. This list of factors was then mapped onto key constructs associated with TPB in order to empirically examine the influencing factors and their impact on intention. Consequently, it was proposed that the construct of subjective norm should be broadened into a social influence construct (i.e. to measure what people in general and important referents thought an individual should do). This was done in order to overcome the narrowness of the idea of subjective norm in TPB (Miniard & Cohen, 1981); and can be justified on the basis of existing empirical evidence (Klobas & Clydes, 2000; Bhattacherjee, 2000).

To the above-modified TPB, the aspect concerning consumer perception of unfairness about firms was added. This helps to address a particular interest of the current study, namely the relationship between consumers and business when explaining some incidents of ACB. As will become evident in what follows this construct is shown to be of significant value to our overall understanding of ACB. Consumer perception of unfairness concerning business clearly has an impact on consumer behavior. With regards to business ethics, Seligman and Schwartz (1997, p. 581) points out that 'consumers might be willing to inconvenience themselves in order to punish unfair firms'. This perception of fairness sometimes functions as a constraint on firms' abilities to maximize profit (Pave, Pava, & Hochman, 1999). According to Equity theory, 'if customers feel they are being treated unfairly in an exchange relationships, perception of inequity will emerge. The inequity can be resolved with various actions' (Alexander, 2002, p. 226). In the context of the current study, such resolution may indeed be in the form of ACB.

Tennyson (1997, p. 250) explains that attitude toward insurance fraud in particular is related to consumer perceptions of insurance institutions; indeed a significant influence on consumer perceptions in her study is consumer evaluation of the fairness of firms. When having negative perceptions of insurance institutions, consumers tend to rationalize their fraudulent claims as acceptable. This is because consumers tend to justify their own questionable behavior in response to firms' unfairness, and so rest liability upon the firms, rather than themselves. Furthermore, findings of some studies (e.g. Seligman & Schwartz, 1997, p. 581; Tennyson, 1997) show that consumer judgments of their own behavior are determined less strictly than in relation to their judgments of firms. Hence, consumers tend to use evaluations of firms' unfairness to account for and moderate their own behavior, reasoning that their aberrant behavior is in fact acceptable behavior; which firms should expect as the negative consequence of their own 'unfair' business practices. Similarly, consumers may excuse their aberrant behavior as the consequence of a tradeoff with firms' unfair behavior: typically 'it's their fault; if they had been fair with me, I would not have done it'; and 'It's a joke they should find fault with me, after the ripoffs they have engineered' (Strutton, Pelton, & Ferrell, 1997, p. 254).

Having discussed here the potential significance of the impact of corporate unfairness, the current study focuses on the concept of perceived fairness of firms behavior in order to investigate its influence on decisions to engage in ACB – in other words, as discussed in the Literature Review, adopting this factor enables an examination of the characteristics of marketing institutions as they impact on consumer perceptions of ethical issues. In brief, in the current study of intention to engage in ACB is said to be influenced by the following factors: attitude, social influence, perceived behavioral control and perceived unfairness.

METHOD

Given the potential sensitivities in investigating ACB, a self-completion questionnaire was adopted based on scenarios adapted from Wilkes (1978, p. 154) and Muncy and Vitell (1992). To examine the varying impact of factors across a range of ACB, five diverse scenarios were created (1) changing a price tag, (2) returning a stained suit, (3) exaggerating an insurance claim, (4) copying software from a friend and (5) taking a quality towel away from a hotel. Each respondent was given a questionnaire containing three of the five scenarios selected at random and then asked to respond to a series of attitudinal questions for each. Clearly, the extent to which scenarios represent actual behavior can be debated (Randall, 1989 cited in Randall & Gibson, 1991). However, their hypothetical nature makes them more suited and less threatening when dealing with sensitive issues (Gattiker & Kelley, 1999) and consequently, they have been widely used in ethics research (Harrington, 1997; Singhapakdi, Vitell, & Kraft, 1996). A full description of the scenarios is provided in Appendix 1.

Scale items drew partly on existing measurement instruments (i.e. Ajzen, 1985, 1991; Chang, 1998) and partly on items developed specifically for the purpose, which were tested through exploratory work. In particular, perceived unfairness was specified to capture unfairness in pricing, business practice and retaliation based on the findings of the preliminary investigation (Fukukawa, 2002). The use of combined measures has been suggested as a way of compensating the weaknesses of newly developed scales with the strengths of established scales (Hinkin, Tracey, & Enz, 1997). This is the approach adopted here. The descriptive scales used in the current questionnaire are provided in Appendix 2.

Finally, the questionnaire also included the BIDR impression management scale (Paulhus, 1991) to examine the possible effect of socially desirability responding and a variety of classification questions. Socially desirable responding is calculated using the BIDR score. A higher score suggests that an individual is more inclined to overstate his/her response. The BIDR score mean for the current study was 7.8 and did not differ across the scenarios. The BIDR score mean was slightly higher in comparison with the means generated in the confirmatory study of BIDR by Paulhus (1991); where the mean ranged from 5.3 to 6.7. This may reflect the fact that the current sample shows a slight bias toward an older population which tends to generate a greater BIDR score (Paulhus, 1991).

A total of 1,250 questionnaires and self-addressed pre-paid envelopes were anonymously hand delivered to residents in a large metropolitan area in the United Kingdom. The target streets were selected systematically to ensure that a range of different residential environments was covered and questionnaires distributed where possible to every house in those streets. Out of 1,250, 344 (27.52%) usable responses were returned over a period of 5 weeks (in June–July 2001) producing 1,030 scenario responses, which were used for subsequent analysis. The full demographic information is included in Appendix 3 and shows a good mix of gender and education, although, as noted, there is evidence of a slight bias toward older respondents.

FINDINGS

Intention to engage in ACB was measured by a 7-point scale (1 extremely likely, 7 extremely unlikely). The number of the respondents was unevenly distributed across the seven categories. Three groupings of the data were created. The first group was comprised of three categories indicating the respondent is unlikely to engage in ACB (1 extremely unlikely, 2 quite unlikely and 3 slightly unlikely) and so labeled as unlikely ($n = 828$). The second group was comprised of three categories of responses likely to engage in ACB (7 extremely likely, 6 quite likely and 5 slightly likely) and so labeled as likely ($n = 174$). The response 'neither' was categorized as the third group because the respondents' intention was uncertain ($n = 28$). Table 1 shows the frequency of intention to engage in different kinds of ACB and highlights notable variations across the different ethical situations. Scenarios 1 and 2 are concerned with changing a price tag and returning a stained suit; most respondents appeared to have no intention to engage in these behaviors. Scenarios 3 and 5 are concerned with exaggerating an insurance claim and taking a quality towel from a hotel; a small but significant number of respondents indicated that they were likely to engage in these behaviors (20.4 and 10.6% of the total respectively). Scenario 4 is concerned

Table 1. Intention to Engage in Aberrant Consumer Behavior.

	Scenario 1: Changing a Price Tag	Scenario 2: Returning a Stained Suit	Scenario 3: Exaggerating an Insurance Claim	Scenario 4: Coping Software from a Friend	Scenario 5: Taking a Quality Towel away from a Hotel	Total
Unlikely	201	212	164	74	177	828
Likely	3	4	42	104	21	174
Neither	5	3	4	11	5	28
Total	209	219	210	189	203	1,030

with copying software from a friend and here the greatest number of respondents (58.4%) indicated intention to engage in this behavior.

Given the mix of established and new scale items, exploratory factor analysis (EFA) was conducted across all units of analysis ($n = 1015$) to identify distinctive dimensions explaining ACB. Both the KMO Measure of Sampling and Bartlett's test of sphericity suggested that the data was suitable for EFA. A principal components extraction and orthogonal rotation were used and a number of variables excluded because of low communalities. None of the factors had factor loadings less than ± 0.5, and so can be considered to be 'practically significant' for the subsequent analysis. Table 2 shows the results of EFA.

Four factors, accounting for 71% of total variance, emerged as dimensions of ACB. These factors differed from those proposed in the TPB-based theoretical framework. The first factor, labeled as Evaluation, was comprised of items related to three components: attitude, social influence and perceived behavioral control. Each of these was assumed to be distinct components of ACB prior to the empirical investigation. The items were loaded together to represent an individuals evaluation of their potential to engage in the behavior, thus measuring whether it was good or other people thought it good to engage in the behavior, as well as whether they felt they were able to engage in the behavior. The second factor captured the perception of unfairness relating to business practice and accounted for 11.3% of the total variance. This factor measures the extent to which consumers are motivated to perform aberrant behavior because of a perceived imbalance between consumers and suppliers and so labeled as Perceived Unfairness. The third factor was labeled as Social Participation and accounted for 8.2% of the total variance. It captured external encouragement to behave in a particular way because of the presence of others. The fourth factor captured attitudes toward the consequences that are expected to result from consumer aberrant behavior and accounted for 7.2% of the total variance. Labeled Consequence, this factor measures the extent to which the outcomes of aberrant behavior are seen as beneficial or harmful.

The factor structure which emerged from the current analysis does not match with that originally proposed. In particular, the factor Evaluation combines elements of attitude, social influence and perceived behavioral control. As outlined in the preceding literature review, the current study has sought to abide by the need for a more dynamic understanding of ACB, and in particular calls for a comprehensive and 'simultaneous' exploration of the relationship between ethical beliefs, attitude and behavior (Mitchell & Chan, 2002, p. 23). Subsequently, the four emergent factors, Evaluation, Perceived

Table 2.   Factor Loading.

Factors (% of Variance Explained)	Evaluation (43.6%)	Perceived Unfairness (11.3%)	Social Participation (8.2%)	Consequence (7.2%)
Cronbach Alpha	0.88[a]	0.83	0.86	0.53
Attitude, evaluation good/bad	−0.584			
Attitude, evaluation risk	This variable was excluded due to the low communality (0.388)			
Attitude, evaluation foolish/wise	This variable was excluded due to the low communality (0.243)			
Attitude, outcome to an actor	This variable was excluded due to the low communality (0.309)			
Attitude, outcome to other consumers				0.819
Attitude, outcome to suppliers				0.711
Social influence, peer participation			0.940	
Social influence, societal participation			0.902	
Social influence, peer approval	0.764			
Social influence, societal approval	0.582			0.508
PBC, easy/difficult	0.757			
PBC, opportunity	0.768			
PBC, Control 1	0.786			
PBC, Control 2	−0.684			
PBC, Control 3	This variable was excluded due to the low communality (0.406)			
Perceived unfairness, pricing		0.820		
Perceived unfairness, retaliation		0.809		
Perceived unfairness, business performance		0.693		

Note: KMO Measure of Sampling Adequacy: 0.890, Bartlett's Test of Sphericity: Significant, Extraction Method: Principle Component Analysis, Rotation Method: Varimax with Kaiser Normalization. Total Variance Explained: 71.0%.
[a]The scores of items which load negative factor scores were reversed to calculate Cronbach alpha.

Unfairness, Social Participation and Consequence, were submitted to an analysis of variance (ANOVA) using the scenarios as factors.

The assumption of ANOVA is for homogeneity of variance. This was not assured, thus a minimum impact of violation was assumed.[5] The result of ANOVA (Table 3) indicated that the means of the antecedents differ across the scenarios ($p < 0.05$). The significant differences among the means of the antecedents across the scenarios were examined based on Scheffe post-hoc tests. This test is considered to be the most conservative method (Hair, Anderson, Tatham, & Black, 1998) and is used for *unequal* sample sizes to test if pairs of the means are different (the sample sizes of the current study are between 186 and 214). In addition, Diagram 1 presents the means of the factor scores of the antecedents across the five different scenarios. It is provided to help the understanding of the roles of the antecedents in influencing a specific ACB.

The varying means of the factor Evaluation across the scenarios can be interpreted as the difference of its role and significance in explaining different ACB. For scenario 1 (changing a price tag) and scenario 2 (returning a stained suit) there is a negative means of evaluation shown while scenario 4 (copying a software from a friend) indicates a positive means of Evaluation. The means of scenarios 3 (exaggerating an insurance claim) and 5 (taking a quality towel away from a hotel) turned out to be neutral, close to zero. The pattern of reported intention across the five scenarios corresponds to the pattern of the means of Evaluation (i.e. the number of those who reported intention to engage in ACB increased in ascending order of scenarios 1, 2, 5, 3 and 4, see Table 1).

Table 3.   ANOVA: The Dimensions of ACB and Scenarios.

		Sum of Squares	df	Mean Square	F	Sig.
Evaluation	Between groups	340.479	4	85.120	127.644	0.000
	Within groups	673.521	1,010	0.667		
	Total	1014.000	1,014			
Perceived unfairness	Between groups	29.975	4	7.494	7.692	0.000
	Within groups	984.025	1,010	0.974		
	Total	1014.00	1,014			
Social participation	Between groups	12.920	4	3.230	3.259	0.011
	Within groups	1001.080	1,010	0.991		
	Total	1014.000	1,014			
Consequence	Between groups	20.717	4	5.179	5.266	0.000
	Within groups	993.283	1,010	0.983		
	Total	1014.000	1,014			

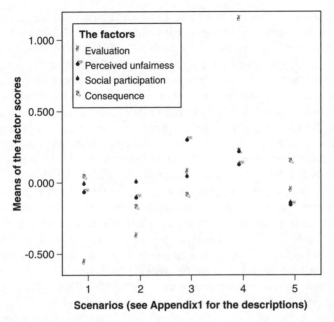

Diagram 1. Drop Chart-means of the Factor Scores across Scenarios.

Interestingly, in terms of Perceived Unfairness, the means for scenario 3 is 0.285, the highest absolute value among the 5 scenarios, and statistically, differs significantly from scenarios 1, 2 and 5. It can be said that Perceived Unfairness is dominant in characterizing an occurrence of the behavior described by scenario 3 (exaggerating an issuance claim). The factor Social Participation defined the difference between scenarios 4 and 5. Software piracy described by scenario 4 is a well-known example of ACB. The impact of Social Participation on this behavior is distinctive. Along with a positive Evaluation, this could confirm – with this behavior being widespread among ordinary consumers and as being a form of social sharing or exchange – that this phenomenon is considered *not* to be wrong. By contrast, scenario 5 (taking a towel away from a hotel) is an act done surreptitiously in the privacy of one's own hotel room. In this case it is a lone act, which arguably is less likely to be discussed publicly. With software piracy, on the other hand, consumers are exposed to an environment where many other consumers conduct software piracy and subsequently learn to follow others' behavior in this respect.

The means of the factor Consequence were statistically different between scenario 2 and scenarios 4 and 5. The negative means for scenario 2 (returning a stained suit) can be interpreted as consumers recognizing possible loss to retailers (e.g. losses of sales and possibly sellable products) and other consumers (e.g. retailers may recover such losses by raising a price). However, the positive means for scenarios 4 and 5 may be more complex. In fact, in line with qualitative data from an exploratory investigation conducted as part of the current study, there is a perception that such behaviors can result in beneficial outcomes to both other consumers and suppliers. It is suggested, for example, that software piracy can help encourage competition over price as well as potentially discourage large multinational companies from operating within monopolies. With respect to taking amenities from hotels and restaurants, this behavior can be thought to function as a form of promotion, since hotels and restaurants often mark their amenities.

Overall, the findings of the current study show that consumer intention of aberrant behavior can be expected to differ according to situations. While consumers present ethical concerns toward various issues in the form of negative evaluation, more than a few consumers demonstrated their willingness to engage in some forms of aberrant behavior. Clearly, consumers are not simply accepting something static as 'unethical' and their behaviors are not even restricted to isolated benefits provided by the illegitimacy of some of the behaviors. In a similar fashion, Carrigan and Attalla (2001) record changeable and fluid consumer ethics within their study on consumer attitudes toward ethical marketing. Despite Nike's 'ethically questionable' engagement with child labor in developing countries, their respondents appeared to continue buying its products. In Carrigan and Attalla's study one of their respondents remarks: 'it is exploitation, but without companies such as Nike, they wouldn't have a job at all' (Carrigan & Attalla, 2001, p. 568). Consumers are proposing-in some cases proactively different standards of ethics and social responsibility and indeed the ethics of consumers can be dramatically changed, depending on the perspectives of individual consumers. Inevitably, with such fluidity in ethical values and behaviors, it is difficult to reach any definitive categorization of the decision-making process of ACB. However, one factor of specific interest to the current study is Perceived Unfairness, which as will be considered in the closing discussion, may provide at least some more tangible insight or talking point against which some practical measures may be taken by individual firms or industries.

The current analysis – following ANOVA – has focused on how factors play distinctive roles across the scenarios. However, in addition to this analysis, t-test was conducted for scenarios 3 and 4 (scenarios 1, 2 and 5 were left out of this test due to the small number of respondents who reported their intention to engage in these behaviors). The purpose of the t-test, which compared those likely to engage in the behavior with those who considered that they were unlikely to engage in the behavior, is that it enables the focus to be placed on a single scenario and examine the extent to which each of the four factors differ across the two groups of respondents (specific to the particular scenario). The result of t-test showed the following: In the case of exaggerating an insurance claim (i.e. scenario 3: Table 4) Evaluation was significantly higher for those intending to engage in the behavior, while Perceived Unfairness demonstrated even greater significance. For this scenario, the means of Perceived Unfairness of the intention group is 1.20 and significantly differed from the non-intention group (the means, 0.06, $p < 0.001$). In addition, Consequence was significantly different between the two groups. Finally, it can be noted Social Participation did not appear to differ across the two groups. In the case of software piracy (i.e. scenario 4: Table 5) positive Evaluation related to an increase in intention to engage in the behavior. It was also apparent that a positive weighting of Social Participation and Perceived Unfairness added significantly to the justification to perform this act. For this scenario, the means of Perceived Unfairness of the intention group is 0.40 and again significantly differed from the non-intention group (the means = –0.35, $p < 0.001$).

As noted in the literature review, previous studies have forwarded the idea that 'consumer traits and disposition' such as positive attitude and social influence (Fullerton & Punj, 1993) do have impact on the occurrence of ACB and our findings are certainly concurrent with such previous studies (i.e. highlighting the strength of importance of Evaluation and Consequence in insurance fraud; and Evaluation, Social Participation and Consequence in software piracy). However, the current study also draws specific attention to the factor Perceived Unfairness which generally has attracted relatively less research interest. The results of *t*-test suggest that the manner in which respondents are perceived to be related to and treated by businesses (i.e.

Table 4. Mean Factor Score of Intention to Engage versus Non-Intention to Engage.

Scenario 3: Exaggerating an Insurance Claim	Intent to Engage in EQB ($n = 42$)	Non-intent to Engage EQB ($n = 163$)	*T*-statistics	Sig.
Evaluation	1.07	–0.20	–10.21	$p < 0.001$
Perceived unfairness	1.20	0.06	–7.06	$p < 0.001$
Social participation	0.18	–0.01	–1.12	ns.
Consequence	0.25	–0.20	–2.72	$p < 0.001$

Note: Equal variances not assumed; ns. = not significant.

Table 5. Mean Factor Score of Intention to Engage versus Non-
Intention to Engage.

Scenario 4: Coping a Software from a Friend	Intent to Engage in EQB ($n = 101$)	Non-intent to Engage EQB ($n = 71$)	T-statistics	Sig.
Evaluation	1.78	0.31	−11.98	$p < 0.001$
Perceived unfairness	0.40	−0.35	−4.47	$p < 0.001$
Social participation	0.43	−0.14	−3.77	$p < 0.001$
Consequence	0.27	0.04	−1.62	ns.

Note: Equal variances not assumed; ns. = not significant.

Perceived Unfairness) also significantly influences whether or not respondents are inclined to engage in the aberrant behavior in question. In other words, this is to say that the relationship between consumers and businesses – at least in specific contexts – should be recognized as playing a distinctive role in forming intention to engage in ACB. While individual perceptions concerning specific ethical issues and ideals may be difficult for firms to understand or indeed influence, the findings concerning Perceived Unfairness is encouraging in that this is something that can be dealt with or examined further by firms themselves, so helping themselves to tackle the negative impact of ACB. Potentially, then, firms' direct channels keeping them in touch with consumers through their marketing activities are highly significant in how the problems of ACB can be addressed. The later part of the following discussion will focus on this specific matter and consider some key practical possibilities for firms.

DISCUSSION

The current study is exploratory in nature and therefore is to be understood as an initial stage in a longer process of theoretical development. It is also important to note that the current sample only relates to UK consumers. In light of which, further research is necessary, only then might it be appropriate to generalize the findings in order to provide practical guidelines for business practitioners and policy makers. However, it is useful at this stage to discuss some more specific issues for those who deal with the impact of ACB on a daily basis.

Fullerton and Punj (2004) suggest that there are two common approaches to tackle ACB: education and deterrence. As has been shown, the current study found that Evaluation toward ethical issues has a significant impact on consumer intention to engage in aberrant behavior. In such circumstance, education may indeed have an impact in raising consumer intolerance toward these types of behavior, as for example represented in this study by scenario 1 (changing a price tag) and scenario 2 (returning a stained suit). Furthermore, where there are already signs of a negative evaluation to engage in ACB, education is likely to help reinforce and/or deepen such a view. However, even if consumers negatively evaluate a situation, where the current study has observed the importance of Consequence (i.e. with scenario 5, taking a towel from a hotel), the more spontaneous, opportunistic kinds of engagement in ACB are less likely to be prohibited by education. In this case, then, deterrence is more likely to be an effective approach. More specifically, in the case of towels being 'taken away' from a hotel, one tactic is to make a clear statement to the effect that the item can be *purchased* as a souvenir, thus, as a form of reverse psychology, highlighting the fact that the item is known by the hotel to be of value to the consumer. In other words, offering a price for the item establishes more clearly that 'taking' it away from the hotel does indeed constitute stealing it.

Of course, in most cases, education and deterrence will be applied in combination. This is likely to be necessary, for example, where Social Participation is shown to be of significance to an intention to engage in ACB. In the current study software piracy (represented in scenario 4, copying a software from a friend) not only showed signs of positive evaluation toward the behavior, but also was found to be influenced by blatant opportunism in combination with a clear sense of social participation (i.e. 'everyone is doing it'). Thus, in this case, neither education nor deterrence on their own are likely to be effective. Instead a combined approach is necessary. Widespread education needs to be achieved in order particularly to raise awareness about intellectual property and the harm that results in piracy, not only to firms and individual (author) copyright holders, but also to the consumers themselves (e.g. jeopardizing the opportunity to benefit from future development of desired goods, and the potential for inflated prices to cover losses). Ultimately there is a need, from such education, to develop a greater sense of ethical belief. In parallel, deterrence is needed not only in a straightforward sense to police behavior, but also to provide a constant reminder (and so reinforce the education) that software piracy is unethical and indeed illegal. Such a combined method may eventually break the 'friendly' and informal economy of software piracy. The recent high-profile cases in which 'ordinary' individual consumers have been prosecuted by the large music companies, after allegedly having illegally download music from the internet, makes for an interesting new trend in measures to curb piracy.[6]

However, a more particular argument that can be made following this current study is that an effective approach to tackle behavior influenced by Perceived Unfairness is likely to need to go beyond the approaches of either education or deterrence, or even their combination. Instead there is a definite need to integrate ethical concern with specific corporate strategy. What is clear from the findings of the current study is that some respondents have negative perceptions about particular industries, in this case the insurance industry, as represented by scenario 3 (i.e. insurance claim exaggeration). While it is not necessarily discernable whether consumer perception here are based on personal experiences or on hearsay and/or stories of victims of common 'aggressive' marketing tactics, it is certainly the case that this scenario prompted a very different set of results to any of the other four projected scenarios. What is apparent with responses to exaggerating an insurance claim is that this behavior is clearly motivated by perception of unfair business practice. Furthermore, if assuming the interrelation of a negative reading for the factor Consequence, respondents in this case are clearly aware that such behavior would result in harm to companies (and, interestingly, other consumers too). Although tentative at this stage, it is suggestible that the potential to redress a perceived unfairness is directly related to retaliatory or ACB. This is a good example of where it is important to understand the interrelationship between factors (in this case between Consequence and Perceived Unfairness) in order to make sense of the behavior in question. In fact, it might even be said that it is the interaction of factors that constitutes the behavior. Again, it should be noted that it is difficult to determine on what basis consumers and potential consumers adjudge their perceptions of companies and whole industries (certainly this is an area ripe for further research). However, what would seem paramount is to take a more strategic view of the problem of perceived unfairness. Outlined below are three main themes through which this might be considered: strategic communication, marketing tactics and customer-business relations. In each case, the point is to reduce the number of opportunities for customers to develop negative perceptions of companies or industries, whether that is through personal experiences or other vicarious means.

For all firms strategic communication is important in tackling perceptions of unfairness held by consumers. However, for large size firms and indeed specific industries as a whole it is perhaps most crucial (it is also a notable concern for those firms which explicitly position themselves as being 'ethical' businesses). Where some industries such as insurance and software industries appear to be more prone to the effects of ACB, these companies may seek to co-operate to improve consumer perception of the industry as a whole. Such an approach can, in part, be seen to have existed for many years with the music recording industry, particularly due to the ubiquity of home-recording. Early industry-led campaigns sought to educate its market, highlighting not only that piracy (even on a domestic level) was illegal, but that it had a direct impact on the development of products – messages such as 'Home recording kills ...' became a standard industry label. Of course, in our present digital and highly synergized environment, such a campaign is now largely out of date. Nonetheless, fundamentally, the problems which beset firms in this industry remain much the same. Companies are likely to need to continue to send out the message that prices may be forced to rise if a minority choose to abuse the process by illegally acquiring software for example. However, such a strategy, which seeks to encourage consumers to be responsible for their own practices, can really only work if the companies themselves can demonstrate their own sense of responsibility. One particular problem in the music industry is that, as Chiou, Huang, and Lee (2005, p. 170) note, '[e]xcessive publicity regarding the exorbitant income of pop singers can only direct consumers to think that the company and the musicians enjoy unreasonable profits and that minor infringement of copyright is acceptable to this wealthy group'. Thus, in these circumstances, it may be ever more important to offer greater transparency to its customers, relating, in this case, the costs and incurring costs of developing and 'manufacturing' software.

Businesses within certain sectors of the economy need to maintain awareness of how consumers perceive the image of the industry as a whole. One concern is that consumers might rarely assess the fairness of the company based on detailed information, but on the vague image of the company or business. Thus, as well as approaching the question of how fairly the company is actually performing, it may be equally important to understand how and to what extent consumer decision-making is influenced by the image and reputation of a company (and not least whether a positive image has greater impact than that of a negative image, or vice versa). As the current findings might suggest, large companies are still frequently perceived as faceless global enterprises for which many consumers have little sympathy. Furthermore, the companies' efforts to try and stop negative perceptions of business have been received cynically by consumers; something which has generally been reinforced with the notable rise in and general acceptance of an anti-globalization protest discourse (cf. Klein, 2000; also more recently with the high-profile 'Make Poverty History' campaign).

Thus, the emergence and managerial use of corporate citizenship and social responsibility as a means for firms promoting both business and consumer ethics may not be entirely effective, or desirable. Skeptical consumers are likely to view such ethical rhetoric as only paying lip service to genuine ethical concerns. In other words, many consumers are unlikely to be receptive to firms' orientations to what is right or wrong when in the first instance they perceive those firms to be not acting fairly. However, rather than simply view this phenomenon pessimistically, it might best be taken as an opportunity to (re-)visit and examine the fairness of corporate conduct. If the relationship between businesses and consumers are causing consumer aberrant behavior, it is perhaps worth examining the nature of the relationship in terms of its communications. In general practical terms, companies can certainly be seen to counter problems by establishing more direct lines of communication with consumers; for instance, providing the means and using technologies (e.g. the Internet) to give customers more opportunity to give feedback. Alternatively, several companies may work together to develop an effective network with sales agents to ensure a sophisticated and dedicated level of customer care and feedback channels. In this way, companies are perhaps able to moderate the impact of being only 'faceless' enterprises. However, in a more complex way, it has to be noted that a corporation's identity is never a single unitary thing, but rather like an individual's subjectivity, is multiple and layered. Balmer and Greyser (2002) identify at least five key types or instances of corporate identity (these differ, for example, depending on whether they are internally or externally manifest, and whether actual, communicated, ideal or predicted); where these identities misalign or fall short the possibilities for consumers to develop misconstrued perceptions toward a corporation increase, which in turn may be the cause of negative perceptions since consumers may feel let down by the company (their expectations no longer meet with their experiences).

At a more fundamental level still there are perhaps serious questions to be asked about the very purpose and mission of a company and its practice. Interestingly, the recent growth in what are termed 'authentic businesses' (Croft, 2005), in which the purpose of a firm is to go beyond simply making profit and instead seek more profound (social and environmental) goals, have shown clear signs not only of communicating well with their customer base, but also of achieving well in financial terms. Finally, however, it is worth noting that where companies assert an increase in commitment to high levels of ethical conduct it generally leads to those companies having 'high expectations of themselves and, by extension, expectations of other firms' (McAlister & Ferrell, 2002, p. 695). Inevitably, then, businesses are ever more concerned with developing successful exchanges with their customers, which in turn, means that ethical dimensions in the business–customer relationship require ever greater attention.

Marketing tactics can also be thought to play a significant role in reducing the propensity of ACB; and this may be as straightforward as examining and revising product offerings and pricing structures. Hotels and restaurants, for example, in order to reduce low-level theft may distinguish the amenities that can be retained by their customers from those which cannot. A simple sign such as 'please take if you like' or 'help yourself' on certain items may be helpful in at least two ways: Not only do customers become aware of goods that are not deemed to be free, but they are also offered other possible souvenirs which may please them. Such a promotional tactic is not just about providing extra benefit to the customer, but equally establishes a tangible or even material means of maintaining the customer–business relationship.

Price is another important issue relating to a consumer's perception of fairness. The relationship between price and product/service attributes (including how price adequately and meaningfully reflects what is on offer) will affect a consumer's willingness to pay for a good. Furthermore, as Ajzen, Brown, and Rosenthal (1996) have shown, willingness to pay for a good can be directly influenced by information given that makes a strong case for the value of that good. Where this flow of information breaks down it is reasonable to suggest there arises greater potential for increased perception of unfairness. As Campbell's (1999) study has argued, where price increases occur, consumer evaluation of price unfairness can be negatively influenced by an inferred and/or misconstrued motive for a price increase; where, for example, the price increase is thought simply to be maximizing firms' profits. Furthermore, as Campbell goes on to explain, the bad reputation of firms can indirectly lead such negative perception. What is apparent from the respondents' remarks in Campbell's study is how consumers are undoubtedly conscious about pricing and profits. Thus, it is reasonable to surmise that consumers may evaluate not only the price of products but also past performance of firms when considering fair pricing. In other words, whether consumers accept a price as fair this might not simply depend on the market offering, but equally be influenced by an overall evaluation of the firm's ethical standing and conduct in the marketplace. One particular problem for the insurance industry, specifically with regards to motor insurance, is that 'honest' customers who pay out for their insurance cover year on year, can hold the view that prices (and price increases) are set in order to subsidize deviant consumers (or even non-policy holders) who otherwise cost the industry hugely. In this case, in order to maintain trust, companies need to consider how they can make pricing structures fair and transparent to their customers. Interestingly, in the UK, the insurance firm Direct Line have run a television advertising campaign which as good as makes a virtue out of this problem. As part of their product offering Direct Line have put great emphasis upon the fact ('unlike many other insurers') that even if you are involved in an accident with a vehicle that is not covered by an insurance policy (i.e. an illegally driven vehicle), they will still uphold the claim in full. The advertisement does not put an emphasis on actual price premiums, but arguably the promotion of a 'fair' product (what you pay for is what you get), is likely to have a positive impact on prospective customers.

Of course, where there are less 'tangible' value aspects to a product or service, consumers have less they can grasp when attempting to evaluate the fairness of price. This can have a great impact on insurance firms for example, since their product is difficult to put a value upon, especially given that theirs is a product that customers generally hope they never actually have to use or 'claim'. Interestingly a recent high-profile advertising campaign by a UK insurance firm, Norwich Union, has centered around the slogan 'Quote me Happy' – the idea being that if you approach the company for their product you will be very happy to find you get a cheaper quote than if you had gone elsewhere. The advertisement also connotes a clear sense of service satisfaction, with prospective customers being shown telephoning for a 'happy quote' in a very relaxed, informal and, as one version of the advertisement puts it, 'over-excited' manner (comparison might well be made with the kinds of advertisements run from time to time by fast food outlets where customers are invited to go up to cashiers in-store and ask for their product in a humorous fashion in order to benefit from a promotion of some kind). The Norwich Union advertising effectively embeds an emotional element to the packaging of their product offering, which combines with a specific message about low price. This is likely to be an effective means of linking a consumer's sense of value for a product with a perception of fairness – indeed, in this case, customers are not only being treated well, they are being 'quoted happy'! However, this tactic is arguably quite risky, since should there be any downfall in the level of the price and/or the quality of its service delivery there is likely to accrue a high level of dissatisfaction and sense of injustice. Reflecting on this point, it is interesting to note a study by Homburg, Koschate, and Hoyer (2005), in which it is demonstrated that longer-term cumulative satisfaction is more strongly related to a willingness to pay than transaction-specific satisfaction. Central to this study is really a point about equity theory, the idea that cumulative satisfaction is a genuine means for exchanging parties to perceive the quality of equitable treatment, i.e. it is only over a period of time and as a result of *more than one* instance of exchange that the ratio of outcome to inputs can be assessed to fair, or just distributed. The implication is that – in terms of maintaining positive perceptions of fairness – it is more important to maintain customer-business relations, than simply trade on ethical concerns.

Relationship management poses certain difficulties with respect to ethical issues, and this perhaps particularly the case for larger firms or where the balance between customer and business is seen to be out of kilter. As Fitchett and McDonagh (2000, p. 218) put it, the discourse of relationship management 'does not travel well into situations where the relative resources, power bases and interests of both parties vary considerably'. Taking this point on board, O'Malley and Prothero (2004) highlight how consumers are often cynical of relational strategies, taking the view that the representation of individuals is not necessarily improved and/or that strategies are really only designed to aid a company's pursuit of profits. Furthermore, larger companies are frequently distrusted in this respect. A common sentiment expressed, for example, is that '[w]hen anything goes wrong all these bigger organizations get very impersonal ... if ever you have a problem nobody wants to know' (Stafford cited in O'Malley & Prothero, 2004, p. 1291). Furthermore, findings by Hagner, Randall, and Geoghegan (1996) support the assertion that consumer evaluations of ethical scenarios are influenced by personal preferences and so differ according to the subject being evaluated. Thus, with respect to the retail setting, indications are that consumer evaluations are not always rational but influenced by consumer preferences for or against the people they are dealing with in the shop. Extending from this line of argument, it might well be expected that consumer evaluations of fairness of market performance can also vary according to preferences.

As a practical measure, retailers must surely seek to further emphasize (and in cases re-orientate) the training of front-line staff. Misleading information and lack of knowledge of in-store staff can cost customers time and effort, and certainly does not aid customer relations, which in turn does make for a particularly positive image of the businesses overall. In some cases the effects of poorly trained staff may not simply be perceived as unhelpful and inadequate, but even as being unfair (McIntyre, Thomas, & Gilbert, 1999). Thus, the improvement in the performance of in-store staff may not just positively aid the building of good relations between staff and customers, but also work toward a more *reliable* partnership between consumer and producer/retailer, i.e. helping naturally discourage customer behavior that might be deceptive and damaging. The literature on service marketing often labels customers who misbehave as 'jaycustomers' (meaning those customers who deviate from acceptable, legal patterns in consumption). Yet, when one considers what might be causing such behavior, it may more often turn out to relate to the behavior of ill-trained staff or poor practices (as it were, 'jay-business'!), in other words due to the failure of marketing implementation (see, for example, Lovelock and Wirtz's (2004, p. 253) note on the 'belligerent' consumer). One study (Smith, 2004, p. 57) of a UK insurance firm reports that when the firm reviewed its claim process, the number of claims were halved after dedicated support was provided to claimants (a theoretical proposition echoing this finding is asserted by Fullerton & Punj, 1993, p. 572). Furthermore, this new practice was implemented without decrease in the firm's customer satisfaction rate. Customers, then, may just want help from firms! Evidently, employees' lack of knowledge and impersonal procedures were just not helping. This particular course of remedial action by a UK insurance firm – which no doubt involved both additional training and staffing costs – may initially sound labor intensive and prohibitively expensive. Nevertheless, with the estimated 1–2 billion loss of potential revenue annually to the UK insurance industry, one must wonder which is more profitable, ignoring insurance claim fraud or training front staff.

CONCLUDING REMARKS

Of course many of the above observations noted for dealing with ACB, in terms which can go beyond simply education and deterrence, can already seen to be in operation in various exchange settings. However, what an enquiry such as this can at least do is refocus our attention on the understanding that lies behind such strategies and principles and so help make further sense of how business ethics in the marketplace translates in terms of marketing practice and in particular with respect to the different qualities the different exchange settings bring about.

As with any such study there is much that can continue to be explored. The growing importance of a number of nascent research interests have been suggested or at least inferred by much that has been discussed above. Key areas of interest include, for example, relationship management and the connection between corporate social responsibly and corporate identity. In seeking to pursue further theoretical advancement in these areas it is surely necessary that consumers be taken account of more fully with respect to their importance as stakeholders. Of course, as it stands, the current study obviously bears more specific or technical limitations which could be tackled in further research. The sample is restricted to UK consumers and the dataset did display some biases, most notably toward the older age groups.

Although the sample was carefully selected to obtain a wide range of consumers, further validation and development with groupings making up an accurate representation of the population of consumers would be desirable. A further limitation might be noted here with respect to the scales for measuring ACB. Ultimately, in order – as is the interest here – to capture the multidimensionality of attributes, it is likely that there is a need to re-visit measurement issues for improved accuracy in future studies.

As a final remark, it is worth stressing that when considering ethical issues in the marketplace, there is evidently a danger in placing too much attention upon only the ethicality of business, or as it were the business of ethics. At best, this can mean missing the importance of the consumer and their interaction with businesses. At worst, this can lead to the myth and precept of a reified consumer: the pervasive doctrine of the consumer as always being right (i.e. 'ethical'). Instead, incorporating more fully a consumer ethics within business ethics can help develop a more balanced and dynamic view of the 'practice' of ethics in the marketplace. Thus, acknowledging how exchange settings are in fact constituted and supported by consumers, businesses and other parties of a society is then important in wanting to understand more fully not only how one action (from these different participants) impacts on the other, but also what effects these interactions have either increasing or decreasing ethical standards in the marketplace.

NOTES

1. Source: National Insurance Crime Bureau, *Materials and Publications*, available online http://www.nicb.org/public/publications/index.cfm, accessed on 5/09/05.
2. Source: Pressbox.co.uk, '$79 Million Counterfeited Worldwide in October!' (2004), available online http://www.pressbox.co.uk/Detailed/20154.html, accessed on 12/08/05.
3. Consumer environmental behavior, Pelletier, Dion, Tuson, and Green-Demers (1999) and Harland, Staats, and Wilke (1999); Wastepaper recycling, Cheung, Chan, and Wong (1999); Software piracy, Chang (1998); Cheating and lying, Beck and Ajzen (1991); Medical profession, Randall and Gibson (1991); Ethical Consumers – Shaw and Clarke (1999) and Shaw, Shiu, and Clarke (2001).
4. The model of Consumer Ethical Dilemmas (Marks & Mayo, 1991) is based on the general theory of marketing ethics (Hunt & Vitell, 1986); the latter based on TRA (which is subsequently extended as TPB).
5. It should be assumed that the size of the groups analyzed is approximately equal. The largest group size divided by the smallest ought to be less than 1.5 (Hair et al., 1998, p. 348). In the current study, it is 1.18.
6. See: *Guardian*, 'Parents count the cost of free music' (25/06/05), available online http://www.guardian.co.uk/uk_news/story/0,,1514148,00.html, accessed on 6/09/05; and

Guardian, 'Music industry cheered by sinking of pirates' (20/06/05), available online http://www.guardian.co.uk/business/story/0,,1510057,00.html, accessed on 6/09/05.

REFERENCES

Ajzen, I. (1985). From intentions and actions: A theory of planned behavior. In: J. Kuhland & J. Beckman (Eds), *Action-control: From cognitions to behavior* (pp. 11–39). Heidelberg: Spring Verlag.

Ajzen, I. (1991). The theory of planned behavior. *Organizational Behavior & Human Decision Processes, 50,* 179–211.

Ajzen, I., Brown, T. C., & Rosenthal, L. H. (1996). Information bias in contingent valuation: Effects of personal relevance, quality of information, and motivational orientation. *Journal of Environmental Economics and Management, 30,* 43–57.

Ajzen, I., & Fishbein, M. (1980). *Understanding attitudes and predicting social behavior.* Englewood Cliffs, NJ: Prentice Hall.

Albers-Miller, N. D. (1999). Consumer misbehavior: Why people buy illicit goods. *Journal of Consumer Marketing, 16*(3), 273–287.

Alexander, E. C. (2002). Consumer reactions to unethical service recovery. *Journal of Business Ethics, 36,* 223–237.

Al-Jabri, I., & Abdul-Gader, A. (1997). Software copyright infringements: An exploratory study of the effects of individual and peer beliefs. *Omega-International Journal of Management Science, 25*(3), 335–344.

Babin, B. J., & Griffin, M. (1995). A closer look at the influence of age on consumer ethics. *Advances in Consumer Research, 22,* 668–673.

Balmer, J. M. T., & Greyser, S. A. (2002). Managing the multiple identities of the corporation. *California Management Review, 44*(3), 72–86.

Beck, L., & Ajzen, I. (1991). Predicting dishonest action using the theory of planned behavior. *Journal of Research in Personality, 25,* 285–301.

Bhattacherjee, A. (2000). Acceptance of E-commerce services: The case of electronic brokerages. *IEEE Transactions on Systems, Man, and Cybernetics – Part A: Systems and Humans, 30*(4), 411–419.

Borna, S., & Stearns, J. M. (1998). The philosopher is not always right: A comment on "the customer is not always right". *Journal of Business Ethics, 17,* 39–44.

British Retail Consortium. (2004). 11th Annual Retail Crime Survey 2003.

Business Software Alliance. (2005). Second Annual BSA and IDC Global Software: Piracy Study.

Campbell, M. C. (1999). Perceptions of price unfairness: Antecedents and consequences. *Journal of Marketing Research, 36,* 187–199.

Carrigan, M., & Attalla, A. (2001). The myth of the ethical consumer – do ethics matter in purchase behavior? *Journal of Consumer Marketing, 18*(7), 560–577.

Chakraborty, G., Allred, A., Sukhdial, A. S., & Bristol, T. (1997). Use of negative cues to reduce demand for counterfeit products. *Advances in Consumer Research, 24,* 345–349.

Chang, M. K. (1998). Predicting unethical behavior: A comparison of the theory of reasoned action and the theory of planned behavior. *Journal of Business Ethics, 17,* 1825–1834.

Cheung, S. F., Chan, D. K.-S., & Wong, Z. S.-Y. (1999). Reexamining the theory of planned behavior in understanding wastepaper recycling. *Environment and Behavior, 31*(5), 587–612.

Chiou, J.-S., Huang, C.-Y., & Lee, H.-H. (2005). The antecedents of music piracy attitudes and intentions. *Journal of Business Ethics, 57,* 161–174.

Cordell, V. W., Wongtada, N., & Kieschnick, R. L., Jr. (1996). Counterfeit purchase intentions: Roles of lawfulness attitudes and product traits as determinants. *Journal of Business Research, 35,* 41–53.

Cox, D., Cox, A. D., & Moschis, G. P. (1990). When consumer behavior goes bad: An investigation of adolescent shoplifting. *Journal of Consumer Research, 17,* 149–159.

Croft, N. (2005). *Authentic businesses: How to create and run your perfect business.* Chichester: Capstone Publishing Limited.

Cummins, J. D., & Tenneyson, S. (1996). Moral hazard in insurance claiming: Evidence from automobile insurance. *Journal of Risk and Uncertainty, 12,* 29–50.

Day, J. (2005). Fraud: Stage fright. *Insurance Brokers' Monthly and Insurance Adviser, 55*(7), 16.

Fitchett, J. A., & McDonagh, P. (2000). A citizen's critique of relationship marketing in risk society. *Journal of Strategic Marketing, 8,* 209–222.

Fukukawa, K. (2002). Developing a framework for ethically questionable behavior in consumption. *Journal of Business Ethics, 41*(2), 99–119.

Fullerton, R. A., & Punj, G. (1993). Choosing to misbehave: A structural model of aberrant consumer behavior. *Advances in Consumer Research, 20,* 570–574.

Fullerton, R. A., & Punj, G. (2004). Repercussions of promoting an ideology of consumption: Consumer misbehavior. *Journal of Business Research, 57,* 1239–1249.

Gattiker, U. E., & Kelley, H. (1999). Morality and computers: Attitudes and differences in moral judgments. *Information Systems Research, 10*(3), 233–254.

Grass, R. S., & Wood, W. A. (1996). Situational determinants of software piracy: An equity theory perspective. *Journal of Business Ethics, 15,* 1189–1198.

Gronroos, C. (1997). From marketing mix to relationship marketing towards a paradigm shift in marketing. *Management Decision, 35*(3/4), 322–340.

Hagner, P. R., Randall, D. M., & Geoghegan, C. (1996). Context effects in ethical evaluations: An experimental study. *Social Behaviour and Personality, 24*(3), 279–292.

Hair, J. F., Anderson, R. E., Tatham, R. L., & Black, W. C. (1998). *Multivariate data analysis* (5th ed.). London: Prentice-Hall International, Inc.

Harland, P., Staats, J., & Wilke, H. A. M. (1999). Explaining proenvironmental intention and behavior by personal norms and the theory of planned behavior. *Journal of Applied Social Psychology, 28*(12), 2505–2528.

Harrington, S. J. (1997). A test of a person – issue contingent model of ethical decision making in organizations. *Journal of Business Ethics, 16,* 363–375.

Hinkin, T. R., Tracey, J. B., & Enz, C. A. (1997). Scale construction: Developing reliable and valid measurement instruments. *Journal of Hospitality & Tourism Research, 21*(1), 100–119.

Homburg, C., Koschate, N., & Hoyer, W. D. (2005). Do satisfied customers really pay more? A study of the relationship between customer satisfaction and willingness to pay. *Journal of Marketing, 69,* 84–96.

Hunt, S. D., & Chonko, L. B. (1984). Marketing and machiavellianism. *Journal of Marketing, 48*(3), 30–42.

Hunt, S. D., & Vitell, S. J. (1986). A general theory of marketing ethics. *Journal of Macromarketing, 6,* 6–15.

Husted, B. W. (2000). The impact of national culture on software piracy. *Journal of Business Ethics, 26,* 197–211.

216 KYOKO FUKUKAWA ET AL.

Klein, N. (2000). *No logo*. London: HarperCollins Publishers Ltd.

Klobas, J. E., & Clyde, L. A. (2000). Adults learning to use the internet: A longitudinal study of attitude and other factors associated with intended internet use. *Library & Information Science Research, 22*(1), 5–34.

Krasnovsky, T., & Lane, R. C. (1998). Shoplifting: A review of the literature. *Aggression and Violent Behavior, 3*(3), 219–235.

Litton, R. (1998). Fraud and the insurance industry: Why don't they do something about it, then? *International Journal of Risk, Security and Crime Prevention*, 193–205.

Lovelock, C., & Wirtz, J. (2004). *Services marketing: People, technology, strategy, international edition* (5th ed.). Upper Saddle River, NJ: Pearson Prentice Hall.

Marks, L. J., & Mayo, M. A. (1991). An empirical test of a model of consumer ethical dilemmas. *Advances in Consumer Research, 18*, 720–728.

McAlister, D. T., & Ferrell, L. (2002). The role of strategic philanthropy in marketing strategy. *European Journal of Marketing, 36*(5/6), 689–705.

McIntyre, F. S., Thomas, J. L., Jr., & Gilbert, F. W. (1999). Consumer segments and perceptions of retail ethics. *Journal of Marketing Theory and Practice, 7*(2), 43–53.

Miniard, P. W., & Cohen, J. B. (1981). An examination of the Fishbein–Ajzen behavioral intentions model's concepts and measures. *Journal of Experimental Social Psychology, 17*, 309–339.

Mitchell, V.-W., & Chan, J. K. L. (2002). 'Investigating UK Consumers' unethical attitudes and behaviors. *Journal of Marketing Management, 18*, 5–26.

Morgan, R., & Hunt, S. (1994). The commitment-trust theory of relationship marketing. *Journal of Marketing, 58*(3), 20–38.

Muncy, J. A., & Vitell, S. J. (1992). Consumer ethics: An investigation of ethical beliefs of the final consumer. *Journal of Business Research, 24*, 297–311.

O'Malley, L., & Prothero, A. (2004). Beyond the frills of relationship marketing. *Journal of Business Research, 57*, 1286–1294.

Paulhus, D. L. (1991). *Paulhus deception scales (PDS): The balanced inventory of desirable responding-7, user's manual*. Toronto Ontario, Canada: Multi-Health Systems Inc.

Pava, M. L., Pava, J., & Hochman, J. (1999). Fairness as a constraint in the real estate market. *Journal of Business Ethics, 19*, 91–97.

Pelletier, L. G., Dion, S., Tuson, K., & Green-Demers, I. (1999). Why do people fail to adopt environmental prospective behaviors? Toward a taxonomy of environmental amotivation. *Journal of Applied Social Psychology, 29*(12), 2481–2504.

Piron, F., & Young, M. (2001). Retail borrowing: Definition and retailing implications. *Journal of Retailing and Consumer Services, 8*, 121–125.

Porter, M. E., & Kramer, M. R. (2002). The competitive advantage of corporate philanthropy. *Harvard Business Review, 80*(12), 56–68.

Randall, D. M., & Gibson, A. M. (1991). Ethical decision making in the medical profession: An application of the theory of planned behavior. *Journal of Business Ethics, 10*, 111–122.

Román, S., & Ruiz, S. (2005). Relationship outcomes of perceived ethical sales behavior: The customer's perspective. *Journal of Business Research, 58*, 439–445.

Seligman, D. A., & Schwartz, B. (1997). Domain specificity of fairness judgments in economics transactions. *Journal of Economic Psychology, 18*, 579–604.

Shaw, D., & Clarke, I. (1999). Belief formation in ethical consumer groups: An exploratory study. *Marketing Intelligence & Planning, 17*(2), 109–119.

Shaw, D., Shiu, E., & Clarke, I. (2001). The contribution of ethical obligation of self-identity to the theory of planned behavior: An exploration of ethical consumers. *Journal of Marketing Management, 16,* 879–894.

Singhapakdi, A., Vitell, S. J., & Kraft, K. L. (1996). Moral intensity and ethical decision-making of marketing professionals. *Journal of Business Research, 36,* 245–255.

Smith, G. (2004). Combating fraud with quality. *Canadian Underwriter, 71*(9), 52–59.

Strutton, D., Pelton, L. E., & Ferrell, O. C. (1997). Ethical behavior in retail settings: Is there a generation gap? *Journal of Business Ethics, 16,* 87–105.

Strutton, D., Vitell, S. J., & Pelton, L. E. (1994). How consumers may justify inappropriate behavior in market settings: An application on the techniques of neutralization. *Journal of Business Research, 30,* 253–260.

Taylor, G. S., & Shim, J. P. (1993). A comparative examination of attitudes toward software piracy among business professors and executives. *Human Relations, 46*(4), 419–433.

Tennyson, S. (1997). Economic institutions and individual ethics: A study of consumer attitudes toward insurance fraud. *Journal of Economic Behavior and Organization, 32,* 247–265.

Tom, G., Garibaldi, B., Zeng, Y., & Pilcher, J. (1998). Consumer demand for counterfeit goods. *Psychology & Marketing, 15*(5), 405–421.

Vitell, J. S. (2003). Consumer ethics research: Review, synthesis and suggestions for the future. *Journal of Business Ethics, 43*(1/2), 33–47.

Wagner, S. C., & Sanders, G. L. (2001). Considerations in ethical decision-making and software piracy. *Journal of Business Ethics, 29,* 161–167.

Wilkes, R. E. (1978). Fraudulent behavior by consumers. *Journal of Marketing, 42*(4), 67–75.

APPENDIX 1. SCENARIOS

Scenario Label	Description
Scenario 1: changing a price tag	A customer notices that certain prices have been lowered in a retail store by crossing out the old price and writing the new price in red ink. The customer has a red pen, so simply crosses out the old price and makes reductions on a few of products she/he wishes to buy. She/he then pays the lower price
Scenario 2: returning the stained suit	A person buys a new suit on Friday to wear for an important party on Saturday. At the party, the suit gets stained with traces of food and perspiration. On Monday, the person returns the suit to the retail store and demands a refund, claiming the suit was not suitable after all

Scenario 3: exaggerating an insurance claim	While on holiday, Sam accidentally dropped a camera worth £100 down a cliff. On return, Sam makes an insurance claim, but gives the value of the lost camera as £200
Scenario 4: coping software from a friend	Chris buys a new computer but chooses not to purchase extra game software priced £50 from the computer shop. Chris then copies the game software from a friend
Scenario 5: taking a quality towel away from a hotel	Sarah/Simon goes on a trip and stays in a hotel. She/he finds a quality towel in her/his room, and thinks it would make nice souvenir. When checking out, she/he takes the towel away with her/him

APPENDIX 2. MEASUREMENTS FOR CONSUMER ABERRANT BEHAVIOR

Antecedents	Variable	Scale (a 7-point scale)
Intention	Intention to perform CAB	In this situation, I would do the same. Extremely unlikely – extremely likely
Attitude	Consequence to others	If I did the same, other shoppers would be: extremely harmed – extremely benefited
	Consequence to suppliers	If I did the same, the retailer/the insurer/the software company/ the hotel would be: extremely harmed – extremely benefited
	Consequence to an actor	If I did the same, I would be: extremely harmed – extremely benefited
	Evaluation, good/ bad[a]	Doing this would be: extremely good – extremely bad
	Evaluation, low risk/high risk	Doing this would be: extremely low risk – extremely high risk
	Evaluation, foolish/wise[a]	Doing this would be: extremely foolish – extremely wise

Social influence	Peer approval	If I did this, my friends would strongly disapprove – strongly approve
	Societal approval	If I did this, other shoppers/other policy holders/ other users/other guests would strongly disapprove – strongly approve
	Peer pressure	If I was faced with this situation, I would do what I think my friends would do. Strongly disagree – strongly agree
	Societal pressure	If I was faced with this situation, I would do what I think other shoppers/other policy holders/ other users/other guests would do. Strongly disagree – strongly agree
Perceived behavioral control	PBC, easy/difficult[b]	For me to do the same would be: extremely difficult-extremely easy
	PBC, opportunity	For me this situation would be too good an opportunity to miss. Strongly disagree – strongly agree
	PBC 1[b]	I could imagine times when I might do the same even if I had not planned to. Strongly disagree – strongly agree
	PBC 2[b]	Even if I had a pressing need, I could not bring myself to do this. Strongly disagree – strongly agree
	PBC 3[b]	I have control over whether or not I would do the same. Strongly disagree – strongly agree
Perceived unfairness	Pricing	Such behavior would compensate for the retailer's/the insurer's/the software company's/the hotel's overcharging. Strongly disagree – strongly agree

| Retaliation | The retailer/the insurer/the software company/the hotel would deserve such behavior. Strongly disagree – strongly agree |
| Business performance | It is OK for shoppers/policy holders/users/ guests to benefit at the retailer's/the insurer's/the software company's/the hotel's expense. Strongly disagree – strongly agree |

[a]Adapted from Ajzen and Fishbein (1980).
[b]Adapted from Chang (1998).

APPENDIX 3. DEMOGRAPHIC INFORMATION

Demographic Categories/No. of the Respondents (Valid Percent) Missing

Gender	Male	154 (45.0%)	Female	188 (55.0%)	2
Age	Under 20			9 (2.7%)	7
	21–30			28 (8.3%)	
	31–40			70 (20.8%)	
	41–50			72 (21.4%)	
	51–60			67 (19.9%)	
	61–70			49 (14.5%)	
	Over 70			42 (12.5%)	
Marital status	Married and living with spouse			243 (71.5%)	4
	Other			97 (28.5%)	
Children	Yes	261 (75.9%)	No	76 (22.1%)	7
Education	O-level/GCSE/school leaving			92 (27.4%)	8
	A-level/university entrance			53 (15.8%)	
	First degree (BA, BSc, etc.)			87 (25.9%)	
	Second degree (MA, PhD, etc.)			34 (10.1%)	
	Other			70 (20.8%)	
Occupation	Self-employed			21 (6.2%)	6
	Senior managerial/professional			24 (7.1%)	
	Middle managerial/professional			80 (23.7%)	

Junior managerial/professional	56 (17.2%)
Skilled/unskilled manual worker	25 (7.4%)
Retired	91 (26.9%)
Full-time student	12 (3.6%)
Housewife	27 (8.0%)
Unemployed	0 (0%)

AT THE MOVIES WITH THE HEALTH INSURANCE INDUSTRY: ETHICAL AND ENVIRONMENTAL ISSUES

Minnette A. Bumpus

ABSTRACT

Motion pictures can serve as an educational tool to shed light on ethical issues in the health insurance industry. To the chagrin of the health insurance industry, this light has oftentimes been unfavorable, as illustrated in such motion pictures as: Damaged Care (Winer, 2002), John Q (Cassavetes, 2002), and The Rainmaker (Coppola, 1997). In reaction to this unfavorable portrayal, health maintenance organizations have taken action to cast themselves in a more positive light. The objectives of this article are: to demonstrate how motion pictures that feature the health insurance industry can serve as a vehicle to illustrate management concepts such as planning, decision making, ethics, and conflict resolution; and to underscore the interrelationships and mutual dependencies of the ethical decisions, the decision-makers, and the context of the ethical dilemmas. Suggestions on how environmental response strategies can be used to improve public perceptions of the health insurance industry are also provided. The teaching method proposed in this article can be used in

Insurance Ethics for a More Ethical World
Research in Ethical Issues in Organizations, Volume 7, 223–236
Copyright © 2007 by Elsevier Ltd.
ISSN: 1529-2096/doi:10.1016/S1529-2096(06)07011-8

undergraduate level and graduate level principles of management, organizational behavior, and ethics courses.

BACKGROUND

The use of movies in business classes to discuss ethical dilemmas, theories, and behaviors has been noted in the literature. The movies highlighted in the literature cover a wide range of industries: real estate, tobacco, automobile, financial, communications, military, education, law enforcement, sports, legal correctional, government, airline, as well as organized crime (Berger & Pratt, 1998; Champoux, 2001a, 2001b, 2001c, 2003a, 2003b; Clemens & Wolff, 1999; Giacalone & Jurkiewicz, 2001; Higgins & Striegel, 2003; Shaw, 2004; van Es, 2003). Although this list of industries is broad, none of these movies examined ethical issues within the context of the health insurance industry, an industry that has oftentimes been viewed in an unfavorable light due to questionable ethical actions.

The objectives of this article are: to demonstrate how movies that feature the health insurance industry can serve as a vehicle to illustrate management concepts such as planning, decision making, ethics, and conflict resolution; and to underscore the interrelationships and mutual dependencies of the ethical decisions, the decision-makers, and the context of the ethical dilemmas.

The following full-length motion pictures can be used to teach ethics in principles of management, business ethics, and organizational behavior courses: (1) *Damaged Care* (Winer, 2002), (2) *John Q* (Cassavetes, 2002), and (3) *The Rainmaker* (Coppola, 1997). The sections to follow provide: an explanation of how to use the aforementioned movies in the classroom, a synopsis of each of the movies, and an analysis of the relevant course content areas. The article concludes with suggestions on how environmental response strategies can be used to improve public perceptions of the health insurance industry.

CLASSROOM USE

Running time. The length of the class period will dictate whether or not the entire movie will be shown during one class period or over two or more class periods. It is also possible to schedule a special showing of the movie in the evening. Alternatively, the viewing of the motion pictures can be assigned as homework since most students have ready accessibility to VCR or DVD players. Another alternative to showing the entire movie is to show selected scenes that depict the particular concepts and theories that the instructor wishes to emphasize. Specific DVD scene numbers (S#) have been provided in the Movie Analysis section for easy reference to the scenes highlighted in this paper.

Introduction. Introduce the movie to the students by using the movie synopsis provided in the next sections. Provide students with a list of the cast of characters and corresponding names of actors. Ask students to view each movie with the goal of observing how the relevant course concepts and theories are depicted in the movie.

Classroom discussion and evaluation. Although each movie contains a host of organizational behavior and management concepts, this paper will limit its discussion to decision-making, planning, and ethics. The DVD version of each movie is accompanied by a list of scenes. Each scene can be analyzed in terms of the stages of the decision making process: (1) identifying and diagnosing the problem, (2) generating alternative solutions, (3) evaluating alternatives, (4) making the choice, (5) implementing the decision, and (6) evaluating the decision (Bateman & Snell, 2004). The formal planning steps, counterparts of the decision making process, can also be explored within each scene: (1) situational analysis, (2) alternative goals and plans, (3) goal and plan evaluation, (4) goal and plan selection, (5) implementation, and (6) monitor and control (Bateman & Snell, 2004). Some of the scenes contain multiple problems, with accompanying situations that can be identified and analyzed.

Examples of the applications of the first steps in the decision-making process and the formal planning process for a select number of scenes can be found in the analysis section for each of the movies highlighted in this paper. Classroom discussions can begin with these first steps and proceed through the remaining steps in the decision-making process and the formal-planning process. Multiple-choice or short answer essay questions[1] can be used to evaluate the students' content mastery (i.e., the students' ability to apply textbook theories and concepts to the "real world events" depicted in the movies).

JOHN Q

Movie Synopsis

John Q (Cassavetes, 2002) stars Denzel Washington, Robert Duvall, James Wood, Anne Heche, and Kimberly Elise (118 min). It is a "socially conscious dramatic thriller about a law-abiding father who after his terminally ill son is denied the transplant he needs by a health-insurance firm, takes a hospital emergency room hostage" (Retrieved 5/9/05 from http://www.reel.com).

Decision Making and Planning Analysis: Identifying and Diagnosing the Problem (Situational Analysis)

The complete list of scenes in the movie, *John Q* (Cassavetes, 2002) can be found in Appendix A. Examples of problems that were identified and diagnosed in a select number of scenes follow.

Scene 5: Diagnosis. Since there were no provisions in the Archibald's insurance policy for major medical, and the Archibald's did not own a house or stocks, Rebecca Payne, decided to treat their case as a cash account, which would require a 30% down payment. A minimum of $250,000 was needed for Mike's heart surgery and the Archibald's were required to make a 30% ($75,000) down payment. This decision by Rebecca Payne would be classified as a *nonprogrammed* decision, because it had been encountered and made before. It had objectively correct answers, and could be solved by using rules and policies.

Scene 6: Runaround. John Archibald's company recently changed insurance carriers from a PPO to an HMO, a less expensive policy. Unfortunately, the new policy restricted coverage of non-management, part-time employees to second tier catastrophic coverage, which had a maximum payout limit of $20,000. Since his employer had reduced John to 20 hours/week, he was considered a part-time employee and thus qualified for second tier catastrophic coverage, despite the fact that for years he had paid for a full coverage policy. *Framing* or the way in which this information was presented to John had an influence on his future decisions.

Scene 8: "Do Something!" After his unsuccessful attempt to raise the $75,000 down payment for his son's surgery, John Archibald received a telephone call from his wife who told him that the hospital was going to release their son since they did not have the full amount for the down payment. John told his wife that he would do something, to which she replied, "You always say you will do something". It appears that John might have suffered from the psychological bias known as *the illusion of control*, which is the belief that one can "influence events even when one has no control over what will happen" (Bateman & Snell, 2004, p. 76).

Scene 17: "Take Mine." In one last attempt to save his son's life, John Archibald instructed Dr. Turner to take out his heart and give it to his son.

This decision by John would be classified as a *satisficing decision* because, although this decision would save his son's life, it was not necessarily the best or perfect decision.

Social Responsibility and Ethics Analysis

The following scenes provide examples of the various moral philosophies that were applied by different individuals when faced with ethical dilemmas.

Scene 7: A Little Help. John Archibald and his best friend, Jimmy Palumbo met with a television anchor at a local television station in the hopes of convincing him to do a public interest story about the Archibald's need of funds to help finance Mike's heart transplant. John and Jimmy were hoping that the television station would accept the *voluntary* form of corporate social responsibility.

Scene 11: Chiefly Concerns. Based upon the information that Mitch shared about the make, model, and year of his car (1986 Mercedes 500); John Archibald concluded that Mitch's explanation for his fiancée's (Julie) injuries was a lie (his airbag went off and her airbag did not) because passenger side airbags were not installed in those type of cars until 1988. It was later learned that Julie had actually sustained her injuries at the hands of Mitch. Mitch might have been able to defend his actions, if according to the "slap-a-ho" tribe, of which he was a "member", it was right, ethical, and acceptable to slap/hit a girlfriend/wife when she "got out of line". Defining one's ethical behavior based on the behaviors and opinions of relevant other people refers to the moral philosophy known as *relativism*.

Scene 12: HMOs and Oaths. While in the ER room, John Archibald questioned why his son's condition had not been detected earlier during one of his regular checkups. Dr. Turner explained that it was quite possible that John's son had not been tested thoroughly. One of the ER doctors provided a further explanation based on the fact that John had an HMO

> HMOs pay their doctors not to test. Its their way of keeping their costs down. Lets say Mikey needed additional testing, but the insurance company says they won't cover him. The doctor keeps his mouth shut and come Christmas the HMO sends the doctor a fat ass bonus check (Cassavetes, 2002).

Based upon the statement by the ER doctor it appears as if the HMOs do not follow the moral philosophy of *deontology*, which focuses on the rights of individuals. These doctors might be able to defend their actions, if they adopted the *relativist perspective* of moral philosophies. That is, a group consensus to comply with the wishes of the HMOs would justify a doctor's decision not to perform a thorough test.

Scene 15: An Open Shot. Lt. Frank Grimes confronted Chief Gus Monroe after learning that Chief Monroe had gone behind his back and decided to implement a plan, which involved sending a sniper into the emergency room through the air ducts to shoot John Archibald. Chief Monroe felt that this course of action was needed because, in his opinion, Lt. Grimes' negotiating was not working well and there was not much time left before John started killing people. Chief Monroe had adopted the *utilitarianism* moral philosophy because he was concerned about consequences that would benefit the greatest number of people.

Scene 21: Three Months Later. It is possible that some of the jurors voted to find John Archibald guilty of kidnaping and false imprisonment because of their beliefs that it is wrong to hold someone against his or her will, regardless of the circumstances or immediate result. This *universalism* ethical system supports the premise that people should hold some values as always appropriate.

THE RAINMAKER

Movie Synopsis

The Rainmaker (Coppola, 1997) stars Matt Damon and Danny DeVito (133 min). In this movie "a novice lawyer finds himself in the midst of a high profile case when the suit he brings against an insurance company uncovers a multimillion-dollar medical insurance scam" (Retrieved 5/9/05 from http://www.reel.com).

Decision Making and Planning Analysis: Identifying and Diagnosing the Problem (Situational Analysis)

The complete list of scenes in the movie, *The Rainmaker* (Coppola, 1997) can be found in Appendix B. Examples of problems that were identified and diagnosed in a select number of scenes follow.

Scene 3: Donny Ray Black. Dot Black decided to finally consult a lawyer after she received the eighth and final letter from Great Benefits Insurance Company, which stated:

Dear Ms. Black: On seven prior occasions the company denied your claim in writing. We now deny your claim for the eighth and final time. You must be stupid, stupid, stupid. Sincerely, Everett Lufkin, Vice President, Claims (Coppola, 1997).

The belief that she could influence events that she actually had no control over could possibly account for Dot's failure to consult a lawyer earlier. This psychological bias is known as the *illusion of control.*

Scene 12: An Offer to Settle. While in Judge Harvey Hale's chambers, Leo Drummond offered Rudy Baylor $75,000 to settle with no admission of liability on the part of Great Benefits Insurance Company. Judge Hale followed up by trying to convince Rudy that the lawsuit was frivolous and that Rudy would be crazy not to accept Drummond's offer of $75,000. Judge Hale and Drummond were taking a *risk* with this tag team maneuver. Rudy's reply to their offer also involved *risk* because the probability of success was less than 100%.

Scene 16: "Do You Remember When You First Sold Out?" Rudy Baylor traveled by bus to Great Benefits Insurance Company's home office in Cleveland, OH to take depositions of four employees. Unfortunately, two of the employees were not present as a result of a resignation and downsizing. Drummond's comments to Rudy about getting pugilistic highlighted the *affective conflict* that existed between the two lawyers.

Scene 19: Looking for Bugs. The attorneys for Great Benefits Insurance Company bugged Rudy Baylor's office in an attempt to stay one step ahead of the plaintiffs. The eavesdropping represented a *crisis.* This unstructured problem required Rudy and Deck to make a *nonprogrammed decision* quickly.

Social Responsibility and Ethics Analysis

The following scenes provide examples of the various moral philosophies applied by different individuals when faced with ethical dilemmas.

Scene 25: Jackie Lemancyzk. Jackie Lemancyzk informed Rudy that the initial claim filed by Mrs. Black had been assigned to her when she was a senior claims examiner. Pursuant to Great Benefits Insurance Company's policy, which was to initially deny all claims, she sent Mrs. Black a letter of denial, then sent Black's file over to underwriting. Per company procedures, the underwriting department sent a memo back to claims that instructed them not to pay the claim until instructed by underwriting. The claims and underwriting departments might be able to defend their actions, if they adopted the *relativist perspective* of moral philosophies, which "bases ethical behavior on the opinions and behaviors of relevant other people" (Bateman & Snell, 2004).

Scene 26: Stolen Papers. Jackie Lemanczyk admitted that she signed the resignation letter and took the $10,000 hush money from Great Benefits Insurance Company because she felt that she had no other options as a broke, single mother of two. She was able to justify her actions with the moral philosophy known as *egoism*, because her decision maximized her own self-interest.

Scene 28: Deny All Claims. The mysterious section U from the Great Benefits' Claims manual states that "claim handlers are directed to deny all claims within receipt of claims – no exceptions" (Coppola, 1997). Wilfred Keeley's rationale for this in-house processing guideline was because sometimes Great Benefits Insurance Company received frivolous and fraudulent claims; this type of language allowed the company to focus on the legitimate and needier claims. *Deontologists* would take exception with this in-house processing guideline because it does not give equal respect to all individuals.

Scene 22: Dot Black Takes the Stand and Scene 28: Deny All Claims. Drummond argued that since only 7,000 bone marrow transplants were performed a year, of which less than 200 were performed in the state of Tennessee, then bone marrow transplants would be classified as experimental procedures and therefore not covered by Dot's Great Benefits Insurance policy. The aforementioned conclusion was contradicted by a report from Great Benefits Insurance Company's own medical committee, chaired by its CEO, Wilfred Keeley, which stated that "since bone marrow transplants have become standard procedure, Great Benefits would be financially justified in investing in bone marrow clinics" (Coppola, 1997). In light of the medical committee's report, some people would view Drummond's arguments as dishonest. Those that support the *universalism* ethical system support the premise that people "should uphold some values, such as honesty, regardless of the immediate results" (Bateman & Snell, 2004, p. 138).

Scene 32: Not Just Another Shark. Shortly after Great Benefits Insurance Company filed for protection under the bankruptcy code, Rudy and Kelly Riker left Memphis to begin a new life. Rudy was contemplating teaching rather than practicing law because after winning such a high profile case, the only place to go was down since all future clients would expect similar results – the same magic. He knew that he could probably do it again, but he did not want to become another Drummond, "a shark in the dirty water who doesn't care about how he wins a case" (Coppola, 1997). Based on the aforementioned, *Kohlberg's model of cognitive moral development* would classify Rudy as being in the *principled stage* of moral judgment.

DAMAGED CARE

Movie Synopsis

Damaged Care (Winer, 2002) stars Laura Dern and James LeGros (114 min). In this movie "a woman working for an HMO discovers the dark side of managed care. She risks her career by speaking out against what she believes to be unethical practices" (Retrieved 5/10/05 from http://www.reel.com/movie).

Decision Making and Planning Analysis: Identifying and Diagnosing the Problem (Situational Analysis)

The complete list of scenes in the movie, *Damaged Care* (Winer, 2002) can be found in Appendix C. Examples of the problems that were identified and diagnosed in a select number of scenes follow.

Scene 3: The Bottom Line. While at Humana, Dr. Linda Peeno received a phone call from a surgeon in Los Angeles who was requesting immediate approval of a heart transplant for his patient. A donor heart had just become available and a decision needed to be made quickly. The constraint of this *time pressure* represented a barrier to effective decision making.

Scene 10: Kindness and Courage. While at Brothers Managed Care, Dr. Linda Peeno received a request for a voice assist machine for Dawn Debose. After a presentation of the voice assist machine by Dr. Kitano to her colleagues at Brothers, Dr. Peeno approved the request. This decision could be viewed as a *maximizing decision* because it would result in the best possible outcomes for Dawn.

Scene 11: Words into Action. Mrs. Adams was faced with a *crisis* when she called the Kaiser Permante of Georgia Triage Center at 3:30 a.m. because her infant son, James had a temperature of 104 degrees. Kaiser responded to Mrs. Adams' *crisis* by referring her to a hospital in the Kaiser network that was located almost 50 miles away from her home.

Scene 13: Special Needs. When the West Palm Peach Florida Sheriff's Department switched health insurance policies to Humana, Mark Chipps was told that everyone, including those with special needs would be covered and that his special needs daughter, Caitlyn, would be put in a state of the art case management program that would provide her better care than under the old plan. Although Humana lived up to this promise, 10 months later Humana dropped Caitlyn from the plan. The West Palm Peach Florida

Sheriff's Department's decision to switch plans might have been biased by the psychological bias known as *discounting the future*. "That is, in [its] evaluation of alternatives, [it] weighted short-term costs and benefits more heavily than longer-term costs and benefits" (Bateman & Snell, 2004, p. 76).

Social Responsibility and Ethics Analysis

The following scenes provide examples of the various moral philosophies applied by different individuals when faced with ethical dilemmas.

Scene 3: The Bottom Line. In a conversation between Sam Verbach and Avery Principle, Avery stated that now that he had his own medical practice, he finally understood the beauty of capitation

> With the money the managed care companies allot for each subscriber's care all you have to do is find a lot of patients and keep them healthy – you get to keep the money .... The brilliance of capitation is that it actually provides doctors with an incentive not to order up expensive procedures (Winer, 2002).

Avery and other doctors could justify their actions, if they adopted the *relativist perspective* of moral philosophies, which "bases ethical behavior on the opinions and behaviors of relevant other people" (Bateman & Snell, 2004).

Scene 3: The Bottom Line. While at Humana, Dr. Linda Peeno received a phone call from a surgeon in Los Angeles who was requesting immediate approval of a heart transplant for his patient. A donor heart had just become available and a decision needed to be made quickly. Dr. Peeno wanted to approve this procedure because she did not see any medical or technical basis for a denial. Her colleagues, on the other hand, were against the transplant on the basis of resource allocation. That is, payment for the heart transplant might be at the expense of: a cleft pallet operation for a child, chemotherapy for a cancer patient, and a lung biopsy for a father of three small children. It appears as if Dr. Peeno's colleagues had adopted the *utilitarianism* moral philosophy, which states "that the greatest good for the greatest number should be the overriding concern for decision makers" (Bateman & Snell, 2004, p. 139).

Scene 7: 100% Denial. The *ethical climate* of an organization is greatly influenced by top management. This influence was illustrated in a conversation between Dr. Linda Peeno and Dr. Gersham outside Dawn Debose's hospital room. Dr. Gersham reminded Dr. Peeno that Brothers Managed Care was losing money. He strongly encouraged her to find a way to move

Dawn Debose from the hospital to a rehabilitation center because her prolonged stay at the hospital was costing Brothers Managed Care a great deal of money. An indefinite hospital stay could hurt Brothers' bottom line.

Scene 8: The Runaround. Dr. Linda Peeno learned that Jemma Koones had denied a claim for a patient's rehabilitation after Dr. Peeno had approved it. Adequate rehabilitation at the time of the accident could have made a difference between the patient functioning in society or spending the rest of his life in social services. When Dr. Peeno learned about Jemma overruling her, she exclaimed, "This is so unethical" (Winer, 2002). Her response probably stemmed from her belief in the *universalism* ethical system which supports the premise that people "should uphold some values, such as honesty, regardless of the immediate results" (Bateman & Snell, 2004, p. 138).

Scene 10: Kindness and Courage, Scene 11: Words into Action, Scene 12: At Risk, Scene 14: Personal Injuries, and Scene 16: Day of Justice. Dr. Linda Peeno became an advocate for those adversely affected by the practices of the HMOs. Her actions illustrated the *principled stage in Kohlberg's model of cognitive moral development.*

ENVIRONMENTAL RESPONSE STRATEGIES

Environmental response strategies can be used to improve public perceptions of the health insurance industry. These response strategies include: Adapting to the Environment – Changing Yourself, Influencing Your Environment, and Changing the Environment You Are In (Bateman & Snell, 2004).

The health insurance industry has already taken action to influence its environment. For example, recognizing the power and influence of movies, the American Association of Health Plans (AAHP) hired a talent agency "for access to key writers, power brokers and directors, as well as for advanced work about coming movies and television shows that might paint the insurers in an unfavorable light. The hope [was] that the health-insurance lobby [might] be able to have some influence over how HMOs are portrayed in the future" (Martinez, 2002, July). One outcome of this partnership was the purchase of full-page ads in *Variety* and the *Hollywood Reporter.* "The ad [read in part]: 'John Q. It's not just a movie. It's a crisis for 40 million people who can't afford health care. The ad [went] on to blame [Denzel] Washington for failing to address the problem of the uninsured and – like the fictional character John Q – the underinsured' ". Dougher (2004, September) provides another example of how the AAHP has influenced its environment: "the

American Association of Health Plans posted a statement on its Web site in response to *Damaged Care*, dismissing it and movies like it as a poor substitute for 'the real debate about health care we ought to be having'".

RECOMMENDATIONS

Did the public view HMOs more harshly in one movie vs. the other? If yes, then what influenced perceptions? One possible explanation could be the main character's level of interaction with the legal system. Varying levels of interaction with the legal system were demonstrated in the movies highlighted in this paper. For example, in the movies, *John Q* (Cassavetes, 2002), *Damaged Care* (Winer, 2002), and *The Rainmaker* (Coppola, 1997), the main characters took action against HMOs by working outside, in conjunction with, and inside of the legal system, respectively. Perceptions could also have been influenced by the moral intensity of the situation. These movies "presented variations in the moral issues, or moral intensity of the ethical dilemma, ranging from clearly unethical/ethical choices to moderately ethical/unethical decision choices" (Glover, Bumpus, Sharp, & Munchus, 2002, p. 221). Future decisions about environmental response strategies might possibly benefit from an examination of correlations between perceptions of HMOs and varying levels of interaction with the legal system and perceptions of HMOs and the moral intensity of the situation.

NOTE

1. Sample multiple-choice exam questions can be obtained from the author upon request.

REFERENCES

Bateman, T. S., & Snell, S. A. (2004). *Management: The new competitive landscape* (6th ed.). Boston: McGraw-Hill/Irwin.

Berger, J., & Pratt, C. B. (1998). Teaching business - - communication ethics with controversial films. *Journal of Business Ethics, 17*(16), 1817–1823.

Cassavetes, N. (2002). *John Q* [Film]. (Available from New Line Home Entertainment, ASIN: B00005JKWX).

Champoux, J. E. (2001a). Animated films as a teaching resource. *Journal of Management Education, 25*(1), 79–100.

Champoux, J. E. (2001b). *Management: Using film to visualize principles and practices.* United States: South-Western College Publishing.

Champoux, J. E. (2001c). *Organizational behavior: Using film to visualize principles and practices.* United States: South-Western College Publishing.

Champoux, J. E. (2003a). *At the movies: Management.* United States: South-Western College Publishing.

Champoux, J. E. (2003b). *At the movies: Organizational behavior.* United States: South-Western College Publishing.

Clemens, J., & Wolff, M. (1999). *Movies to manage by: Lessons in leadership from great films.* NY: Contemporary Books.

Coppola, F. (1997). *The Rainmaker* [Film]. (Available from Paramount Studio, ASIN: 63051818100).

Dougher, C. (2004). Life death and the bottom line. *CityLink Magazine*, September 8.

Giacalone, R. A., & Jurkiewicz, C. L. (2001). Lights, camera, action: Teaching ethical decision making through the cinematic experiences. *Teaching Business Ethics*, 5(1), 79–87.

Glover, S. H., Bumpus, M. A., Sharp, G. F., & Munchus, G. A. (2002). Gender differences in ethical decision making. *Women in Management*, 17(5), 217–227.

Higgins, S. O'L., & Striegel, C. (2003). *Movies for business: Big-screen lessons in corporate vision, entrepreneurship, logistics, and ethics.* Spokane: New Media Ventures.

Martinez, B. (2002). Tired of being cast as the villain, HMOs hire talent agency. *Wall Street Journal*, July 9.

Shaw, B. (2004). Hollywood ethics: Developing ethical issues ... hollywood style. *Journal of Business Ethics*, 49(2), 167–177.

van Es, R. (2003). Inside and outside *The Insider*: A film workshop in practical ethics. *Journal of Business Ethics*, 48(1), 89–97.

Winer, H. (2002). *Damaged Care* [Film]. (Available from Paramount Home Video, ADIN: B00006RCNB).

APPENDIX A. SCENES FROM MOVIE *JOHN Q* (CASSAVETES, 2002)

1.	Main Titles	12.	HMOs and Oaths
2.	One Family	13.	Payback and Releases
3.	Overqualified	14.	Waiting on a Miracle
4.	Fateful Sunday	15.	An Open Shot
5.	Diagnosis	16.	The Public Eye
6.	Runaround	17.	"Take Mine."
7.	A Little Help	18.	A Last Message
8.	"Do Something!"	19.	"Let's Do It."
9.	Tension and Trauma	20.	Surrender
10.	Demands	21.	Three Months Later
11.	Chiefly Concerns	22.	End Credits

APPENDIX B. SCENES FROM THE MOVIE *THE RAINMAKER* (COPPOLA, 1997)

1.	Rudy Baylor	18.	A Wrongful Death
2.	Bruiser Stone and Associates	19.	Looking for Bugs
3.	Donny Ray Black	20.	Jury Tampering
4.	Miss Birdie's Will	21.	Divorce Papers
5.	Ambulance Chasing	22.	Dot Black Takes the Stand
6.	Kelly Riker	23.	"Give me the bat."
7.	He'll Kill Me	24.	Everett Lufkin's Testimony
8.	Hustlers	25.	Jackie Lemancyzk
9.	Personally Involved	26.	Stolen Papers
10.	Subpoenas and Hacksaws	27.	Carmine DeSoto vs. Club Ruby
11.	Sworn in by a Fool	28.	Deny All Claims
12.	An Offer to Settle	29.	Closing Arguments
13.	Judge Tyrone Kipler	30.	The Jury's Verdict
14.	Donny Ray's Deposition	31.	Everybody Loses
15.	I Just Wanted to See You	32.	Not Just Another Shark
16.	"Do You Remember When You First Sold Out?"	33.	Titles
17.	Kelly Leaves Cliff		

APPENDIX C. SCENES FROM THE MOVIE *DAMAGED CARE* (WINER, 2002)

1.	The Small Still Voice	9.	Serving the Company
2.	A New Job	10.	Kindness and Courage
3.	The Bottom Line	11.	Words into Action
4.	Bad Medicine	12.	At Risk
5.	Welcome to Brothers	13.	Special Needs
6.	Darkening Forrest	14.	Personal Injuries
7.	100% Denial	15.	Gathering Storm
8.	Runaround	16.	Day of Justice

WALKER PERCY: A PROPHET FOR PROFIT-MAKERS

Rev Robert E. Lauder

A LIFE AND AN ILLNESS BLESSED

A slight acquaintance with the writings of Walker Percy probably would not lead someone to link his thought to the world of business. Indeed this Catholic existentialist might seem as far from the market place as possible. Nor would Percy's life immediately suggest that this Southern doctor turned writer was either interested in the world of business or had anything of significance to say to those who labor in the business vineyard. It would seem that Percy never had a regular job that enabled him to support himself, his wife, and their two daughters. Can someone so distant from and perhaps disinterested in the world of commerce have anything important to say to those who labor daily as business people? Indeed he can, perhaps precisely because, in his life, circumstances distanced him from the world of commerce and gave him the leisure time to reflect on just what is and what is not important in life.

Born on May 28, 1916 in Birmingham, Alabama, Walker had two brothers. When Walker was 13 years of age, his father committed suicide and it seems reasonable to suspect that this event influenced Walker's entire life. In several of Percy's novels suicide figures importantly in the plot. Two years after the suicide Walker's mother died in an automobile accident. William Alexander Percy, a planter and author and the first cousin of Walker's

Insurance Ethics for a More Ethical World
Research in Ethical Issues in Organizations, Volume 7, 237–251
Copyright © 2007 by Elsevier Ltd.
All rights of reproduction in any form reserved
ISSN: 1529-2096/doi:10.1016/S1529-2096(06)07012-X

father, adopted Walker and his two brothers. This cousin, known as "Uncle" Will, brought up the three boys and Walker lived with him in Greenville, Mississippi until Walker went to the University of North Carolina at Chapel Hill from which he graduated in 1937. His next degree was a medical degree from Columbia University's College of Physicians and Surgeons. During an internship at Bellevue, young Dr. Percy, who at this time was enamored of science, contracted tuberculosis. That was in 1942. It may well be that before he contracted tuberculosis Percy basically embraced the philosophy of scientism.

It is impossible to be an educated person in the 21st century and not be enamored of science. From improving and preserving people's health to putting them into outer space, science's accomplishments are awesome. Percy, whose college courses and courses in medical school strongly emphasized science, described his admiration of science:

> It was the elegance and order, and, yes beauty of science which attracted me. It is not merely the truth of science that makes it beautiful but its simplicity. That is to say, its constant movement in the direction of ordering the endless variety and the seeming haphazardness of ordinary life by discovering underlying principles which as science progresses become ever fewer and more vigorously and exactly formulated – at least in the physical sciences (Percy, 1991, p. 187. In future notes the book "Signposts in a Strange Land" henceforth will be referred to as *Signposts*).

Scientism however is a philosophy that shrinks both reality and the human mind's capacity to grasp reality. The philosophy of scientism says that only statements of positive science are meaningful and true. Many people, probably large numbers of college students, who may never have heard the word "scientism," believe in its tenets. This is what Percy wrote of a person who embraces scientism:

> ... I am speaking of a rather more typical denizen of the age who believes, as part of the very air he breathes, that natural science has the truth, all the truth, and that the rest – religion, humanism, art – is icing on the cake; attractive icing, yes, but icing nonetheless, which is to say, noncognitive icing, emotional icing. Notice that I distinguish here between scientism as an all-pervading ideology and the scientific method as a valid means of investigating the mechanisms of phenomena.[1]

If Walker Percy, before he was stricken with tuberculosis, was not a proponent of scientism, he was almost a proponent. He claimed that when he was stricken with tuberculosis he felt as Kierkegaard felt after he had read Hegel. Percy wrote, "Hegel, said Kierkegaard, explained everything under the sun, except one small detail: what it means to be a man living in the world who must die."[2]

Percy thought that science had handled all questions except the same one that Hegel had not handled. The illness marked a dramatic turning point in the young doctor's life. In his recuperative period he read very serious novels such as those by Dostoevsky, Mann and Tolstoy. He also read the existentialist philosophers such as Kierkegaard, Heidegger, Sartre, Camus, and Marcel. These philosophers, I believe especially Kierkegaard and Marcel, had a profound influence on Percy. He came to see human person differently. It is impossible to overemphasize the importance that his illness played in the re-direction of the young doctor's life. Martin Luschei sees this time of illness in Walker's life as crucial in Percy's self-understanding. Luschei wrote:

> In his middle twenties, Walker Percy, like Dante midway in life's journey, found himself in a dark wood. He had come into it a medical student, bound for a career in psychiatry, he went out from it a novelist. What he encountered there seems to have been a realization like the one Binx Bolling arrives at in *The Moviegoer* that though the universe had been disposed of, he himself was left over. If the birth of Walker Percy the novelist can be dated, it is from the moment of that recognition, for what drove him forth was the awareness that he was still obliged to draw one breath and then the next and had best be charting his course (Luschei, 1972, p. 6).

After he recuperated, he never returned to the practice of medicine. He went home, married in 1946 Mary Bernice Townsend and with her studied religion for a year. At the end of the year both of them became Catholics. That Percy did not return to the practice of medicine, that he never earned a living as a medical doctor, would seem to make him an unlikely person to provide assistance for people in business. The opposite is true. The philosophical and religious reflection that took place during Walker's illness started him on a life of reflection and a kind of mission to share the fruits of his reflection with others. That mission led him first to write some scholarly philosophical articles and eventually six novels and what he called the last of the self-help books.

In 1950 Bernice and Walker moved to Covington, Louisiana, opened a bookstore and raised two daughters. Though Walker was delighted that his philosophical essays were published, he wanted to reach out to a wider audience. In a note to me in 1990 Bernice wrote, "He always said: I have something to say and I will say it" (Luschei, 1972, pp. 3–4). In order to reach the wider audience he desired he began to write novels and all six of his fictional tales were praised critically. By the time he died of cancer in 1990, Percy was widely judged to be one of the most important American novelists of the second half of the 20th century.

Why do I call Percy a prophet? I see a prophet as someone who calls attention to some important truths, perhaps truths that have been forgotten or are being neglected. Percy believed that many people in the contemporary world were adrift without a spiritual compass. He wrote to remind them, to awake them, even to provoke them so that they would see the meaning of person and understand that to be a person is to be a wayfarer, a pilgrim who has not reached his or her home. The first great intellectual discovery of Percy's life was the beauty of science but he had a second discovery. He described it as follows:

> If the first great intellectual discovery of my life was the beauty of the scientific method, surely the second was the discovery of the singular predicament of man in the very world which has been transformed by science. An extraordinary paradox became clear: that the more science progressed, and even as it benefited man, the less it said about what it is like to be a man living in the world. Every advance in science seemed to take us further from the concrete here-and-now in which we live. Did my eyes deceive me, or was there not a huge gap in the scientific view of the world (scientific in the root sense of 'knowing')? If so, it was an oversight which everyone pretended not to notice or maybe didn't want to notice.[3]

Serious Questions for Reflection

In an important essay entitled "The Delta Factor" Percy poses some questions to stimulate reflection. What the questions deal with are dramatized in Percy's six novels. The following are some of the questions that Percy poses in "The Delta Factor":

> Why does man feel so bad in the twentieth century?

> Why does man feel so bad on the very age when, more than in any other age, he has succeeded in satisfying his needs and making over the world for his own use?

> Why has man entered in an orgy of war, murder, torture, and self-destruction unparalleled in history and in the very century when he had hoped to see the dawn of universal peace and brotherhood?

> Why have more people been killed in the twentieth century then in all other centuries put together?

> Why is war man's greatest pleasure?

> Why is man the only creature that wages war against his own species? (Percy, 1975, pp. 4–5)

These questions reveal some of Percy's preoccupations throughout his writing career. Something had happened to people in the 20th century and like a good diagnostician Percy believed he knew the spiritual illness and had an idea of the cure. According to Percy many have fallen into what he calls the malaise. By the malaise Percy meant an inauthenticity, a lack of vitality. A person stricken by the malaise lacks awareness of what is important and may experience both anxiety and numbness. Though people may have many roles and wear many masks somehow their true self, the depth of the self, is lost or forgotten. In Percy's mind the first step toward finding a path out of the malaise was to realize that you are lost. The scientist turned author was a prophet in that he set about trying to help people gain insight into their situation and to offer a remedy to retrieve the lost self.

RELIGIOUS EXISTENTIALISM: TWO PHILOSOPHERS

I have been teaching the philosophy of existentialism for over 35 years. In any social gathering as soon as it is learned that I teach existentialism someone will ask me, "Just what is existentialism?" I can understand why the question is asked. In the latter half of the 20th century I heard the word used to describe almost anything. Putting a tag on any philosopher is always risky and many of the famous philosophers who have been tagged existentialists such as Martin Heidegger and Gabriel Marcel have shunned the title. I believe that there is a common strain that can be found in all the thinkers who have been grouped by many historians of philosophy under the title "existentialism." What distinguishes members of this group is a very strong emphasis on human freedom. There may be huge differences among many existentialists in their interpretation of reality but what is common to all of them is the freedom, and hence the responsibility, of the human person. If an existentialist is an atheist, such as Jean Paul Sartre was, then the vision of the human person is that he or she is alone in a godless universe, creating himself or herself by free choices. If an existentialist is a theist, such as Gabriel Marcel was, then the vision of the human person is that he or she is co-creating himself or herself with God. Whether atheist or theist, the existentialist insists on the freedom of human persons and that we are responsible for who we are and for our choices. The existentialist is totally opposed to any philosophies that argue for determinism or behaviorism. One of the most dramatic depictions of freedom is in Sartre's play *The Flies*. The main character, Orestes, who I believe is a spokesperson for Sartre, is talking to Zeus, who I believe is a stand-in for the traditional God of Western classical philosophy. Zeus is angry with Orestes because Orestes refuses to bow down and worship Zeus.

Orestes, I created you, and I created all things. Now see those planets wheeling on their appointed ways, never swerving, never clashing. It was I who ordained their course, according to the law of justice. Hear the music of the spheres, that vast, mineral hymn of praise, sounding and resounding to the limits of the firmament. It was my work that living things increase and multiply, each according to his kind. I have ordained that man shall always beget man, and dog give birth to dog. It is my work that the tides with their innumerable tongues creep up to lap the sand and draw back at the appointed hour. I made the plants grow and my breath fans round the earth the yellow clouds of pollen. You are not in your own home, intruder, you are a foreign body in the world, like splinter in flesh, or a poacher in his lordship's forest. For the world is good, I made it according to my will, and I am Goodness.

ORESTES: Let it crumble! Let the rocks revile me, and flowers wilt at my coming. Your whole universe is not enough to prove me wrong. You are the king of gods, the king of stones and stars, king of the waves of the sea. But you are not the king of man.

ZEUS: Impudent spawn! So I am not your king? Who, then, made you?

ORESTES: Yes. But you blundered; you should not have made me free (Sartre, 1946, pp. 119–120).

While embracing the existentialist emphasis on freedom that is so evident in Sartre, Percy chose a freedom whose origin and goal is God. For Percy relationship with God does not become an obstacle or a hindrance to the freedom of human person but rather leads to the flowering and fulfillment of human freedom. The emphasis on human freedom and its fulfillment in God Percy finds in the vision of the first existentialist Soren Kierkegaard (1813–1855) and the Roman Catholic existentialist Gabriel Marcel (1889–1973).

Kierkegaard's influence on Percy is so pervasive in the Southern writer's novels that I describe Percy as a 20th century Roman Catholic version of the 19th century Lutheran Protestant Kierkegaard. Commenting on Percy's early career as an essayist exploring philosophical issues and the malaise that has infected citizens of the contemporary world, psychiatrist Robert Coles clearly describes Percy's mission, indeed apostolate, as a novelist:

Dr. Percy, the essayist, wished for listeners, but worried all during the 1950s that he was not quite able in his various articles, to spell out his particular, American, and Christian existentialism. He tried and tried; he put words into sentences, paragraphs, short or long statements. But he was searching for the way to bring home, tellingly, to his listeners (readers) what has happened to them – to him, of course, as well: spiritual homelessness. With each essay he explored a facet of that 'problem,' that 'condition.' But he sensed himself in a maze: how to make his 'message' come closer to the lives of others – connect with their human sensibilities. By the late 1950s he had come upon an answer: escape the maze, leap over the wall, write novels (Coles, 1978, p. 137).

In an interview, talking about his choice of the novel as the means to convey his message and of the advantage that a novelist has over the scientist, Percy said:

> In fact, I see my own writing as not really a great departure from my original career, science and medicine, because ... where science will bring you to a certain point and no further, it can say nothing about what a man is or what he must do. And then the question is, how do you deal with man? And if you are an anthropologist in the larger sense, interested in man, how do you study him? And it seemed to me that the novel itself was a perfectly valid way to deal with man's behavior (Carr, 1985, p. 60).

Neither the writings of Soren Kierkegaard nor Gabriel Marcel are easy reading. Both thinkers probe deeply into the human mystery. One of Percy's marvelous accomplishments is to take the philosophical insights of these two giants and weave them into his novels. Thousands who might neither be inclined nor have the background to read either Kierkegaard or Marcel may be exposed indirectly to some of the wisdom of these two philosophers through Percy's readable novels. In each of his six novels Percy tells a story but he also deals with the ultimate meaning of human person.

HUMAN PERSON AND GOD

My interpretation of Percy's six novels is that the structure is Kierkegaardian but the resolution of the plots, with one apparent exception, relies on Marcel's notion of love.

According to Percy, Kierkegaard was the one who enabled him to see beyond scientism and secular humanism. Stunned by Kierkegaard's insistence that the only way to be yourself was to be yourself before God, Percy wrote of the Danish Christian existentialist:

> So what was important about Kierkegaard for me was that he was a man who was trying to open up a whole area of knowledge to me in the most serious ways, in the most precise way – and quite as serious as any science, or more serious. And, of course, it is religious too. This was a far cry from the other alternative that I had always read about, that the alternative to science is art, play, emotion. I saw for the first time through Kierkegaard how to take the alternative system seriously, how to read it as a serious thinker, a serious writer. I hadn't seen any way to think about it. Kierkegaard gave me a way to think about it (Dewey, 1985, pp. 109–110).

According to Kierkegaard there are three spheres of existence or three stages on life's way. They are the aesthetic, the ethical and the religious. Each is an enclosed, isolated, independent sphere of life (Jolivet, 1950, p. 113). Movement from one stage to the next cannot take place through

mere development. Living to the full either of the first two will not necessarily lead to the third nor will living with total dedication to the aesthetic
lead to the ethical (Jolivet, 1950). No one of the stages is understandable
unless the other two are known.

The aesthetic stage is a romantic preoccupation with and dedication to
pleasure. The person on the aesthetic level knows only the moment. The
Rodgers and Hart song title comes to my mind: "Falling in Love
with Love." The aesthetic is committed to the enjoyment of enjoyment.
Self-interest is predominant. Living on the aesthetic level is a superficial way
of living. The aesthetic recognizes no obligation or duty except the duty of
self-enjoyment. It would seem that the aesthete is doomed to frustration.
Preoccupied with the momentary and the passing, the aesthete's life seems
to be based on mood and the person on this level may be overcome by
boredom and even long for death (Kierkegaard, 1959, pp. 235–236).

In the ethical stage are present the purpose and direction that are lacking
to the aesthete. The person on the ethical stage is preoccupied not with what
he wants to do but with what ought to be done. The preoccupation is with
duty. Looked upon as a constant and reliable guide to conduct are the laws
governing social behavior.

Looking at the religious stage as presented by Kierkegaard in *Concluding
Unscientific Postscript* will clarify the limitations of the two previous stages.
Four notions that are characteristic of the religious stage are: subjectivity,
inwardness, the leap, and the absurd. By subjectivity Kierkegaard meant
dedication to Christ, a passion and deep personal concern for truth. Christian truth was not objective in the sense of being something "out there" that
could be examined impartially. No, Christian truth was to be lived. For
Kierkegaard the subject is an active, self-choosing, and self-renewing energy
(Brown, 1956, p. 42).

At its highest, subjectivity is a passionate interest in one's eternal salva-
tion (Kierkegaard, 1941, p. 33). Inwardness emphasizes the importance
of the subject turning toward the manner of the relationship. Inwardness
suggests depth. The leap is linked to the risk that is essential to the religious
stage. Because no proof for Christianity was possible, to become a Christian
a leap was necessary (Kierkegaard, 1941, pp. 90–97). That eternity
had entered time, that God had become human, Kierkegaard felt almost
added an absurd element to Christian belief (Kierkegaard, 1941, p. 345).
What was important for Kierkegaard was the existential meaning of the
Incarnation, what subjective significance the Incarnation had in the life of
the believer.

Percy's six novels are Kierkegaardian in structure and by that I mean the hero of each is on one of the first two stages and is choosing either to move toward the religious stage or choosing not to move toward it. In the novels the religious stage is achieved through love of a woman and finding God through loving a human person is typical Gabriel Marcel. The French existentialist has been described as a more personal existentialist than Kierkegaard (Coles, 1978, p. 15). Marcel wrote of his own philosophy:

> It is not enough to say that it is a metaphysic of being; it is a metaphysic of *we are* as opposed to a metaphysic of *I-think*. (Holland, 1990, p. 3)

I have long thought that the easiest and quickest way to enter into Marcel's thought is through his distinction between a problem and a mystery. According to the Roman Catholic philosopher there are four key differences between a problem and a mystery. A problem is external to the self, generates curiosity, has a solution, and is available to be worked on by anyone. A mystery always includes thought about the self, generates wonder and awe, has no final solution and can only be reflected upon by the individual himself (Gallagher, 1962, pp. 30–40).

Percy's heroes are initially immersed in the world of problems but the dimension of mystery enters. Reading Marcel's reflections on technocracy calls to my mind the struggles that Percy's heroes have with the malaise. Marcel links technocracy to the smothering of the spiritual in a human person. Marcel wrote:

> The world of the problematical is the world of fear and desire, which are inseparable; at the same time, it is the world of the functional – or what can be functional ... ; finally it is the kingdom of technics of whatever sort. Every technique serves, or it can be made to serve, some desire or some fear, conversely, every desire as every fear tends to invent its appropriate technique. From this standpoint, despair consists in the recognition of the ultimate inefficacy of all technics, joined to the inability or the refusal to change over to a new ground – a ground where all technics are seen to be incompatible with the fundamental nature of being, which itself escapes our grasp (insofar as our grasp is limited to the world of objects and to this alone). It is for this reason that we seem nowadays to have entered upon the very era of despair; we have not ceased to believe in technics, that is to envisage reality as a complex of problems, yet at the same time the failure of technics *as a whole* is as discernible to us as its partial triumphs. To the question: what can man achieve? We continue to reply: He can achieve as much as his technics; yet we are obliged to admit that these technics are unable *to save man himself*, and even that they are apt to conclude the most sinister alliance with the enemy he bears within him (Marcel, 2002, pp. 30–31).

In addition to opposing secular humanism, determinism and any type of behaviorism, Percy was concerned about the dualism that has plagued

Western man's self-understanding since Descartes split man into two entities, a soul which carries around a body. In stressing the unity of human person, Percy found a champion in Marcel. The existentialist personalist, regretting the legacy philosophy inherited from his 16th century fellow countryman, wrote:

> It is evident that there exists a mystery of the union of the body and the soul. The indivisible unity always inadequately expressed by much phrases as *I have a body, I make use of my body, I feel my body*, etc., can be neither analyzed nor reconstituted out of precedent elements. It is not only data, I would say that it is the basis of data, in the sense of being my own presence to myself, a presence of which the art of self-consciousness is, in the last analysis, only an inadequate symbol (Marcel, 2002, p. 19).

But the mystery of human person is very much linked in Marcel's philosophy to the mystery of God. One way of approaching God according to Marcel is through hope. Hope goes beyond the world of problems and reaches the mystery at the heart of personal existence. Marcel wrote:

> Hope consists in asserting that there is at the heart of being, beyond all data, beyond all inventories and all calculations, a mysterious principle which is in connivance with me, which cannot but will that which I will, if what I will deserves to be willed and is, in fact, willed by the whole of my being (Marcel, 2002, p. 28).

In addition to hope another human experience that can lead to the Divine is love. When one person loves another he or she discovers that the beloved will live forever, not just in the lover's memory, but really live. Kenneth Gallagher, a foremost commentator on Marcel, wrote an excellent summary of how love points beyond the grave and also opens the lover to the presence of God. Gallagher wrote:

> Not only perfect love but all love insofar as it *is* love, is haunted by this illimitable presence. That is the meaning of the prophetic 'thou shall not die': through my love I grasp you as a participant in a presence which cannot fail. The more I love you, the surer I am of your eternity: the more I grow in authentic love for you, the deeper becomes my trust and faith in the Being which founds your being. There is no question of loving God or creature, since the more I really love the creature the more I am turned to the Presence which love lays bare. That is why Marcel believes that there is a 'subterranean connection' between faith in its ontological plenitude and the unconditional love of creature for creature: even where there is no explicit faith in God, this love is not thinkable, is not possible except in being capable of such faith, but in whom it is not yet awakened, it is, as it were, the prenatal palpitation of that faith (Gallagher, 1962, p. 80).

In doing research on Marcel as a source of Percy's philosophical vision, I came upon Mary Deems Holland's book analyzing Marcel's notion of person as it can be found in Percy's novels. The author provided an excellent summary of the philosophical vision in Marcel's plays. As I read the summary I came to realize that if instead of Marcel's plays we substituted the novels of Percy the summary would be an apt description of the vision of person in Percy's novels. The following is the summary commentary:

In both his philosophical essays and plays, Marcel focuses on the day to day encounters that the individual has with other individuals. Pointing to our tendency to cut ourselves off from others and our concomitant need for other people, Marcel stresses the value of the ordinary interchanges that people experience in the family, the business world and the church. No individual is ever completely cast off from others, even though to live an authentic existence is to struggle, requiring real effort on the part of the individual to remain open, to search out those others who can be loved. As Marcel sees it, one never ceases to be *homo viator*, one who must search for ways to become more open to the ambiguous but real ontological presence that surrounds an individual like a sea. The victory for Marcel lies in the search itself, a search made in the company of other people (Holland, 1990, pp. 4–5).

Amazing how the description fits Percy's writing. All six of Percy's novels are about *homo viator* searching for meaning while existing on Kierkegaard's aesthetic or ethical level. The drama in all six of the novels is clearly a religious drama as Percy, like an Old Testament prophet, tries to call readers to a new self-awareness, one that echoes St. Augustine's profound insight that our hearts are restless until they rest in God.

THE CATHOLIC NOVELS

By the term "Catholic novel" I wish to indicate a novel whose theme is based in some Catholic teaching and the teaching is dealt with positively. This does not mean that every Catholic or priest or nun in the novel is a saint or that the sinful aspects of the church are overlooked or concealed. John Henry Cardinal Newman was correct when he said that real literature had to deal with people as they are and that means sinful. However a novel whose theme rejects or attacks Catholic teaching would not qualify as a Catholic novel in my view. So James Joyce's *Portrait of the Artist as a Young Man*, while it is an excellent novel, is not a Catholic novel. Graham Greene's *The Power and the Glory*, while it depicts a cowardly priest, a drunkard who has fathered an illegitimate child, is a magnificent Catholic novel because, through its weak protagonist, Greene illuminates the beauty and depth of Catholic teaching about the priesthood.

Percy's six novels are *The Moviegoer* (1961), *The Lost Gentleman* (1966), *Love in the Ruins* (1971), *Lancelot* (1977), *The Second Coming* (1980), and *The Thanatos Syndrome* (1987). In each the main character is on a quest and the reader, through Percy's excellent writing, is invited to self-reflection. I think it is accurate to call Percy's works novels of ideas. They are serious and deal with important issues, though they contain a considerable amount of humor. *Love in the Ruins*, whose subtitle is *Confessions of a Bad Catholic Near the End of the World*, is an extremely funny satire that pokes fun at just about every aspect of contemporary life including some of the confusion that exists in the contemporary Catholic Church. Still it contains a beautiful vision of how commitment to Christ changes daily experience.

An early paragraph in *The Moviegoer*, which I think is Percy's finest novel, gives a portrait of the typical Percy protagonist, sunk in the malaise. Binx Bolling describes himself accurately and the picture we get is of someone lost in a consumer culture.

> Life in Gentilly is very peaceful. I manage a small branch office of my uncle's brokerage firm. My home is the basement apartment of a raised bungalow belonging to Mrs. Schexnaryde, the widow of a fireman. I am a model tenant and a model citizen and take pleasure in doing all that is expected of me. My wallet is full of identity cards, library cards, credit cards. Last year I purchased a flat olive – drab strongbox, smooth and heavily built with double walls for fire protection, in which I placed my birth certificates, and my inheritance: a deed to ten acres of a defunct duck club down in St. Bernard Parish, the only relic of my father's many enthusiasms. It is a pleasure to carry out the duties of a citizen and to receive in return a receipt or a neat styrene card with one's name on it certifying, so to speak, one's right to exist. What satisfaction I take in appearing the first to get my auto tag and my brake sticker! I subscribe to Consumer Reports and as a consequence I own a first-class television set, an all but silent air conditioner and a very long lasting deodorant. My armpits never stink (Percy, 1961, pp. 6–7).

Even re-reading this paragraph makes real the claim of some existentialists, such as Jean Paul Sartre and Albert Camus, that the basic philosophical question in an absurd world is why not commit suicide! Binx however knows that something is wrong. He undertakes a search and describes it as follows:

> The search is what anyone would undertake if he were not sunk in the everydayness of his own life. This morning, for example, I felt as if I had come to myself on a strange island. And what does such a castaway do? Why he pokes around the neighborhood and he doesn't miss a trick.

> To become aware of the possibility of the search is to be onto something. Not to be onto something is to be in despair (Percy, 1961, p. 13).

This passage is typical of the search and questioning that occupy the main characters in Percy's novels. This is even true of Lancelot, the murderer in the novel that has his name. Lancelot Lamarr, who has murdered his wife and her lover is in an asylum called the Center for Abnormal Behavior. He is visited by a boyhood friend who has become a priest-psychiatrist. The entire novel, except for the last two pages is Lancelot telling his story and why he committed murder to Father John. About to be released from the institution, Lancelot tells the priest that he has a plan to remove the evil from the contemporary scene through violence when he is released. Finally the priest speaks, though only 13 words. The last two lines of the novel, a question from Lancelot and a response from Father John are:

> Very well. I've finished. Is there anything you wish to tell me before I leave?
>
> Yes (Percy, 1977, p. 257).

The priest is going to speak the good news of Jesus Christ to Lancelot!

Scenes and dialogue from every novel could be quoted to underline the presence of both Kierkegaard's and Marcel's religious vision in Percy's writings. There is one section in *Love in the Ruins* that I especially love. It is a vivid articulation of Percy's Catholic vision. Dr. Thomas More is looking back on the life he and wife had and he is reflecting on how good it was.

> Sunday morning I'd leave her and go to mass. Now here was the strangest exercise of all! Leaving the coordinate of the motel at the intersection of the interstates, leaving the motel with standard doors and carpets and plumbing, leaving the interstates extending infinitely in all directions, abscess and ordinate, descending through a moonscape countryside to a town! Where people had been living all these years, and to some forlorn little Catholic church up a side street just in time for the ten-thirty mass, stepping up on the porch as if I had been doing it every Sunday for the past twenty years, and here comes the stove-up bemused priest with his cup (what am I doing here? says his dazed expression) upon whose head hands had been laid and upon this other head other hands and so on, for here off I-51 I touched the thread in the labyrinth, and the priest announced the turkey raffle and Wednesday bingo and preached the Gospel and fed me Christ.
>
> Back to the motel then, exhilarated by – what? By eating Christ or by the secret discovery of the singular thread in this the unlikeliest of places, this geometry of Holiday Inns and interstates? Back to lie with Doris all rosy-flashed and creased of cheek and slack and heavy-limbed with sleep, cracking one eye and opening her arms and smiling.
>
> "My God, what is it you do in Church?"
>
> What she didn't understand, she being spiritual and seeing religion as spirit, was that it took religion to save me from the spirit world, from orbiting the earth like Lucifer and the angels, that it took nothing less than touching the thread off the misty interstates and eating Christ himself to make me mortal man again and let me inhabit my own flesh and love her in the morning (Percy, 1971, p. 254).

More than 2000 years ago Aristotle admitted that philosophy did not bake bread. However the Greek genius would have insisted on the indispensable role that philosophy plays as persons try to make sense of their lives. Even when you deny the value of philosophy, you are engaging in it. Even the most famous skeptic in the history of philosophy, David Hume, when he denied that philosophy could establish anything, was embracing a philosophical vision, namely the philosophy of skepticism. There is really no escaping philosophy. I believe there is no escaping the questions that Walker Percy raised in both his essays and his novels.

Does Walker Percy have value for those in the business world? If by value we mean how to succeed in business and improve your economic situation, Percy will be of no value. This prophet will not help us make monetary profits. However if by value we mean helping us to live meaningfully and authentically, then Percy can serve as a prophet for us. His writings call us to reflect on who we are, why we are here and where we are going. No small service!

NOTES

1. See, Percy, Physician as Novelist, *Signposts, op. cit*, p. 192.
2. See, Percy, Culture, the Church and Evangelization, *Signposts, op. cit.,* p. 297.
3. In a note to me from Walker's widow dated October 12, 1990.

REFERENCES

Brown, J. (1956). *Kierkegaard, Heidegger, Buber and Barth: Subject and object in modern theology.* New York: Collier Books.
Carr, J. (1985). An interview with Walker Percy. In: L. A. Lawson & V. A. Kramer (Eds), *Conversations with Walker Percy.* (p. 60). Jackson: University Press of Mississippi.
Coles, R. (1978). *Walker Percy: An American search.* Boston: Little, Brown and Company.
Dewey, B. R. (1985). Walker Percy talks about Kierkegaard: An annotated interview. In: L. A. Lawson & V. A. Kramer (Eds), *Conversations with Walker Percy* (pp. 109–110). Jackson: University Press of Mississippi.
Gallagher, K. (1962). *The philosophy of Gabriel Marcel.* New York: Fordham University Press.
Holland, M. D. (1990). *The gift of the other: Gabriel Marcel's concept of intersubjectivity in Walker Percy's novels.* Pittsburgh, Pennsylvania: Duquesne University Press.
Jolivet R. (1950). In: W. H. Barber (Trans.), *Introduction to Kierkegaard.* (p. 113). London: Frederich Muller, Ltd.
Kierkegaard, S. (1941). In: D. F. Swenson (Trans.), *Concluding unscientific postscript* (p. 33). Princeton: Princeton University Press. (Completed after the death of Swenson and provided with Introduction and Notes by Walter Lowrie.) Original book was in Danish.
Kierkegaard, S. (1959). In: W. Lowrie (Trans.), *Either/Or* (Vol. II, pp. 235–236). New York: Anchor Books, Doubleday and Company. (Revisions and a foreword by Howard A. Johnson.)
Luschei, M. (1972). *The sovereign wayfarer: Walker Percy's diagnosis of the malaise.* Baton Rouge: Louisiana State University Press.

Marcel, G. (2002). In: M. Harrari (Trans.), *The philosophy of existentialism* (pp. 30–31). Secaucus, NJ: The Citadel Press.

Percy, W. (1961). *The moviegoer.* New York: Alfred A. Knopf.

Percy, W. (1971). *Love in the ruins: The adventures of a bad Catholic at a time near the end of the world.* New York: Farrar, Straus and Giroux.

Percy, W. (Ed.). (1975). The Delta Factor. In: *The message in the bottle: How queer man is, how queer language is, and what one had to do with the other* (pp. 4–5). New York: Farrar, Straus and Giroux.

Percy, W. (1977). *Lancelot.* New York: Farrar, Straus and Giroux.

Percy, W. (Ed.). (1991). *Signposts in a strange land* (p. 187). New York: Farrar, Straus and Giroux. (An introduction by Patrick Samway, S. J.)

Sartre, J. P. (1946). *The flies and no exit and three other plays.* New York: Vintage Books.

WORKPLACE ROMANCES: A PLATONIC PERSPECTIVE

Martin J. Lecker

ABSTRACT

This paper examines the corporate policies on workplace relationships in the insurance industry. It consists of identifying whether the 48 insurance companies found in the Fortune 500 have any policies that restrict employees from dating each other within their organization and if so, what were these restrictions. In addition, 235 employees in the insurance field were surveyed to determine their perceptions of the positive and/or negative effects of romantic relationships had in their workplace environment. These results were examined from a Platonic perspective with a recommendation for a code of ethics developed from policies existing in other insurance companies and suggested by the current literature.

INTRODUCTION: ROMANCE IN THE WORKPLACE

On March 5, 2005, Boeing Company's C.E.O. Harry C. Stonecipher was asked to resign after refusing to end his relationship with a subordinate (Henry, France, LaVelle, Brandy, & Weber, 2005, p. 94). With a 2% increase in the number of hours worked within the last 10 years by those engaged in the finance, insurance, and real estate industry, workplace

Insurance Ethics for a More Ethical World
Research in Ethical Issues in Organizations, Volume 7, 253–279
Copyright © 2007 by Elsevier Ltd.
ISSN: 1529-2096/doi:10.1016/S1529-2096(06)07013-1

romances may be the only option for many to fraternize beyond the traditional working relationship (Wilson, Filosa, & Fennel, 2003; U.S. Dept. of Labor, 2005). Perhaps, longer working hours may be one of the reasons why one-third or more of all relationships commence at work, as well as why more than one-half of those office liaisons result in marriage or long-term relationships (Wilson et al., 2003; Navarro, 2005). It may be no wonder why workplace romances are on the rise.

Referring back to the Stonecipher situation, one may raise the question, does a corporation have the right to establish rules of conduct for its employees in their interpersonal relationships? Although the review of literature will address the various issues found as a result of workplace romances universally, the primary research will focus on the insurance industry. After reviewing the literature, the 48 insurance companies found in the 2004 Fortune 500 (Fortune, 2005) were contacted to determine whether any written or unwritten policies existed regarding the prohibition of workplace romances. This was followed up by surveying 235 insurance employees and identifying whether they had ever observed a workplace romance, and if so, what were its effects on their organization. Upon an examination on several of the written works by Plato, in terms of his philosophies on moderation, pleasure, happiness, and the good life, various ethical implications surrounding workplace romances were then developed. Finally, conclusions were drawn and recommendations were made to identify which corporate policies on workplace romances would be most beneficial to those in the insurance industry.

Before commencing our discussion on workplace romances, it would be best if the term was first defined. According to R.E. Quinn, one of the first researchers to publish an article on the topic, workplace romances was defined as "a relationship between two members of the same organization that is perceived by a third party to be characterized by sexual attraction," (Quinn, 1980). For purposes of this study, workplace romances will be confined to only monogamous relationships occurring between employees working within the same company, even though it could include relationships outside the organization such as suppliers or customers. Furthermore, this study was limited to only insurance companies.

The first question to be considered is how prevalent are workplace romances? Although the studies vary, it has been reported that up to 80% of Americans have experienced some type of romantic relationship at work either through personal experience or by observation (Schaefer & Tudor, 2001; Powers, 1999, p. 1; Mainiero, 1989, p. 278). In fact, in one Human Resource Management survey, it was reported that of the 617 respondents,

55% of these workplace romances resulted in marriage (Hammonds, 1998). In a survey by the Society of Human Resource Management, 57% of the 663 corporate executives reported that an office romance led to marriage over the previous 5 years (Franklin, 2002, online).

A second question to be considered is, are workplace romances advantageous to the organization? In some studies it was found that being involved with a co-worker may lead to a more inspired, creative individual, as well as enrich personal relationships (Jones, 1999; Karl & Sutton, 2000, p. 432; Mainiero, 1989, p. 5173). In one study it was found that by watching two co-workers in an office romance, it could actually be uplifting to the observers and may even result in a more energized, exciting, and stimulating working environment (Karl & Sutton, 2000, p. 432). In a second study conducted by Mainiero, there was evidence that indicated the attitude of the couple involved in the relationship actually improved in areas of their motivation and productivity (Karl & Sutton, p. 432).

On the other hand, a preponderance of the literature suggests that there are numerous detrimental consequences associated with a workplace romance. As a result of these consequences, the issue exists on whether an employer should have a policy prohibiting such workplace relationships will be discussed throughout this article, along with the diversity of opinions, which has been generated by this topic.

In her landmark book, *Office Romance: Love, Power & Sex in the Workplace*, Mainiero (1989, pp. 77–98) identifies seven potential negative outcomes that may arise for the individual or corporation when a relationship between two co-workers exists. The adverse consequences include: (1) jeopardizing career advancement; (2) negatively impacting professional relationships; (3) enduring other colleagues observing the relationship, as if it was in a fishbowl; (4) reducing a couple's work performance; (5) exacerbating potential gossip, office politics, self-doubt, as well as compromising ones objectivity; (6) creating an unhealthy competition between those in the relationship; and (7) developing the potential for a conflicts of interest involving the couples in the relationship (Mainiero).

Another potential problem can be the possibility for sexual harassment charges or other acts of retaliation by one of the participants, if the relationship is not amicably terminated (Pierce & Aguinis, 1997, p. 198; Jones, 1999). In a 1998 study by the Society for Human Resource Management, it was predicted that 24% of workplace romances may result in sexual harassment claims (Wilson, 2003; Powell, 2001). In fact, if the relationship is between a superior and a subordinate, it is highly likely that the possibility for a claim of sexual harassment claims can be even greater. In addition, if an employer decides to discipline, demote, or terminate an individual involved in a workplace romance, a claim of sexual harassment may be alleged, even if it is not the case in the given situation (Wilson et al., 2003).

A further ethical issue is the perception of a conflict of interest. Often, there are allegations of favoritism toward one of the parties in the workplace romance, by those who are not in the relationship (Foley, 1999; Mainiero, 1989, p. 250; Jones, 1999; Frank, 1984, p. 37). For example, if one of the parties involved in the workplace romance is promoted, assigned a sought after project, or any other perquisite is attained, the perception of favoritism exists (Foley & Powell, 1999). Not only does this affect the entire workplace, it could also lead to a collectively, reduced productivity and a lower group morale within the organization or department (Foley and Powell).

One such case that demonstrated that a conflict of interest based upon favoritism could leave a company liable for damages occurred in a recent California Supreme Court ruling. In July 2005, it was decided that workers can sue an organization if a subordinate is given preferential treatment with a superior who s/he is in a romantic relationship with (Navarro, 2005, 1,9; Edna Miller v. Department of Corrections, 2005). In this case, a prison warden had a sexual relationship with three female employees, but one was given preferential favoritism over the others (Navarro, 9; Edna Miller). The California justices ruled that in cases of pervasive sexual favoritism, it was tantamount to sexual harassment since the message conveyed to the women subordinates was that they were viewed by management as being inferior (Navarro, 9; Edna Miller). The justices further supported this ruling by stating that the only way these women were able to get ahead in this particular workplace was by having sexual relations with their supervisor, which in essence was sexual harassment (Navarro; Edna Miller). Consequently, this ruling can now be used as a precedent for other romantic situations, where perhaps the explicit intent may not have been a "quid pro quo," but the perception of such a situation may be interpreted in the same manner.

Another negative consequence is the potential for confidential information to be discussed between the parties involved in the relationship (Foley & Powell, 1999). Whether or not such a breach occurs is immaterial, but because there is always the potential that this may occur further undermines the professionalism of those in the relationship, as well as creating an unhealthy environment in the workplace (Foley & Powell, 1999). In fact, when conflicts of interest are believed to take part between the parties involved in the relationship, colleagues are more inclined to see punitive managerial action toward the offenders (Powell).

LEGALITIES: EMPLOYEES VS. EMPLOYER RIGHTS

One area of controversy that pervades workplace romances is to what extent the employer has the right to monitor or prohibit employee relationships. Oddly enough, when it comes to corporate policies prohibiting romances in the workplace, the laws and the courts seem to be somewhat divided in their decisions. In New York State, under its 1993 Labor Law Section 201-d, companies are prevented from developing policies which prohibit dating among co-workers, since employees cannot be discriminated against for any recreational activities that are lawful (Jones, 1999; New York Labor Law Section 201-d, 2005). In Colorado, under its Revised Statute 24-34-402.5, its laws are similar in nature to New York, regarding employers who prohibit their employees from dating each other in the same organization, however, if there is a conflict of interest, the employer may terminate an employee (Colorado Revised Statutes, 2005).

But even the New York State Labor Law Section 201-d has an exception. In a 1995, State of New York v. Wal-Mart Stores Incorporated case, it was decided that the employer, Wal-Mart, did not violate New York State Labor Law Section 201-d, for discharging two of its employees who violated its fraternization policy (State of New York v. Wal-Mart Stores, 1995). In this case, one of the employees was married to someone else and marital infidelity had broken matrimonial statutes, the courts interpreted this infidelity as an illegal activity and ruled that Wal-Mart was not violating the New York Labor Law Section 201-d (State of New York v. Wal-Mart).

In some situations, Constitutional Law plays an indirect role in protecting a government employee's right to privacy, in that the state may not restrict an individual's right to privacy, including workplace relations without some sort of justification (Paul & Townsend, 1998). In William O. Shuman, Jr. v. City of Philadelphia, a police officer, was dating an 18 year old, and because her parents did not want their daughter dating an older man, they pressured the Philadelphia Police Department to fire Shuman for inappropriate behavior (Shuman v. City of Philadelphia, 1979). However, Shuman, the plaintiff won and was reinstated, with back pay, under the protections of the First, Fifth, and Fourteenth Amendments (Shuman; Amendments to the Constitution, 2005). By petitioning the government (City of Philadelphia) for a redress of his grievances, Shuman was exercising his rights protected by the First Amendment (Shuman; Amendments). Secondly, when Shuman refused to testify against himself, which was a Philadelphia Police Department policy, given that his self-testifying involved off-duty, personal activities, his Fifth Amendment rights were breached (Shuman; Amendments).

Finally, under the Fourteenth Amendment, which proclaimed that no state might deprive any person of life, liberty or property, without due process of law, Shuman proved that the City of Philadelphia also breached this right (Shuman; Amendments).

But, Shuman v. City of Philadelphia was not the only case when the courts had decided in favor of the employee. In Waggoner v. Ace Hardware Corporation, in the State of Washington, two employees, who were dating each other, were terminated due to its anti-nepotism policy (Wayne Waggoner v. Ace Hardware Corporation, 1997). Under the Revised Code of Washington State (RCW 49.60.180), an employer cannot discharge individuals because of their marital status (RCW 49.60.180, 2005). By discharging Wayne Waggoner and Kathy Cyr for dating each other, since married couples could not be discharged under this law, by not being married, this unmarried couple was being discriminated due to their marital status, of lack thereof (Waggoner v. Ace Hardware). The court found that discrimination against single employees based upon their dating relationship was a prohibited employment practice, just as it is against married couples (Wayne Waggoner v. Ace Hardware). Interestingly enough, according to the literature, almost half of all states have laws prohibiting discrimination against workers on the basis of marital status (Williams, Giuffre, & Dellinger 1999).

In addition, many employers have lost lawsuits involving the invasion of privacy (Foley & Powell, 1999). In these cases, the courts have held that the constitutional right to privacy prohibits unregulated employer inquiries into personal sexual matters that are not related to job performance (Paul & Townsend, 1998). Therefore, if the surveillance of private activities was involved, the violation of privacy laws may exist, thus opening the employer's liability for a lawsuit (Schaefer & Tudor, 2001).

Yet, the majority of the court cases, where companies have either no-spouse laws (in states that do not prohibit them) or "no fraternization" polices, generally will favor the employers. In many states, it is legal for a company to prohibit dating as long as the employees are forewarned, and the policy is applied consistently (Schaefer and Tudor; Williams et al., 1999, p. 79). Therefore, if the policies are not discriminatory and single out a particular gender or even marital status, it is extremely likely that the employer will prevail. In fact, in some cases, employers have been permitted to require their employees to disclose information about intimate relationships that involve actual or perceived conflicts of interest and can be discharged for failing to do so (Williams et al., 1999).

One reason for strict "no fraternization policies" may be due to the agency principle, established by the Meritor v. Vinson case, where employers were found to be liable for the acts of their employees (Karl & Sutton, 2000, p. 431; Meritor Savings Bank, FSB v. Vinson et al., 1986, online). In this case, a supervisor was having unwelcome sexual relations with a subordinate (Meritor v. Vinson; Neese, Cochran, & Bryant, 1989). Yet, the Supreme Court ruled that whether or not the employer Meritor Savings Bank, knew about the situation, it was still liable for sexual harassment since the superior was an agent of the bank (Meritor v. Vinson; Neese et al., 1989). Furthermore, this Court ruled that even when sex-related conduct is "voluntary," even if the relations were not forced, under Title VII of the Civil Rights Act of 1964, if the alleged sexual advances were claimed to be unwelcome, it was categorized as sexual harassment (Meritor v. Vinson; Neese et al.).

In several cases, many married couples have tried to attempt to use the laws to protect them from job loss or transfer, but in most cases the employees have been unsuccessful since they had been unable to prove that their employer was discriminating against them (Williams et al., 1999). One strategy used by the employees is by attempting to use federal laws to protect them from marital status discrimination, but unless sexual discrimination is proven under Title VII of the Civil Right Act, the employers have been successful in maintaining their "no-spouse rules" (Wolkenbreit, 1997). In fact, in several of these cases, the employer was able to prove that these discharges or transfers had been based upon job performance or the company reallocation of personnel, rather than due to any discriminatory practices.

For example in Sanguinetti v. United Parcel Service (U.P.S.), the employer, U.P.S., had a "no-dating" rule which discouraged managers from maintaining personal, sexual relationships with other U.P.S. employees (Sanguinetti v. United Parcel Service, 2000). Although the woman he was dating, a subordinate, was not fired Sanguinetti was unable to prove that he was discriminated against based upon his gender (Sanguinetti v. United Parcel Service).

In the 1993 case, Sarsha v. Sears, Roebuck & Company, an operating manager, who was second in command, was dating a subordinate and was warned by his supervisors not to date any co-workers (Sarsha v. Sears, Roebuck & Company, 1993). Like Sanguinetti, in the case previously discussed, Sarsha sued for gender discrimination because his female subordinate was not fired, and age discrimination because the person who replaced him was 8 years younger (Sarsha v. Sears). The courts found in favor of Sears Roebuck and Company since Sarsha could not prove discrimination and because he failed to adhere to his employer's policy of not dating any co-workers (Sarsha v. Sears).

In a 1980 case against International Business Machines (I.B.M.), John Rogers, an I.B.M. employee was fired for dating a subordinate employee, but he claimed wrongful termination and invasion of privacy (Rogers v. International Business Machines, 1980). Upon I.B.M.'s own internal investigation regarding the job performance of Mr. Rogers, it was discovered that his own fellow employees substantiated that Rogers' productivity had declined and that his relationship with the subordinate had affected the workplace adversely (Rogers v. I.B.M.). Furthermore, since Rogers himself gave permission for I.B.M. to investigate his productivity and the affect it had on the workplace, his claim for an invasion of privacy could not be proven (Rogers v. I.B.M.). Given his poor job performance and that he could not prove that I.B.M. invaded his privacy, Rogers lost his case (Rogers v. I.B.M.).

Given the ambiguity of the laws and the courts, many firms believe the best defense is to have non-fraternization policies, which prohibit managers from having intimate relationships with their subordinates. One such company is Lloyd's of London, who has a very strict non-fraternization policy and will not allow couples to work in the same area, especially if one is in a position of power over the other (Schaefer & Tudor, 2001). Many other major companies have similar policies limiting or prohibiting workplace romances which includes: General Motors, AT&T, Intel and Staples (Symonds, Hamm, & DeGeorge, 1998; Schaefer & Tudor, 2001; Hammonds, 1998, online; Stanton, 1998, online).

Although in many states these non-fraternization policies are illegal, given the Sarbanes-Oxley Act of 2002, several employers are reverting to these types of policies to protect themselves further if a potential lawsuit evolves. According to Section 406 (a), companies are required to adopt a code of ethics for their financial officers (Sarbanes-Oxley Act of 2002, 2002, online). Furthermore, Section 406 (c) states,

> In this section, the term 'code of ethics' means such standards as are reasonably necessary to promote- (1) honest and ethical conduct including the ethical handling of actual or apparent conflicts of interest, between personal and professional relationships (United States Sarbanes-Oxley Act of 2002).

University of Denver Associate Professor of Business Ethics and Legal Studies, Kevin O'Brien believes that although the Sarbanes-Oxley code of ethics requirement is for executives, many companies have made it applicable to all employees (O'Brien, 2005). When there is a workplace romance involving a superior and a subordinate who may benefit by more remuneration, a better work schedule, or a sought after work assignment, it would behoove a firm to have some conflict of interest policy. In the long run, a non-fraternization policy could mitigate the potential for such a conflict of interest.

RESEARCH QUESTION AND HYPOTHESIS

After reviewing the literature, it may be concluded that there appears to be an inconsistency between the laws governing the rights of both the employees and the employers regarding workplace romances. In addition, the literature further reveals that many companies do not have any clear or formalized set of policies governing the workplace romances. Therefore, the research question posed is, should insurance companies have formal policies regarding workplace romances?

The hypothesis of this research is that insurance companies should have a set of formalized policies, in order to protect themselves from potential lawsuits arising from workplace romance relationships, which are becoming more prevalent in the business world.

EMPIRICAL METHODOLOGY AND RESULTS

In order to test the hypothesis, a twofold empirical research study approach was used. First, the 48 Fortune 500 insurance companies identified in the 2004 edition of *Fortune Magazine* were contacted to determine whether their organization had any corporate policies which restricted employees from dating each other within their company and if so, what these restrictions were (Fortune, 2005, F-46-49). Secondly, 235 insurance employees were asked to complete a survey (found in the Appendix A) to determine: if they had ever observed a workplace romance as an insurance employee; what their perceptions were in terms of the positive and negative affects it may have had on their organization and whether their companies had any policies prohibiting these type of relationships.

Fortune 500 Insurance Firms Survey

The first facet of the research was conducted through an e-mail and/or a telephone survey, where the 48 Fortune 500 insurance companies were contacted. Forty insurance companies responded to the survey, which was an 83% response rate, while eight insurance companies refused to

Table 1.   Fortune 500 Company-Insurance Firms $N = 40$ Responses.

Response	Number	Percentage
Formal policy	13	32.5
Informal policy	8	20.0
No policy	19	47.5

participate in it. The companies were asked: (1) whether they had any policies which restricted their employees from dating each other (i.e. being
married) within their organization; (2) if they had a restrictive policy,
whether it was formal or informal; and (3) if there were any policies which
restricted their employees from dating (or being married), what the restrictions were. Table 1 shows the results regarding whether or not these companies had instituted a policy on workplace romances.

Of the 40 Fortune 500 insurance firms surveyed, 21 companies (52.5%)
had a formal or informal policy on workplace romances. Eighteen (86%) of
these 21 firms restricted their supervisors from dating subordinates and had
either an informal or formal workplace romance policy. Yet, all 21 insurance companies with workplace romance policies prohibited either dating or
being married to anyone who had budgetary control or the power to issue
any significant assets over the individual whom they had a romantic/marital
relationship with. In general, the informal policies discouraged employee's
workplace relationships, if their productivity was compromised, as compared to the formal policies, which discouraged workplace romances or
corporate married coupled relationships, and if any financial, scheduling,
supervising, or resource control was under the auspices of one of the individuals involved in the relationship.

On the other hand, 19 insurance companies, representing 47.5% of those
surveyed, lacked a policy on employee dating. In a January 1998 survey by
the Society for Human Resource Management, it was found that less than
30% of the companies had a policy on workplace relationships between
senior executives and their subordinates (Hammonds, 1998, online). Comparing the results from the Society for Human Resource Management survey (30.0%) with the author's Fortune 500 insurance company survey
conducted 7 years later (52.5%), there was an increase of almost 23% realized as more companies had developed policies on employee dating. One
reason, which may be attributed to this increased difference, disregarding
the sample size, is the expensive litigation, which may result if the workplace
relationship is terminated. For example, the Miami Law Firm of Steel,
Hector and Davis averaged 10–15 cases annually because one of the parties

of a terminated relationship would claim charges of sexual harassment (Hammonds, 1998). Each of these charges would result in costing their clients from $500,000 to $1 million per case (Hammonds, 1998). Furthermore, in a United Kingdom survey, it was found that 20% of the businesses had formal policies relating to workplace romances, compared to 32.5% of the insurance companies surveyed from the Fortune 500 research conducted by this writer (Love Contract Needed, 2005). Obviously, the issue of workplace romances is universal and is not only confined to the United States.

Insurance Employee Survey

The second facet of the survey focused upon the employees of selected insurance companies and their perceptions regarding: whether there is a company policy on workplace romances; their effectiveness in terms of productivity, and the effects that workplace romances have on other employees. Due to the sensitive nature of the survey, company policies prohibiting participation in any research survey, and the difficulty in locating insurance employees willing to take the time to complete the survey, the convenience sampling was believed to be the most optimum collection method for this research. Although most statisticians prefer a more probabilistic sampling method, given the small number of insurance employees willing to participate in this survey, the convenience sampling method was the most optimum approach in successfully conducting this type of a survey (Anderson, Sweeney, & Williams, 1993).

A random sample of 235 employees who worked for insurance companies in the states of New York or Florida was distributed and returned. In several cases, the surveys were distributed to insurance employees, in various administrative positions ranging from a receptionist to a President or CEO of the corporation. For this reason, only the number of those respondents who elected to return the survey is known, not those refusing to participate. Originally the survey was to be limited to the New York State area, but when the opportunity to survey employees from the State of Florida was presented, the geographic scope of the survey sample was extended. The actual survey appears in Appendix A and only the pertinent summarized data will be discussed, as well as some selected, applicable literature review, which was used as a comparative basis.

Four main issues were analyzed and will be discussed in this article. These issues were: (1) perceived prevalence of office romances in the workplace; (2) observations of office romances and reactions or perceptions of its affect on the workplace; (3) perceived risks involved for the participants of a workplace romance; and (4) whether there were any informal or formal policies relating to workplace romances and any specifics regarding these policies.

The first focus of the research was to answer the question, how prevalent are workplace romances in the insurance industry? Evidently, workplace romances are fairly pervasive in the insurance industry, as well as in other industries. Based upon those surveyed, 43.8% reported that they observed a workplace romance. This supports several earlier cited studies reporting that up to 80% of Americans have observed an office romance (Schaefer & Tudor, 2001; Powers, 1999, p. 1; Mainiero, 1989, p. 278; Westoff, 1985, p. 19). In a recent 2005 survey, it was found that approximately 60% of the respondents admitted to being involved in an office relationship (Conlin, 2005, p. 91).

On the contrary, of those who participated in the insurance survey, only 13.6% believed that workplace romances were very common. Yet, when asked if a workplace romance existed where they worked, 40.8% responded that although they may have been aware of the office romance, not everyone else had been cognizant. In actuality, there may be more office relationships occurring than is known or reported, especially if the participants are discreet enough or their fellow employees are oblivious to these relationships. This assumption, that office romances are actually rising, was evident in Mainiero's research, where 37% believed that these relationships were occurring more often (Mainiero, 1989, p. 279). In another study by the National Federation of Independent Business, which concurred with the Mainiero's study, an increase of 14% more workplace romances occurring in 2005 than in 2003 was found (Conlin, 2005, p. 91). These studies support the assumption that there appears to be an increase in workplace romances.

In terms of the workplace romance participants and their respective hierarchical relationships to each other, the research survey found that 28% were in a subordinate–superior relationship, while 66% of them were co-workers without any hierarchical difference. The other 6% of those surveyed were aware that the workplace romance existed, but were unsure of their ranked position.

At this point it would behoove us to analyze what affects the office romance had on the workplace. Almost 69% of those surveyed were not affected in the least by the workplace romance, with less than 14% feeling uncomfortable, and almost 18% experiencing happiness for the couple.

However, an analysis of the co-workers' perceptions of the couple in the workplace romance was inconclusive regarding their productivity and collegiality. In 57.3% of the cases, employees reported that they felt no difference in terms of their feelings for the couple in the office relationship, nor noticed any change in their productivity or demeanor. Although, 9% found the individuals in the relationship easier to get along with, almost 5% believed that these "romantics" (those in a workplace romance) were more difficult to be with. In over 18% of the workplace romances observed, their co-workers found them to be less productive, but yet almost 5% of those surveyed found them to be more productive. In 16.5% of the situations, fellow employees lost respect for them because of the romance, and almost 11% resented the romantics because they showed favoritism to each other.

The next issue to discuss is whether there are any inherent risks when involved in an office romance. To begin with, in almost 84% of the observed office romances, it was reported that management took no action at all. Still, in almost 9% of the workplace romances, the management either forced one of those in the workplace romance to be transferred, dismissed, or were issued a reprimand or a warning. For almost 6% of those individuals in a workplace romance, it was reported that they were asked to voluntarily transfer from the department where their partner worked or to leave the company. In summary, 15% of those involved in a workplace romance faced some punitive risks.

But, what other risks was involved for those in a workplace romance? Almost 60% of those surveyed believed if an individual is involved in an office romance, his/her career could be threatened. Fifty-seven percent believed those in an office relationship might be compromising their professional relationships by being in a workplace relationship. Fifty-two percent believed the couple's work performance could decline, while 49% of those surveyed felt that other co-workers could lose respect for them. On the other hand, 19% believed that there were no inherent risks if the individuals, who were in an office romance, could act professionally.

Given that there were risks for those in a close office relationship, were the risks (or benefits) greater for men or women? Sixty-one percent of those surveyed believed that the risks or benefits were applied equally regardless of the participant's gender. However, almost 29% of those surveyed believed that the risks were greater for the women compared to the 6% who felt that the risks were greater for the men. Perhaps, the 29% of those surveyed believed that females were at a greater risk than their male counterparts due to the large number of males in supervisory positions, and the political power that they wielded within the organization. On the other hand, those believing that the male was at greater risk could be attributed to the threat of sexual harassment lawsuits. However, it should be noted that with the increase of women in managerial and executive positions the risks will depend upon the corporate culture and the organization's policies, rather than the gender of the individual in the workplace romance.

The final facet of the survey examined the existence or non-existence of company policies regarding workplace romances. Thirty-nine percent of the employees worked for an insurance company who had an informal policy regarding workplace romances. In 55% of those respondents' firms, office romances were discouraged. Another 41% of those surveyed responded that office romances were neither encouraged nor discouraged, while only 1% felt that the informal policies in the firms were inconsistent (3% declined to respond). Nevertheless, for those in an office romance where their companies *had* an informal policy, 44% were discouraged if they were in a supervisor–subordinate position, 38% were discouraged if they were co-workers who worked in the same department, and 22% were discouraged even if they were co-workers in another department.

The last section of the survey focused upon whether there was a formal policy regarding workplace romances. Based upon the survey, 21% of those responding had a formal policy; 75% did not have a policy, and 2% did not know whether such a policy existed (while the remainder did not respond). The formal policies which were in existence varied with each company surveyed and included: discouraging employees from dating each other; restricting the dating of employees if the relationship involved a supervisor and subordinate; not tolerating any workplace romance; not viewing any office romance favorably; or requiring the individuals to take a seminar on sexual harassment which included what should be done if the romance is terminated by one of the "romantic" partners.

Based upon the survey, there appeared to be ambivalence on the part of the company's management to develop any formalized policy, which would prohibit or discourage these workplace relationships. In addition, in most cases (84%), the management would not interfere with those in a workplace romance, possibly because their co-workers felt no difference toward them for being in an office relationship (57%) or were not affected (69%) by the relationship. However, the majority of those observing such a relationship believed that there were some risks involved with the participants.

PLATONIC PERSPECTIVES

After reviewing the literature and results of the research surveys, the next step was to analyze the merits or drawbacks of a workplace romance from a broad, classical philosophical approach. Since Plato was one of Greece's greatest philosophers, some of his selected, classical works were analyzed. The Platonic sources examined were *The Republic, Symposium, Philebus,*

Gorgias, Lysis, and *Protagoras.* The philosophies of these sources were then interpreted in terms of moderation, pleasure, happiness, and the good life and their relationship to contemporary workplace romances. In addition, the critiques of several Platonic scholars have been included.

Plato's *Republic* was the first source to be examined. In Book IV, the tripartite of the soul was examined with special attention given to the appetitive part. It was stated in section 445b, "Even if one has every kind of food and drink, lots of money, and every sort of power to rule, life is thought to be not worth living when the body's nature is ruined" (Cooper, 1997, p. 121). Furthermore, it is stated in 444d, "Virtue seems then, to be a kind of health, fine condition, and well-being of the soul, while vice is disease, shameful condition, and weakness" (Cooper, p. 120). Given that a workplace romance is tantamount to the appetitive part of the soul, one may conclude that the individuals who are willing to enter an office romance without any regard to how it would affect others in the workplace, would apparently not be placing themselves in a virtuous role.

But, is it possible to deny oneself a romantic pursuit so as not to compromise the professional reputation of the individual? In other words, can an individual control the appetitive urges of the soul in order to make a more rational decision regarding the workplace? In section 437d of Plato's *Republic* it is stated:

> insofar as it is thirst, is it an appetite in the soul for more than that for which we say it is the appetite? For example, is thirst thirst for hot drink or cold, or much drink or little, or in a word, for a drink of a certain sort? Or isn't it rather that, where heat is present as well as thirst, it causes the appetite to be something cold as well, and where cold for something hot, and where there is much thirst because of the presence of muchness, it will cause the desire to be for much, and where little for little? (Cooper, 1992, p. 113)

Evidently, according to Plato, one can control the appetitive urges. So, if you compare the desire of a superior to be in a workplace romance with a subordinate when it is not professionally advisable, can the rationale decision not to be involved with a subordinate supersede the motivation to have such a romance? According to the passage, it is feasible for an individual to control his/her thirst so that in the summer he/she would drink an iced cold beverage, rather than a hot one. Using the same rationale, then why cannot a supervisor control his/her urge to date a subordinate and find someone else to date out of his/her organization?

In Plato's *Symposium,* moderation is alluded to in section 196c when Agathon states, "For moderation, by common agreement, is power over pleasures and passions and no pleasure is more powerful than Love-..."(Cooper, 1992, p. 479). However when Diotima discusses love, according to Platonic critic Thomas Gould, Diotima is defining love "as desire to possess the good, and the good is the name which give things when possessed, will lead to happiness" (Gould, 1963, p. 47). Gould believes that Diotima's role in this passage is to define love according to Plato, which is the universal longing for happiness (p. 101). In sections 208c–209a, Diotima differentiates being pregnant in body from being pregnant in the soul, which is a metaphor for wisdom (Cooper, p. 491). Furthermore, as she explains it "part of wisdom deals with the proper ordering of cities and households, and that is called moderation and justice" (p. 491).

In the *Republic*, Plato again addresses this moderation with respects to virtue. As he puts it simply, "moderation is surely a kind of order, the mastery of pleasures and desires"… (430e) "the desires of the inferior many (,) are controlled by the wisdom and desires of the superior few.." (431d). After addressing courage and wisdom, Plato examines moderation and states that these are three of the four virtues in his utopian city, which is a metaphor for the soul. Just as an aside, later on justice, the fourth virtue, is discussed in section 433b (Cooper, 1992, p. 106, 108).

In section 66e of the *Philebus*, the issue of reasoning which can lead to moderation and virtue is addressed. As Socrates stated, "reason is far superior to pleasure and more beneficial to human life" (Cooper, 1992, p. 456).

Even in his critique of the *Gorgias*, Gould pointed out that according to Socrates (Plato's spokesperson) intelligence was the desire for the best (Gould, 1963, p. 70). Gould further stated that Socrates felt that only good men were happy and goodness was really knowledge (pp. 70–71). Further analyzing this point, Gould believed that intelligence meant having the right desires (p. 71). Therefore, moderation was considered a virtue in Platonic terms, which will ultimately lead to the good life.

In reviewing section 520c in the *Republic*'s Book VII, a reference was made to the Cave.

> Therefore, each of you in turn must go down to live in the common dwelling place of the others and grow accustomed to seeing in the dark. When you are used to it, you'll see vastly better than the people there. And because you've seen the truth about fine, just, and good things, you'll know each image for what it is and also that of which it is the image. (Cooper, 1992, p. 192)

Plato believed that it was the obligation of the wise ones, who knew the truth and were *just,* to return to the area where it was unjust. In other words, instead of experiencing this newfound metamorphous, for the good of the community, the wise ones had to return to their original place and lead the others with their newly acquired knowledge. It is the same thing in regards to the working world, each supervisor, as well as employee, has to have an allegiance to their company and sometimes must sacrifice personal gratification for the communal workplace.

When critiquing section 220a7–b5 of the *Lysis*, Terence Irwin notes that Socrates claims that whatever is loved for the sake of some further end is not really what is loved (Irwin, 1995, p. 67). He then relates it to the Instrumental Principle when he refers to secton 468b7–c5 of the *Gorgias* where Socrates claims "that when we do x for the sake of y, what we want is not x but y" (p. 67). Here lies an interesting conundrum: is the subordinate using the superior for advancement or is the superior being given an opportunity to be with someone because she/he is in a position of power to do so? Although this issue is beyond the legal responsibility of the organization, the ethical implications, which this question raises does seem to address the issue of leading a just life.

In Book X, Plato further supports his view when he states in sections 618e and 619a, that by leading a just life (which could lead to a good life), one can attain happiness for its own sake.

> to reason out which life is better and which worse and to choose accordingly, called a life worse if it leads the soul to become more unjust, better if it leads the soul to become more just…And we must always know how to choose the mean in such lives and how to avoid either of the extremes, as far as possible, both in this life and in all those beyond it. This is the way that a human being becomes happiest. (Cooper, 1992, p. 290)

Platonic critic, S.T. Lowry would concur with the above *Republic* passage, since in his analysis of the *Protagoras*, he points out that Socrates insists that knowledge of future pain will lead men to forgo current pleasures that are inadequate to justify the price paid in the future (Lowry, 1987, p. 37). Lowry's analysis in part may be found in section 353d of the *Protagoras*, "bad things are bad not because they bring about immediate pleasure, but rather because of what happens later…" (Cooper, 1997, p. 783).

Lowry's viewpoint is further supported by Irwin's analysis of the *Protagoras* when he points out how Socrates believes that "it is plausible to suppose we gain more of the same thing (pleasure) in the long term by giving up some of it (pleasure) in the short term" (Irwin, 1995, p. 113). Irwin's analysis of sections 353 and 354 in the *Protagoras* is developed by demonstrating the analogy of how an individual with a toothache is willing to endure the short-term pain experienced by the filling of the tooth cavity when the long-term gain is not feeling anymore pain (113). Sometimes employees must give up something, which may cause us pain or inconvenience in the short term for pleasure in the future.

In summary, most employees know what is acceptable behavior in the workplace, and if having a workplace romance creates a conflict of interest or if favoritism is manifested as a result of the relationship, not only is it unethical, but as Plato believed, it will create unhappiness in the long run for the individuals involved in the relationship.

RECOMMENDATION

Based upon the literature, the primary research, and the review of selected works from Plato, it is recommended that although a company should respect the individual rights of each employee, it has also a moral responsibility to its employees collectively, as well. So, if having a workplace romance affects the majority of the employees, the productivity of the company, and the potential for lawsuits, it may behoove the company to have a formal policy, which restricts certain workplace relationships. Therefore, in the opinion of this writer, the insurance industry should be a benchmark for other industries in professionalizing the conduct of its employees when it could lead to an unhealthy working environment by codifying its ethical expectations, especially in the area of workplace romances.

Although there are several possible approaches in developing a corporate or industry-wide code of ethics on workplace romances, this writer is recommending that one of the following four policies are considered. These four recommended policies to be considered are: (1) consensual relationship policy; (2) non or anti-fraternization policy; (3) superior–subordinate prohibition policy; and (4) conflict of interest policy.

The first one, a consensual relationship policy contract, has also been termed a "love contract," and was first created by Jeffrey Tanenbaum, a partner at Littler Mendelson in San Francisco (Schaefer & Tudor, 2001; Chen & Sambur, 1999, online). The consensual relationship policy contract is a document where employers will require any supervisor who is involved in a romantic relationship with a subordinate to sign a contract acknowledging the relationship and includes other clauses to protect the company from potential lawsuits. It is really intended for higher level employees such as CEOs and officers, top-level executives, and in some cases, directors (Flynn, 1999, online). Yet, in some cases, it will be used if two employees of the same rank are having an office romance. This contract may be used as an alternative to the forced resignation or transfer of one or both employees and reduces the potential liability for an employer (Schaefer and Tudor). A sample of a consensual relationship policy contract is found in Appendix B.

The essentials of a consensual relationship policy include: notifying the human resource director that a workplace relationship exists; acknowledging the review of the company's policy prohibiting sexual harassment; agreeing to possible reassignment if the social relationship involves a subordinate employee; avoiding indiscreet behavior while at the workplace; notifying the human resource director should the social relationship terminate; and mandating the employees in the workplace relationship to sign the company's consensual relationship policy (Gutierrez, Preciado, & House, LLP, 2005, online).

However, it should be pointed out that there may be some drawbacks to this type of contract. These include: perception that the employer is coercing the employees to sign it; issues of privacy, especially that the third party employer is privy to the knowledge of the relationship; no guarantee of immunity from sexual harassment charges; being construed as overkill and the potential to be destructive to the employee morale; and that it may be considered to be a possible form of discrimination (Chen & Sambur, 1999, online). Nevertheless, based upon several cases cited earlier in this study, the organizations who have a consensual relationship policy on workplace romances were more successful when faced with a lawsuit than the organizations without any policy or contract.

The second recommendation is to have an anti-fraternization policy between any two employees of the company (Wilson et al., 2003, online). In other words, employees within the same company are prohibited from dating each other. The one drawback is in several states, this practice is outlawed for the public sector. However, in the case of the private sector, if the employees have advanced notice of a company's anti-fraternization rule, their claim in the courts is significantly weakened (Wilson, Filosa, and Fennel). In fact, a few of the Fortune 500 insurance companies contacted in the research survey had such anti-fraternization policies.

The third recommendation is a deviation of the anti-fraternization policy which prohibits superiors and subordinates from dating. A sample of this policy is found in Appendix C. Again, in some states it may not be legal to have such a policy, but in those states not prohibiting such a policy, it is another option.

The fourth recommendation is to have a written policy that expressly prohibits any employee from being engaged in a romantic relationship if it will result in a conflict of interest. Examples of such a conflict includes any situation where one party has the authority to distribute resources, schedule or supervise personnel, or is responsible for the budgeting of the individual who she/he is involved with in the workplace romance. In addition, companies should have sexual harassment policies in place, should the workplace romance terminate and one party decided to retaliate against another party as a result of the broken relationship.

Although it is incumbent upon employers that the privacy of its employees is never compromised, nevertheless, the workplace should be one in which everyone can flourish without any unnecessary distractions. The insurance industry has traditionally been a leader in demonstrating its belief in the value of its employees and this should never change. After examining the literature and the responses of the surveys, it appears that the insurance companies which lack formal policies regarding workplace romances may be more apt to face potential lawsuits than those companies with clearly written and consistently applied guidelines, especially those lacking policies which prohibit supervisor–subordinate dating (Meyer, 2005, online). Perhaps, short of mandating one of the four recommended policies, the insurance industry might recommend that every insurance firm develop some type of policy regarding workplace romances.

It is true, that an insurance corporation cannot dictate the values of its employees without their support, but its management can model by example in identifying the principles which is conducive to a productive and satisfactory working environment. However, it still is up to each individual employee to exercise prudent judgment in making ethical or just decisions. Perhaps Plato stated it best in Book X, section 617e of the Republic, "Virtue knows no master; each will possess it to a greater or less degree, depending on whether he values or disdains it. *The responsibility lies with the one who makes the choice*" (Cooper, 1992, p. 289).

REFERENCES

Amendments to the Constitution. (2005). U.S. House of Representatives Website. http://www.house.gov/Constitution/Amend.html viewed November 16, 2005.

Anderson, D. R., Sweeney, D. J., & Williams, T. A. (1993). *Statistics for business and economics*. Minneapolis/St. Paul, Minnesota: West Publishing Company.

Conlin, M. (2005). Good divorce, good business: Why more husbands and wife teams keep working together after they split up. *Business Week*, October 31(3957), pp. 90–91.

Chen, A. J., & Sambur, J. A. (1999). Are consensual relationship agreements a solution to sexual harassment in the workplace? *Hofstra Labor and Employment Law Journal*, LexisNexis. Suffern, NY: SUNY Rockland. http://ezproxy.sunyrockland.edu viewed October 23, 2005.

Colorado Revised Statutes: 24-34-402.5. (2005). LexisNexis Academic. Suffern, NY: SUNY Rockland. http://ezproxy.sunyrockland.edu viewed November 14, 2005.

Cooper, J. M. (Ed.) (1997). *Plato: Complete works*. Indianapolis, IN: Hackett Publishing Company.

Edna Miller *et al., Plaintiff and Appellants v. Department of Corrections et al., Defendants and Respondents.* 36 Cal. 4ᵗʰ 446. (2005, July 18). LexisNexis Academic. Suffern, NY: SUNY Rockland. http://ezproxy.sunyrockland.edu viewed October 23, 2005.

Flynn, G. (1999). Love contracts help fend off harassment suits. *Workforce, 78*(3), 106–108. http://www.workforceonline.com viewed October 19, 2005.

Foley, S., & Powell, G. N. (1999). Not all is fair in love and work: Coworkers' preferences for and responses to managerial interventions regarding workplace romances. *Journal of Organizational Behavior, 20*(7), 1043–1049. Proquest. New York, NY: New York University. http://proquest.umi.com/pdqwebhttp://proquest.umi.com/pdqweb?did = 48248512&Fmt = 3&clientID = 9269&RQT = 309&V Name = PDQ viewed August 28, 2005.

Fortune 1000. (2005). *Fortune,* Special Issue, April 18, F-46–F-69.

Frank, C. (1984). Office romances: Dating grows, so do worries. *ABA Journal, 70*(8), 37, Business Source. NYU, New York, NY. http://search.epnet.com/login.aspx?direct = true&db = buh&an = 4738 viewed November 15, 2005.

Franklin, R. (2002). Office romances: Conduct unbecoming? *Business Week Online,* February 13. http://www.business.week.com viewed August 2, 2005.

Gould, T. (1963). *Platonic love.* New York: The Free Press of Glencoe.

Gutierrez, Preciado, & House, L. L. P. Website. (2005). Office romance policy and Contract. http://www.gutierrez-preciado.com viewed October 19, 2005.

Hammonds, K. H. (Ed.), (1998). Sex on the job. *Business Week Online,* February 16. http://www.businessweek.com/archives/1998/b3565063.arc.htm viewed October 2, 2005.

Henry, D., France, M., LaVelle, L., Brady, D., & Weber, J. (2005). The boss on the sidelines. *Business Week,* April 25, 86–96.

Irwin, T. (1995). *Plato's ethics.* New York, NY: Oxford University Press.

Jones, G. E., (1999). Hierarchical workplace romance: An experimental examination of team member perceptions, *Journal of Organizational Behavior, 20*(7), 1057–1072. http://proquest.umi.com/pdqwebhttp://proquest.umi.com/pdqweb?did = 48248552&Fmt = 3&clientId = 9269&Rname = PQD viewed August 29, 2005.

Karl, J. A., & Sutton, C. L. (2000). An examination of the perceived fairness of workplace romance policies. *Journal of Business and Psychology, 14*(3), 429–442.

Love Contract Needed in the Workplace. (2005). *British Journal of Administrative Management, 46*(April/May), 8. Business Source Premier. Suffern, NY: SUNY Rockland. http://ezproxy.sunyrockland.edu viewed December 12, 2005.

Lowry, S. T. (1987). *The archaeology of economic idea: The classical Greek tradition.* Durhan, NC: Duke University Press.

Mainiero, L. A. (1989). *Office romance: Love, power, & sex in the workplace.* New York: Macmillan Publishing Company.

Meritor Savings Bank, FSB v. Vinson et al. 477 U.S. 57. (1986, June 19). LexisNexis Academic. Suffern, NY: SUNY Rockland. http://ezproxy.sunyrockland.edu viewed November 17, 2005.

Meyer, H. (2005). Love and romance in the workplace. *BusinessKnowHow.* http://www.businessknowhow.com/manage/romance.htm viewed November 27, 2005.

Navarro, M. (2005). Love the job? What about your boss? *The New York Times,* July 24, Section 9, 1, 9.

Neese, W. T., Cochran, D. S., & Bryant J. A. (1989). Should your firm adopt an anti-fraternization policy? *SAM Advanced Management Journal,* Autumn, 25–28.

N.Y. CLS Labor Section 201-d. (2005). LexisNexis Academic. Suffern, NY: SUNY Rockland. http://ezproxy.sunyrockland.edu viewed October 23, 2005.

O'Brien, K. (2005). Associate Professor of Business Ethics and Legal Studies, University of Denver, Daniels College of Business. E-mail. November 2, 2005.

Paul, R. J., & Townsend, J. B. (1998). Managing the workplace romance: Protecting employee and employer rights. *Review of Business, 19*(2) 25–30. http://proquest.umi.com.pqdwebhttp://proquest.umi.com.pqdweb?did = 33738435&sid = 2&Fmt = 4&clientId = 9269&RQT = 309 &VName = PDQ viewed August 29, 2005.

Pierce, C. A., & Aguinis, H. (1997). Bridging the gap between romantic relationships and sexual harassment in organizations. *Journal of Organizational Behavior, 18*, 197–200.

Powell, G. (2001). Workplace romances between senior-level executives and lower-level employees: An issue of work disruption. *Human Relations, 54*(11), 1519–1544. http://proquest.umi.com/pdqwebhttp://proquest.umi.com/pdqweb?did = 91079212&Fmt = 4& clientId = 9269&RQT = 309&Vname = PDQ viewed August 29, 2005.

Powers, D. M. (1999). *The office romance.* New York: American Management Association.

Quinn, R. E. (1980). Coping with cupid: The formation, impact, and management of romantic relationships in organizations. Cited in Schaefer and Tudor (2001).

RCW   49.60.180.   (2005).   http://www.leg.wa.gov/RCW/index.cfm?fuseeaction = section& section = 49.60.180 viewed November 26, 2005.

Rogers, P., v. International Business Machines Corporation. 500 f. Supp. 867. (1980, November 13). LexisNexis Academic. Suffern, NY; SUNY Rockland. http://ezproxy.sunyrockland. edu viewed October 23, 2005.

Sanguinetti, P., v. United Parcel Service, Inc., Defendant. 114 F. Supp. 2d 1313. (2000, August 20). LexisNexis Academic. Suffern, NY: SUNY Rockland. http://ezproxy.sunyrockland. edu viewed October 23, 2005.

Sarsha, P-A., v. Sears, Roebuck & Company, Defendant-Appellee. 3 F. 3d 1035. (1993, August 20). LexisNexis Academic. Suffern, NY: SUNY Rockland. http://ezproxy.sunyrockland. edu viewed October 23, 2005.

Schaefer, C. M., & Tudor, T. R. (2001). Managing romances. *S.A.M. Advanced Management Journal, 66*(3), 4–10. http://proquest.umi.com/pdqwebhttp://proquest.umi.com/pdqweb?did = 7974418&Fmt = 3&clientId = 9269&RQT = 309&Vname = PQD viewed August 29, 2005.

Shuman v. City of Philadelphia. 470 F. Supp. 449. (1979, April 18). LexisNexis Academic. Suffern, NY: SUNY Rockland. http://ezproxy.sunyrockland.edu viewed October 25, 2005.

Stanton, M. (1998, October 1). Courting disaster. Govexec.com. http://www.govexex.com/ features/1098/1098s4.htm viewed October 23, 2005.

State of New York, Respondent-Appellant v. Wal-Mart Stores, Inc., Appellant-Respondent. 621 N.Y.S. 2d 158. (1995, January 5). LexisNexis Academic. Suffern, NY: SUNY Rockland. http://ezproxy.sunyrockland.edu viewed October 23, 2005.

Symonds, W. C., Hamm, S., & DeGeorge, G. (1998). Sex on the job. *Business Week*, February 16, 3565. Academic Search Elite, NY: SUNY Rockland. viewed September 7, 2005.

United States Sarbanes-Oxley Act of 2002. An Act to Protect Investors by Improving the Accuracy and Reliability of Corporate Disclosures Made Pursuant to the Securities Laws, and for Other Purposes. Washington, DC US G.P.O. Supt. Of Docs. Public Law 107-204. http://purl.access.gpo.gov/GPO/LPA229345 viewed November 27, 2005.

U.S. Department of Labor Bureau of Statistics. (2005). *Employment, Hours, and Earnings from the Current Employment Statistics Survey (National).* http://data.bls.gov/cgi-bin/ surveymost, viewed August 30, 2005.

Wayne Wagoner, et al., Appellants, v. Ace Hardware Corporation. 927 P.2d 251. (1997, June 3). LexisNexis Academic. Suffern, NY: SUNY Rockland. http://ezproxy.sunyrockland. edu viewed November 20, 2005.

Westoff, L. A. (1985). *Corporate romance: How to avoid it, live through it, or make it work for you.* New York: Random House, Incorporated.

Williams, C. L., Giuffre, P. A., & Dellinger, K. (1999). Sexuality in the workplace: Organizational control, sexual harassment, and the pursuit of pleasure. *Annual Review of Sociology, 25*(1), 79–80.

Wilson, R. J., Filosa, C., & Fennel, A. (2003). Romantic relationships at work: Does privacy trump the dating police? *Defence Counsel Journal, 70*(1), 78–88. Proquest. New York, NY: New York University. http://ezproxy.library.nyu.eduhttp://ezproxy.library.nyu.edu:2062/ pdqweb?index = 0&sid = 2&srchmode = 1&vinst = PROD&f viewed August 28, 2005.

Wolkenbreit, R. (1997). In order to form a more perfect union: Applying no-spouse rules to employees who meet at work. *Columbia Journal of Law and Social Problems.* http:// exproxy.sunyrockland.edu viewed November 17, 2005.

APPENDIX: A. SURVEY ON INSURANCE COMPANY EMPLOYEE DATING POLICIES $N = 235$

1. Which best describes the approximate number of employees in your organization (at the location where you work, not the total number of employees nationwide)?

   25 or less **63.4%**   26–100 **20.0%**   101 + (more than 100) **16.6%**

2. Have *you* ever observed an office romance in your organization (i.e. two employees who are dating each other)?

   Yes **43.8%**   No **56.2%**   (If not, please skip questions #3-7)

   For questions #3 – 7; think of one particular office romance that you observed at work

3. Which best describes the organizational relationship between these employees? (Please respond to only one)

   (Responses do not total 100% as numbers were rounded off to the nearest tenth of a percent)
   30.1% Peers at the same level in different departments
   35.9% Peers at the same level in the same closely related department
   18.4% Superior (boss)- subordinate relationship in the same department
   9.7% Superior-subordinate relationship in other department
   5.8% Did not know their position or which departments they were in

4. How *visible* were the participants regarding their "office romance?" (Please respond to only one)

   18.4% Very visible; everyone knew about the romance
   40.8% Somewhat visible; some people knew but others did not
   40.8% Not at all visible even though we all knew about the romance

5. What happened to the participants as they pursued their "office romance?" (Check to all that apply)

    (Totals exceed 100% due to multiple responses)

    8.7% They were easier to get along
    4.9% They were more difficult to get along with
    4.9% They were more productive in their jobs
    18.4% They were less productive in their jobs (1 "if problems in relationship")
    16.5% Co-workers lost respect for them because of their romance
    10.7% Co-workers resented the romance because they showed favoritism to each other
    57.3% No difference

6. What actions by management were taken, if any? (Choose one)

    83.5% No action at all; management turned a blind eye
    4.9% Management forced a transfer or dismissal of one party
    3.9% Management issued reprimands and warnings
    5.8% One party willingly transferred or left the company
    1.9% No response

7. What were *your* feelings/reactions to this office romance?

    13.6% Felt uncomfortable
    17.5% Was happy for them
    68.9% Not affected either way

8. In *your* opinion, what are the perceived risks for those who participate in an office romance? (Please check all that apply)

    (Totals exceed 100% due to multiple responses)

    59.6% Careers would be threatened
    57.0% Professional relationships could be ruined
    52.3% Work performance may decline
    48.9% Co-workers may lose respect
    19.1% I don't believe there are any risks if they could act professionally
    2.1% No response

9. In *your* opinion, do the risks (or benefits) depend upon gender?

    28.9% Risks are greater for women
    6.4% Risks are greater for men
    61.3% Risks and benefits are applied equally regardless of gender
    3.4% No response

10. In *your* opinion, how common are office romances in your organization?
    13.6% They are very common
    47.7% They occur rarely
    34.0% They never occur
    4.7% No response

11. Does your company have an *informal* norm or policy in your organization's culture regarding office romances?

    (Responses do not total 100% as numbers were rounded off to the nearest tenth of a percent)

    > **39.1%*** Yes (If yes, answer questions # 12 and 13)
    > **57.4%** No(If no, go to question #14)
    > **3.0%** Did not respond
    > **.4%** Don't know

    ***10.6%** checked "no informal policy" but responded to questions 12 and 13 indicating an informal policy *does* exist so the response was changed from "no" to "yes"

12. How would *you* describe the informal office policies in your organization?

    > **55.4%** Office romances are discouraged
    > **41.3%** Office romances are neither discouraged or encouraged
    > **1.1%** Inconsistent (checked both)
    > **2.2%** Did not respond

13. If an informal policy exists, it is applied differently to the rank position or level of those involved in an office romance? (Check to all that apply)

    (Totals exceed 100% due to multiple responses)

    > **38.0%** Office romances are discouraged for members working within the *same* department
    > **21.8%** Office romances are discouraged for members working in *different* departments
    > **43.5%** Office romances are discouraged for those in a supervisor (boss) subordinate position
    > **43.5%** Difficult to say, depending on the individual situation
    > **6.5%** No response

14. Does your company have a formal *policy* on office romances (dating) as distinguished from a policy on sexual harassment?

    (Responses do not total 100% as numbers were rounded off to the nearest tenth of a percent)

    20.9% Yes   **74.5%** No   **1.7%** Don't Know   **3.0%** Did not respond

15. If yes, what is it? (Please feel free to attach the policy or write below and on the other side of this survey, if necessary)

    (a) sexual harassment policy; seminar required held every six months by independent
    (b) attorney; individuals free to do what they want on personal time; policy references if
    (c) romance goes bad
    (d) confidential
    (e) its discouraged
    (f) dating is acceptable if not visible within office environment and does not interfere
    (g) with normal business activities

(h) against company rules
(i) not looked upon favorably
(j) unknown
(k) prohibits fraternization between exempt (management) and non-exempt
     (subordinate) regardless of departmental segmentation also exempt (management)
     and exempt (subordinate) prohibited
(l) no sexual harassment
(m) not acceptable
(n) not tolerated
(o) cannot date if report to each other or if can influence performance evaluation; if so,
     transfer is an option

Survey Questions (modified) from Mainiero (1989), Appendix D: Office Romance 16
Question Survey Results pp. 278–81.

APPENDIX: B. SAMPLE CONSENSUAL RELATIONSHIP CONTRACT

Employee A, employed by the ABC Insurance Company as an insurance agent, and Employee B, employed by the ABC Insurance Company as an insurance agent supervisor, hereby notify ABC Insurance Company that we wish to enter into a voluntary and mutual consensual social relationship.

In entering into this relationship, we both understand and agree that we are both free to end the social relationship at any time. Should the social relationship end, we agree that we will not allow the breakup to negatively impact the performance of our duties.

Before we signed this Consensual Relationship Contract, we received and reviewed the Company's Sexual Harassment Policy, a copy of which is attached hereto. By signing below, we acknowledge that our social relationship does not violate the Company's Sexual Harassment Policy, and that entering into this social relationship has not been made a condition or term of employment.

By signing below, we acknowledge that, under the Confidential Medical Information Act, the ABC Company is prohibited from releasing to one of us any information regarding the other's medical condition, disability or communicable disease.

_____ Employee A
_____ Employee B

Source: Gutierrez, Preciado & House, L.L.P. Website. http://www.gutierrez-preciado.com viewed October 19, 2005.

APPENDIX: C. SAMPLE ANTI-FRATERNIZATION POLICY FOR SUPERVISORS AND SUBORDINATES

ABC Insurance Company prohibits supervisors or managers from engaging in romantic relationships with their subordinates within the company. Relationships between management personnel and employees raise issues of equity, fairness, favoritism and potential legal liability for the company and, therefore, will not be permitted. If management becomes aware of any such relationship, both parties will be confronted and unless they are willing to terminate the relationship, management will ask the supervisor to leave the company. This policy does not apply to employees not in management. If, however, a relationship not covered by this policy causes disruption within the workplace or any other performance problems, discipline may be imposed.

Source: Wilson, Filosa, and Fennel. Defence Counsel Journal. Jan. 2003. Vol 70, Issue 1. http://ezproxy.library.nyu.edu viewed August 28, 2005.